CELLULOID NATIONALISM AND OTHER MELODRAMAS

THE **SUNY** SERIES

CULTURAL STUDIES IN CINEMA/VIDEO

WHEELER WINSTON DIXON | EDITOR

and

SUNY series in Feminist Criticism and Theory
Michelle A. Massé, editor

CELLULOID NATIONALISM AND OTHER MELODRAMAS

From Post-Revolutionary Mexico
to *fin de siglo Mexamérica*

SUSAN
DEVER

STATE UNIVERSITY OF NEW YORK PRESS

Published by
State University of New York Press, Albany

Printed in the United States of America

For information, address State University of New York Press,
90 State Street, Suite 700, Albany, NY 12207

Production by Marilyn P. Semerad
Marketing by Michael Campochiaro

Library of Congress Cataloging-in-Publication Data

Dever, Susan, 1955–
    Celluloid nationalism and other melodramas : from post-revolutionary Mexico to fin de
siglo Mexamérica / Susan Dever.
        p. cm. — (SUNY series, cultural studies in cinema/video) (SUNY series in feminist
    criticism and theory)
    Includes bibliographical references and index.
    ISBN 0-7914-5763-X (alk. paper) — (ISBN 0-7914-5764-8 (pbk. : alk. paper)
        1. Motion pictures—Mexico—History. 2. Melodrama in motion pictures. 3. Mexican
Americans in motion pictures. I. Title. II. Series. III. Series: SUNY series in feminist
criticism and theory

PN1993.5.M4 D48 2003
791.43'0972—dc21
                                                                                    2002030972

10 9 8 7 6 5 4 3 2 1

I dedicate this book to my father,
for bequeathing his love of Los Angeles,
and to my mother,
for giving her all so that
I could love Mexico.

CONTENTS

◫

ILLUSTRATIONS

ACKNOWLEDGMENTS

The renewing miracles of family, friends, filmmakers, critics, colleagues, students, archivists, activists, a publishing house, several institutions, four cats, and the blessings of chocolate have sustained and inspired me throughout the writing of this book. I cherish all with infinite wonder and gratitude.

Early versions of the manuscript, based in part on my dissertation written at Stanford University with the guidance of Mary Louise Pratt and UC-Santa Cruz's Julianne Burton-Carvajal, were completed thanks to generous grants and teaching fellowships through the Department of Spanish and Portuguese, the Programs in Chicano and Feminist Studies, the National Women Studies Association, the Minton Fund for Studies in Popular Culture, the Mabel Wilson Richards and Andrew Mellon Foundations, and the Walter J. Gores Prize. A rendition of Chapter Two was published in Spanish by *Archivos de la Filmoteca* 16 (Feb. 1994) [Valencia, Spain]: 36–49, thanks to editor Gastón Lillo. Chapter One saw a previous incarnation in *Spectator: The University of Southern California Journal of Film and Television Criticism* 13.1 (fall 1992): 52–69, edited by Chon Noriega. Assistance from my current institution, the University of New Mexico (site of the world's most engaging students), has included crucial support from a University teaching award, College of Fine Arts research grants, and timely backing from my home department, Media Arts. Other organizations and their administrators in Mexico and the United States have also offered essential help. My thanks especially to the Cineteca Nacional de México and to the Universidad Autónoma de México's Filmoteca for opening their archives and screening rooms and for providing me with numerous production stills. *Gracias mil* to Rogelio and Xóchitl Agrasánchez for stills from their Mexican Film Archive, recaptured electronically with other visual material by the wizardry of Dennis DeHart and Dan Herbert. My thanks to muralist Charles Freeman for permission to print my photo of his inspiring mural, *Return to the Light*. I am indebted to the Cine Media Project at UC-Santa Cruz, the Film and Television Archive at UCLA, and Stanford University for funding my participation in a series of conferences on Mexican cinema and culture that significantly influenced my post-thesis work.

Over the long haul I've benefited inestimably from readers who have transfused my thinking and writing with their knowledge and skill. Julianne Burton-Carvajal was fundamental in exciting my interest in the field she has worked to establish and promote. I am also grateful for her permission to cite from her English translation of her *Matilde Landeta: Hija de la Revolución* (Mexico City: IMCINE and CONACULTA, 2002). As imaginative mentor and incisive dissertation co-chair, she has my everlasting gratitude, as does co-chair Mary Louise Pratt, who instrumentally shaped my ideas about intercultural arenas. The melodramas discussed in this book form part of, and comment upon, the domain she calls "contact zones"—those "social spaces where disparate cultures meet, clash, and grapple with each other, often in highly asymmetrical relations of domination and subordination. . . ." My understanding of transculturation as a dynamic that works on all members of the contact zone owes much to her work. Carlos Monsiváis, whose patient instruction illuminated me on many occasions and in many cities, has both my thanks and awe: only the most dedicated cinephile would accompany me to double features *after* the last half-dozen conference screenings. Elena Poniatowska welcomed me into her home and offered stimulating conversations during my initial summer of research in Mexico that I shall always recall with delight. While in Northern California, I profoundly appreciated the scholarship and responses of professors Tomás Ybarra Frausto, the late Arturo Islas, Norma Alarcón, Michael Predmore, Chon Noriega, and Claire F. Fox. Southern California lent me an ocean and Daniel Moreno's political savvy with which to enrich my life and work. In New Mexico I found the indispensable wisdom and commentaries of mentors and colleagues *extraordinare:* theorists Ruth Salvaggio (who read the manuscript multiple times), Minrose Gwin, Diana Robin, and Kim López (doubling as penultimate copyeditor); filmmakers Deborah Fort, Ann Skinner-Jones, and Nina Fonoroff. My (excessive?) passion for the genre of excess notwithstanding, Department Chief Ira Jaffe, scholar of quiescent films, has read and discussed my work with a wonderful willingness to walk on the wild side, where colleague Gus Blaisdell has already been shouting his encouragement. Readers for SUNY Press, including Cynthia Steele and two anonymous readers, offered supremely useful suggestions for revisions whose manifestations I hope will cheer them in some measure. The wit and vision of SUNY Press Editor-in-Chief, James Peltz, as well as the excellent guidance from his assistant Lisa Chesnel, copyeditor Nancy Dziedzic, and Production Manager Marilyn P. Semerad, have made the production process thoroughly enjoyable. My home support team, Teaching Assistants James Stone, Stephanie Becker, Shawn Hayward, and Colin Gunckel, together with librarian Dave Herzel, know (too well) how much their responses to my work, as well as their making room for me to do it, have earned my abiding appreciation.

As will be evident in the text, I would not only lack a book were it not for filmmakers Matilde Landeta, Marcela Fernández Violante, and Allison Anders, but I would have enjoyed vastly fewer pleasures in this life. What great gifts these artists have shared!

Other protagonists who have played key roles in the sublime and quotidian dramas of writing and life include an *abecedario* of the splendid: Priscilla Archibald, Roger and Mandy Boesche, Sergio de la Mora, David and Jackie Dever, Onofre di Stefano, Sam Edwards, Ann Eldredge-Burns, Elena Feder, Kris and Pedro Galindo, Jeanne Houser, Allen Issacs, Ruth Lucas, los López San Caralampio, Kathy McKnight, Nancy H. Owen, Deborah Plumley, Linell Roccaforté, and Esperanza San Miguel *y mis comadres* of the neighborhood.

Adored confidants with sharp blue pencils and matching razor intellects are agents of the divine. I'm graced with the most angelic, who will forgive even the trespasses against which they warn me. Fathomless love and thanks to Susan Anderson, who weathered the journey with me *Al filo del agua* and beyond; to Nathan Vail, who first taught me to listen to words on a page; to Rachel Stocking, who miraculously never tires of making me make sense of those words; to Greg Strickland, who expertly holds me to the lessons learned; to Shawna, who wickedly lets me off scot-free; and to Magali Roy Fequiere, who exuberantly puts me through my paces in learning other languages and other cultures that someday may even fall within my ken.

PROLOGUE

—————— N ——————

Emblazoned on the wall of a three-story subsidized retirement complex in North East Los Angeles, an indigenous Mesoamerican seems to gaze at me as I snap his picture from a dozen different angles (Fig. p.1). His head tilts back into an enormous halo of a hat and he regards the barrio through half-closed eyes. Arms outstretched in emphatic gesture, he embraces—or challenges—everyone: the neighborhood's majority Latinos, the newly arrived Asians, the black family next door, and the few aging white folks whose families have been in Highland Park since the late nineteenth century. Beyond my old front porch where my *comadre* Esperanza now reigns, beyond the Chinese couple's front-yard vegetable garden, beyond the senior citizens' minuscule lawn, the native man's image also dominates the ever-hardening freeway artery that borders the east side of our turf. Pasadena suburbanites en route downtown rest in his gaze as they wait for commuter traffic to thin. People stopping around the corner to tour El Alisal, home of the turn-of-the-penultimate-century city booster Charles Fletcher Lummis, cannot escape his sight.[1] On the other side of the freeway, visitors at the Heritage Square Victorian structures exchange glances with a man who silently but powerfully addresses us all.

The barrio has changed in the years since I've lived here. Friends greet me like an errant wayfarer, chiding me and describing the new *ambiente*. While I was away thinking about art in graduate school, art came to the neighborhood. While I've abandoned their children's education for mine—and worse, been enjoying a university job in another state—our little corner of North East L.A. has prospered culturally, if not economically. The change, it appears, is due to the arrival and presence of the newest "migrant soul,"[2] the indigenous protagonist of Charles Freeman's 1994 mural, *Return to the Light*. My former neighbor, Mr. Ramírez, regards the figure as a personal friend. *"Es de Chiapas,"* he proudly tells me, *"mexicano de a verdad."* This "real Mexican" turns out

1

FIGURE p.1. *Return to the Light.* Mural by Charles Freeman, 1994. Courtesy Freeman and SPARC.

to be a Tzotzil spiritual healer, whom African American muralist Freeman employed as his focal point after seeing the Swiss Mexican émigré Gertrude Blom's 1974 photograph of the Lacandón religious man.

Blom's print is well known in Mexico and the United States. Featured on the front cover of a 1993 catalogue for the traveling photographic exhibition "México: Through Foreign Eyes," it can also be seen stenciled on tee-shirts worn by Mexico City mestizas expressing their solidarity with the Zapatista liberation movement.[3] On the border between the Los Angeles communities of Highland Park and Montecito-Lincoln Heights, a place where people struggle daily against the violent effects of urban poverty, the gently authoritative central figure presents a revitalizing force. Freeman's painting has inspired the kind of community solidarity that has put neighbors in touch with each other in planning the mural, employed local teens in its completion, and encouraged senior citizens to come outside to enjoy it. As I approach such a group of residents chatting on the sidewalk, friendly faces nod hello. Although some don't recognize me, and some have no idea that I still think of this barrio as home, nobody appears to mind the presence of a white stranger with a camera. When the group ambles down the street, I am left alone with a Tzotzil shaman from Chiapas and other transculturated beings whose prominent portraits almost seem to emerge from the east wall of the Carlota Park Apartments.

However much I press my back against the chain-link fence that separates the "service" road from the freeway, it is difficult to squeeze the thirty-five by twenty-two foot mural into my viewfinder. If I vertically frame northern Mexican revolutionary Pancho Villa on the left, I erase southern war hero Emiliano Zapata on the right. Too much upward tilt to my horizontal camera and I miss union leader César Chávez, disappearing along with the Vietnam vet who "will work for food." Focusing on portraits of the local Latino poets and mid-century labor leaders obscures the likeness of an elderly homeless person asleep on a bench advertising "affordable" senior citizen housing. Shooting at the wrong angle I lose sight of the image of a young man bleeding to death in the arms of his weeping mother.

I have a perspective problem here. Since I can't change the focal length on the lens of my disposable camera, only by shifting my literal standpoint can I take in the mural in all its diverse unity. Moving from close-ups that honor the specificity of each narrative, I have to step back to see the whole picture. The ideal vantage point appears to be somewhere in the middle of the freeway.

Negotiating "global" and "local" spaces becomes charged with new meaning as I throw Esperanza's ancient truck into gear to get a feel for freeway viewing. It is fitting that in Los Angeles, the motorized hub of this Mexamérica, cultural interactions take place between complex sites of "home" and "route." Sitting at the wheel of the barrio's most familiar vehicle creates a third context: "transport." The anonymity of lone photographer and ubiquitous motorist fades when old neighbors laugh with recognition as I rumble by. "*Quihúbole, gabacha!*" a young mother and former student calls out to her "honky" Spanish teacher, who is pleased to feel at home. "Looking good!" I reply, preparing to take one last good look at the mural that renders theories about transcultural representation into art. I edge slowly into the morning's calm rush hour, pausing not five miles from the world's most traversed freeway intersection, and consider the pleasures and problems of looking.

INTRODUCTION

―――――――――――― N ――――――――――――

Of Melodrama and Other Inspirations

This book is about citizenship and enfranchisement in an increasingly transnational world. It examines the strategies and effects of cinematic and political representation by analyzing melodramas as manifestations of a genre or a sensibility. It is about camera-wielding artists and their subjects in Mexico and in what I consider one of its principal satellite cities: Los Angeles. Depending on your point of view, the book regards "México y el México de afuera," a sort of extended Mexican nation; "Greater Aztlán," reclaimed Latino territory; or "Mexamérica," a composite transnation. The more my own points of view and my own points of departure and arrival have shifted, the more I have used the third term for its cultural, political, and geographical inclusivity. At once native and emigrant, tourist and resident alien of this region, I write "through foreign eyes" about places I have thought of as "home." Consequently I am concerned less about identity politics than I am about the politics of identities. I see subjectivity as constituted in time and place through transaction: ethnicity, culture, age, ability, class, religion, gender, and sexuality compose the currency of exchange whose "value" fluctuates with various "markets." What interests me is how arbiters of national and cultural citizenship seek to fix or topple market values by reifying or dismantling notions of authenticity and worth, thereby incorporating or disenfranchising particular members of the body politic. How marginalized citizens respond to such discursive (trans)nationalism and claim their own places in diverse communities defines the widest scope of my inquiries.

Like Charles Freeman's mural, this book juxtaposes post-revolutionary Mexico with post-rebellion Los Angeles. Where Freeman draws from the iconography of the Mexican muralist movement to link mid-century Mexican patriotism with 1990s expressions of community solidarity, I look to the Mexican movies of the 1940s to inform my analysis of Mexican nationalism and its influence on *fin de siglo* cinema of Mexamérica. The protagonists and premises of our projects are strikingly similar. Freeman's attention to Latina/o artists and activists, Mesoamerican natives, and Mexican revolutionary generals is echoed by my examination of filmmakers and their subjects from this same company. His call for inclusive participation in rebuilding post-1992 Los Angeles resounds in my advocacy of the democratic incorporation of all residents as citizens. The muralist's insistence on transcultural representation is present in my thesis that representation is as much about politics as it is about art.[1]

A word here about the political realm before we move into its art(istry). Throughout the book I understand the Mexican Revolution as *event, condition,* and *ideology.* As armed conflict, the Revolution lasted from 1910 to 1920, with precursors dating back as early as the 1906 mine strike in Cananea, supported by the Partido Liberal Mexicano (PLM) against the foreign-friendly economic policies of dictator Porfirio Díaz (who held office from 1876–1880 and from 1884–1911, the period known as the "Porfiriato").[2] As a web of social, political, and economic conditions, the "Revolution in Power" can be positioned along a continuum from the progressive to the reactionary. If the 1930s saw some radical ideals enacted, though unevenly, until nearly the end of that decade,[3] with the inception of monopoly capitalism in 1940, Mexico entered an ultraconservative era characterized in the 1950s by an increasingly virulent fear of communism. By the end of the '50s, paranoia metamorphosed into action. In 1958, his last year in office, President Adolfo Ruiz Cortines's administration brutally put down a workers' movement for union independence that anticipated the 1968 government-ordered massacre of students and their supporters in Tlatelolco under President Gustavo Díaz Ordaz.[4] This moment signals "the almost formal interment of the Mexican Revolution. . . ."[5] Mexico does not see the moribund Revolution resurrected until January 1, 1994, when the implementation of NAFTA (North American Free Trade Agreement) caused a world-changing uprising. Militating against the trade accord, seeking democracy and economic equality, members of the Mexican Zapatista National Liberation Army (EZLN) revitalized the image and ideals of Revolutionary leader Emiliano Zapata in support of their efforts to reform the nation. The revolt, which had found favor in Mexico and the international community, was countered by President Carlos Salinas de Gortari's fierce reprisals that resulted in the massacre of Zapatista insurgents as well as civilians.[6] Though this movement radically altered the beliefs of a civil society that may have inherited a mythical idea of an enduring Mexican Revolution, it was not a completely isolated event. Throughout the century we can trace radical and liberal activity, including a variety of urban strikes, other indigenous uprisings, women's movements, battles for sexual and gender equality, and class struggles that respond to and intertwine with reactionary and neoliberal practices leading directly to those of the right-of-center government now in power, President Vicente Fox's Partido de Acción Nacional (PAN). Only as an *interrupted ideology*, with varying rhetorical power dependent upon various proponents, has the Revolution survived the century and beyond, embodied not just in seventy years of single-party rule (the "Institutional Revolutionary Party" [PRI]), but also in its multifaceted opposition.

Using similar characterizations—event, condition, and ideology—I examine the incendiary turn-of-this-century Los Angeles. If what has become known as the "Rodney King Incident" (rather than the "Koon, Wind, Powell, and Briseno Brutality Scandal," including the trial of those white policemen in white Simi Valley and the subsequent reaction in the streets) was obviously not as cataclysmic as a revolution, as a classic "bread riot" or a "rebellion" the burning of the city has recalled and extended civic debates of the revolutionary 1960s when the Watts "Riots" ignited a national response to the politics of privilege. As political scientist Cedric Robinson so clearly sees in the 1990s example of civil disobedience, the "pavement lynching of Rodney King" has sparked another conversation about power and representation.[7] The televised reprise of the beating on videotape reflects "public performances . . . orchestrated by the powerful in America" both within the nation and upon the world stage. Where the assault was "a reverberation from the disintegration of civil society in America," it was also a "local reiteration of a national social agenda," characterized by the "civilizing discipline" that the dominant impose globally.[8] "The scenes from this unmistakably real cop show," writes Robinson, "cascaded backward to the recent and not-so-distant past as an inadvertent mimicry of the info-tech war in the Persian Gulf and prior instances of Pax Americana." Though the mainstream media's dramatization of Rodney King and the L.A. Rebellion may have served to shroud the policy and practices of what Robinson calls "an amoral ruling elite," critical readings like his re-dramatize events. King is not blamed as the perpetrator of his own victimization; the Rebellion is not seen as an isolated, apolitical occurrence. Instead, Robinson describes a "foreign policy [that] substitut[es] nationalism, militarism, and neoimperialism for international law and the community of nations." At the same time he decries domestic policy, unveiled by the assault and its mediation in the news, that "conjur[es] racism, sexism ('family values'), authoritarianism, and . . . patriotism to drown out hopes for equality, justice, and individual dignity." In my own alignment of Revolution and Rebellion, like Robinson I am less concerned about the duration of *events* than I am about *conditions* and *ideologies* that force and categorize uprisings. At issue for me is how public discussions, political discourse, and art function to legitimate or unmask the faces of power.

Given the stakes of today's global capitalism, the sovereignty of nations and citizens has never been more at issue. Superpowers forge third-class, extra-national citizens both within and outside their political borders in order to extract tribute to the multinational, corporate state through the exploitation of labor. Representation, both in the sense that "my people are represented in the movies" and "my congresswoman represents me in the capital," increasingly has to do with how power is articulated, consolidated, legitimated, and proportioned. Questions of agency and strategy are crucial here: Who represents whom? What is at issue? How is meaning made? How, for example, does a Mexican '40s film retrospective about natives and nationalism—complete with former film diva as neo-native—serve a '90s Tijuana audience, made up of, say, middle-class Mexican mestizos, Chicano Studies scholars, impoverished indigenous people, transnational art critics, border-dwelling diva impersonators, government officials, and cultural nationalists? As I argue in my first chapter regarding the icon that is María Félix, the significance of such an affair is clearly multivalent. Text only speaks in context. Filmmakers, museum curators, politicians, movie stars, and chroniclers may appear to establish a cohesive context for cultural events, but differently located patrons interrupt cohesion, making sense of their experience from their own perspective. At the same time, context is established through community conversation. Though organizers' conservative intentions might be received by some spectators as camp, for instance, other viewers' subversive translations, filtered through a critic perhaps, might cease to be seditious.

If *what* signifies is up for grabs, *how* meaning is constituted becomes of paramount concern. High drama in Tijuana—from newspaper headlines heralding the arrival of legendary actress María Félix months before her live appearance, to transvestites' multiple manifestations of *la Doña* "in the flesh"—reminds us that melodrama is more than movies. The mode's principals act not only for stage and screen; melodrama's protagonists also create the conditions of cinematic production by acting in the political arena.

From its theatrical displays in post-revolutionary France to its cinematic expressions in post-revolutionary Mexamérica, melodrama persists as a discursive strategy to organize and support power—or to contest power imbalances—in strife-torn societies. As a mode, or as a *modus operandi*, it functions to right worlds irrupted by personal, civil, and foreign conflicts. That an outpouring of national sentiment so often characterizes the genre is a consequence of one of its functions as mediator and redresser of social injustices. Peter Brooks's description of how this "mode of excess" surfaced at the moment of transition between sacred and secular rule in early nineteenth-century France well informs observers of other bellicose eras. Whether the melodramatic rhetoric of social transformation harmonizes politicians' or artists' theme songs, its polarizing mechanisms "legislate the regime of virtue" in a variety of national contexts.⁹ Mexico's denunciation of conservative Catholicism in the revolutionary years desacralized the State and left it in need of laic consecration. Moral authority to govern became dependent on national discourses, like those of post-revolutionary France, which represented "the Republic as the institution of morality." Activists in post-rebellion Los Angeles denounced the right wing's demonization of the poor and ordained their own moral high ground by dramatizing the evils of less-than-compassionate, one-size-fits-all "family values." "Righteousness," once the domain of the sacred, resounded afresh in street vernacular as a potent term to describe the secular worthiness of any citizen willing to stand up for "the cause." Such a citizen became enfranchised by "the people," a discursive idea (more than an entity) that constituted a resecularized and democratic force proposing values by which a new "moral majority" might be defined.

However didactic or therapeutic, melodrama is not universally prescriptive. As cinematic art or civic ardor, melodrama aims to address spectators who represent a wide range of convictions while permitting spectacle-makers great latitude in orienting their political and moral compasses. While commercial movie melodramas may be enlisted to model the rights and responsibilities of citizenship in redefined national domains, both mainstream and more independently conceived melodramas can provide ways for newly enfranchised citizens to reflect—both cognitively and affectively—on the significance of their participation in nation-states whose sacred legitimacy revolution has called into question. Because of its operation in both aesthetic and political realms, melodrama's tactical maneuvers are necessarily overt. Again, its texts speak in context, in community conversations, and with utmost clarity. The genre's accessibility facilitates the decoding and encoding of its lessons; its intelligibility invites the deconstruction of its practices.

That such a self-reflexive, grandiloquent strategy expresses the concerns of daily life is fitting for a genre with democratic terms of address and the conviction that personal ethics can be made to represent the morals of "the people." Quotidian existence is at once prosaic and sublime; melodrama finds meaning in the mundane and elevates its significance to transcendent proportions. If the mode's excesses succeed to the extent that they cogently "argue the logic of the excluded middle,"¹⁰ they also take as their *causes célèbres* the very arena of the "excluded middle": transitional space. Melodramatized binaries in the liminal zones between nations, cultures, classes, and genders incorporate exclusion. The idea of a cultural (if not a political) "Mexamérica," for example, both dramatizes the tension extant between Mexico and the United States and offers a kind of resolution of that tension. "Trespassers Welcomed," its border signs read, "Proof of Identity Not Required." What does matter, as the region's banking institutions have forcefully proclaimed from their multicultural billboards, is not identity but moral rectitude:

"Character Counts!" they admonish. In melodrama's gaze it is not just the examined life, but the life examined and certified as deserving that becomes the life worth living.[11]

At one century's end and another's beginning, transnational, transcultural, transclass, and transgender negotiations are just beginning to be examined. Their worth as objects of study seems to be valued on a sliding scale commensurate with their perceived importance. (Depending on your point of view, this perception is or is not reflected by the number of texts published in each area.) Whereas the transnational realm now commands the most analysis, perhaps given its complicity with—or its struggle against—the colonizing desires of mega-multinational corporations, transcultural space increasingly captures critical inquiry. These days, cultural critics concerned about citizens and nations almost literally cannot read a text or attend a conference without being asked to think about "border crossings" or "hybrid cultures."[12] In an effort to draw attention to the less-studied transclass and transgender fields, scholars have used these same terms to enlarge the context of their work.

Sharing that critical milieu, this book incorporates and excludes like any other. For example, my analysis of instances of transgender representation and spectatorship may only illuminate the functions of nation and culture somewhat as "borders" and "hybridity" metaphorically characterize gender studies. Yet I hope to move beyond metaphor to stage, instead, some of the everyday transgender stances that filmmakers and spectators assume in order to make meaning of their worlds. Here the daily workings of a generally "excluded middle"—the space between fixed gender positions—will be highlighted to reveal gender as a naturalized category that some filmmakers have tried to use, and others have attempted to disrupt, in coding their movies. I argue that the very democracy of 1940s melodramas, however touted or derided as "películas lacrimosas para mujeres" ("women's weepies"), and however calculated to inculcate women and men as "appropriately" gendered citizens, has offered opportunities for spectators to identify against expectation. And spectators, as the literal border-crossing, San Diegan transvestites in Tijuana so beautifully dramatized in their myriad manifestations of María Félix, have established their own grounds for cross-identification. That the actress as image could not only represent but *be represented by* an abundance of identities suggests both the seductive power of iconography and its permeability. By exploring transgendering as a trope of the melodramatic film apparatus democratically available to us all (and I employ "apparatus" just as democratically to include all agents of production and reception from script to screening event), we can see how the melodrama of the *included* middle helps us read complexity into cinema's manichaean margins. Whether we biological females, males, or anyone else watch films "as women," or "as men," or "as transpeople," our attention to the possibility of fluid spectatorship alerts us to the various uses filmmakers have ascribed to gender as a signifying system. As I discuss in greater detail below, when Mexico's pioneering woman filmmaker Matilde Landeta "performed masculinity" in order to dramatize her exclusion from the all-male ranks of the Directors' Guild, for instance, she acted to denaturalize the perquisites of gender. When the female protagonist of her revolutionary film, *La Negra Angustias* (María Elena Marqués as Black Anguish; 1949), assumed men's clothing to lead her nation into the holy war that was the Revolution, Landeta suggested how women might have a variety of roles in the resacralization of nations. When these and other melodramas of the middle ground serve as primers for citizenship, the homogenizing desires of the State and the heterogeneity of its inhabitants combine to forge a not-untroubled mixing of new world orders. It is the possible if problematic coalition of Mexamérica's migrant souls (trans)forming nation and culture that this book ultimately seeks to address.

THE GOLDEN AGE OF MEXICAN (TRANS)NATIONALISM

How mid-century Mexican melodramas contributed to the establishment of the national imagination as well as to new world orders is best understood in the context of the wide-ranging dissemination of this "Golden Age" of movies. From the mid-1930s to the mid-1950s, Mexican cinema addressed an audience that encompassed not only Mexico, but the rest of Latin America, other Spanish-speaking nations, and the United States as well.[13] Initially supported by U.S. and European technology, the Mexican film industry imported human resources and materials, then "nationalized" both products and aesthetics, and ended up exporting a kind of Mexican-coded *hispanidad* that spoke to Latinos throughout the Americas. The visual vernacular (and especially the 1920s muralist project) that subsequently inspired Soviet filmmaker Sergei Eisenstein[14] was enlarged in the '40s by Mexican directors and actors, added to by other Latinos, and supplemented by the occasional Hollywood filmmaker.[15] This border-crossing cinema was at once a thoroughly national product and a transnational hybrid. As such a multifaceted creation, it simultaneously turned its gaze inward on itself, describing Mexico for Mexicans, and outward on an unevenly assimilated "other," defining *lo mexicano* vis-à-vis Hollywood, or *hispanidad* for Latinos.

This is a crucial characterization of a cinema that has participated in both progressive and retrograde projects. This dual categorization is important especially because it has been the practice of some critics to fix on a single interpretation of its politics. From its inception, Mexican cinema's contemporary critics perceived their national industry as largely "revolutionary" because it supported the ideals of the 1910 Revolution.[16] By the 1970s, with the surge of New Latin American Cinema production and criticism, writers of *Nuevo Cine*'s manifestos regarded Golden Age Mexican film as "reactionary" because the emotional melodramas impeded intellectual lucidity and thus political action.[17] Finally, some film scholars working today contrast Mexican and U.S. filmmaking. For this school, mid-century Mexican movies principally formed a radical, alternative cinema that departed from the conservative, mainstream aesthetic of Hollywood.[18]

Taken as a composite these viewpoints have a great deal to teach us about Mexican film. What's interesting about the theories is that each one focuses on a different aspect of Golden Age Mexican cinema, indicating a variety of directions that we might pursue. The most useful strategy is not to argue absolutes; the 1940s and 1950s saw the production of radical and conservative films within alternative and mainstream cinema. Considered in the light of a polyvalent national project elaborated by a range of post-revolutionary politicians, artists, writers, and intellectuals, Golden Age film projected representations of a national citizenry that was far from a unitary amalgam. Resistant in many ways to the dominant Hollywood paradigm of homogeneity, the Mexican cinematic body politic was conceived of as specifically "raced," gendered, and marked by class. Categories such as "women" and "patriots," for example, proved to be particularly significant (and yet still fluid) in the hands of a variety of chroniclers who produced films with both "revolutionary" and "reactionary" messages.

As many generations of movie-going Latinos can attest, it is especially the movies' female patriots—roles played paradigmatically by stars María Félix and Dolores del Río—who mediated nation and *hispanidad*. Within Mexico these stars negotiated a relationship between spectators and the State, indoctrinating viewers in the rights and duties of Mexican citizenship. (Given the Mexican government's subsidy of the film industry, making the State the producer of Golden Age cinema, this relationship was particularly well defined.[19]) On screen and off the stars followed filmmakers' and federal producers' cues to engage viewers through cinematic lures or commercial advertising, through direct political speeches narrativized on film or delivered in public, and through the usual apparatus of fan-and-stardom constructed in radio and print media.

Outside Mexico spectators were conscripted into a Pan-Latino citizenship when they assigned new meanings to the overdetermined stereotypical signifiers of Mexicanness.[20] Divas like the Cuban Ninón Sevilla, the Spanish-descended Meche Barba, the Czech Miroslava Stern, the Argentine Libertad Lamarque, and border-crossing Katy Jurado (who successfully worked in Mexico and Hollywood) facilitated viewers' cultural enfranchisement. The stars' different national backgrounds helped shift cinematographer Gabriel Figueroa's paradigmatic Mexican skies and director Emilio Fernández's ubiq-

FIGURE i.1. *Flor silvestre's* revolutionary bedfellows. Courtesy Cineteca Nacional.

uitous native cacti to common ground that, if not specifically Mexican, was very definitely Pan-Latino territory. In the States Latinos from various regions could simply dichotomize two worlds: Mexican film represented what Euro-America was not. Affirmation of *hispanidad* might well be gleaned through a Mexican lens.

Given the culturally enfranchising mission of this cinema, it is not surprising that melodrama would be a favored genre. Whether Golden Age film employed the terms of historical, maternal, or paternal/patriarchal melodrama, via the genre of excess it could deliver high-resolution truths.[21] Melodrama's exaggerated symbolic system permitted easy spectator access to a moral universe that was marked by a range of often contradictory ideologies (Fig. i.1).

What interests me are the mechanics of these contradictions. Although Mexican melodramas, along with the State that patronized them, might appear to have represented an impermeable, monolithic unity, there were telling fissures in both structures. The ruling Institutional Revolutionary Party and institutionalized revolutionary melodramas, as a whole, did offer fictions of national unity. But even as post-revolutionary, pre-industrial Mexico struggled to narrowly define the nation through representation or rhetoric, even as freely trading, *fin de siglo* Mexico has conscripted art worlds to present melodramatic displays of its "Thirty Centuries of Splendors," other Mexicos within

Mexico have articulated, and continue to elaborate, different visions of the nation.[22] Within an expanded notion of a plurality of Mexican national projects, it is vital to reexamine some of the monumentalized figures of the status quo in addition to giving attention to Mexico's "other" chroniclers. Pausing now to look at the efforts of so-called mainstream arbiters in light of "alternative" practitioners' works allows us to understand the porous, dialogic nature of representation, and thus its often contradictory logic.

CITIZEN VASCONCELOS (1882–1959); OR,
"I'M NOT MAKING HISTORY; I'M TRYING TO CREATE MYTH"

While the roots of both hegemonic and unorthodox cinematic nationalism were as varied as their fruits, mainstream patriotic melodramas drew deeply from official rhetoric about the nation that emerged in the early 1920s immediately after the decade of armed revolt.[23] These often melodramatic discourses worked to resacralize public space, "imagining communities," as Benedict Anderson theorizes in a parallel context, in concert with "religious imaginings" that attempted to reinstate moral values in irrupted societies.[24] In official discourse the national and the sacred were linked not only by their shared reverential language, but by their common concern with death, rebirth, and especially immortality.

When we consider the bloody chaos with which Mexico emerged into the twentieth century, the nation's discursive drive for eternal life takes on pointed historical significance. Post-revolutionary periods required "a transformation of fatality into continuity, contingency into meaning."[25] The mechanics of the rhetorical practices used to transform a ruptured republic into a continuity can be clearly seen in the messianism of one of the most expressive members of the Mexican political intelligentsia: José Vasconcelos. However successful or problematic were his projects to transform contingency into meaning, this vociferous twentieth-century messiah commanded public platforms and pontificated to mass audiences from his tenure as Mexico's first Secretary of Public Education (1920–1924) to his popular (but thwarted) bid for the presidency in 1929.[26] Even before reaching the apex of his power in the early '20s, he orchestrated public opinion from his influential position in the Ateneo de la Juventud and from his presidency of this cultural organization reformulated as the Ateneo de México. With its simultaneous founding in 1912 of the Universidad Popular Mexicana (for post-war laborers and any other adults who desired an education), this Athenaeum of some of Mexico's most invigorating minds constituted a major force for nationalistic "rehabilitation of thought about the Race."[27] Vasconcelos's strategies in imagining the nation and his techniques in promoting his visions reveal meaningful parts of the infrastruc-

ture of nationalism and the workings of the specifically Mexican cultural artifacts from which his discourses borrowed (particularly muralism) and which
they subsequently influenced (especially cinema). Steeped in a tradition of
patriotism and *indigenismo,* couched in religious terminology, marked by traditional gender expectations, and concretized in images of unusually stable
symbolic value that increased in significance as they were juxtaposed with
other icons, the post-revolutionary hegemonic national project can trace a
strong genealogy to José Vasconcelos's imagined community.

As was the case with this Secretary, who was both a prolific writer and
a major political figure, the creative intelligentsia and the government were
often embodied in one and the same figure. The legacy of the Porfiriato
ensured, if not an absolute congruence of public and private ideology, at least
a comfortable marriage of bourgeois intellectuals with the State. The young
writers in the Ateneo de Juventud could rail against the positivism of an
"Orden y Progreso" government, but this did not contradict the fact that
these middle-class thinkers aligned themselves with the nation to such an
extent that, quite like the most strident positivists, they believed themselves
members of the "civilized class" who incarnated Mexico. But unlike the Porfiriato positivists, the intelligentsia, particularly as spearheaded by Vasconcelos in the new Ateneo, held out for the salvation of the uneducated and
impoverished. "Mexicanos en potencia" ("potential Mexicans"), as he saw
them, the poor could improve at least their moral and ethical lot if they were
uplifted by Culture.

Short of reading French poets or becoming Hellenic scholars, the
masses could become civilized—that is, "nationalized"—through more
direct means. "Culture," for the largely illiterate proletariat, would have to
be rendered iconographic in order to be read. As Minister of Public Education and Rector of the National University, Vasconcelos set out to make his
ideology intelligible. Enlisting the burgeoning muralist movement, his Secretariat (the SEP) commissioned artists—most notably Diego Rivera—to
transform "illegible" culture into an ethic and aesthetic fathomable to the
least learned citizens.[28]

For those already elevated Mexicans who could more easily read their way
into the national project—and thus more ably reproduce themselves in future
citizens—Vasconcelos found other kinds of teachers. The literate would benefit, for example, from the SEP's publication of editions of more than five hundred classics, popularly priced.[29] And in 1922, just as Rivera began painting his
history of Mexico on the first floor of the ministry walls, the Secretary engaged
Chilean poet, future Nobel laureate and "Teacher of América," Gabriela Mistral, to come to Mexico to write and lecture on the significance of education
for the nation's women. Like Rivera, whose task was to position the national
culture within the greater "cultura autóctona hispanoamericana,"[30] Mistral

would unite continental thinking in order to enlarge Mexican nationalism. But while Rivera was invited to address *el pueblo mexicano* in its entirety, Vasconcelos charged Mistral to preach to a somewhat smaller, but key, congregation. She would consecrate the nation's future mothers, who in turn would civilize new generations of citizens. As a part of the Secretary's offer for the Chilean to spend a few years in Mexico so that she might help reform young women's rural "Escuelas-Hogares" (Home-Schools), he requested that Mistral compile a reader for the institution named in her honor. *La maestra* more than obliged. She directed her text to the parishioners permitted her and also cast a promise to the wider world: "to the work I will realize some day, destined to the women of América."[31]

Before considering how Rivera reimagined the national education project he was called upon to illustrate, and before noting how Mistral complied with her assigned mission, we might recall the backdrop of Vasconcelos's patriotic zeal as revealed by his self-fashioning. Narrated in four volumes, the first of Vasconcelos's epic memoirs, *Ulises Criollo* (Creole Ulysses), was published just as the former Education Secretary should have been completing his term of office as President of the Republic.[32] The melodramatic account (which some appreciate as a "sinfonía"[33] and others ridicule as akin to the "syrupy ballads of Agustín Lara"[34]) positions Vasconcelos as the heroic figure in contests great and small. Building up to the story about the evil forces that wrested away the 1929 election only to place the country in the hands of barbarous military might, the autobiographer begins his morality play with portraits of the family and home that constituted his first "Mexico." We see the adult Vasconcelos's idealization of nation and citizenship as directly related to the boy's experiences in the northern border town of Piedras Negras, Coahuila. It was there, contends biographer and cultural critic José Joaquín Blanco, "far from dictatorial institutions like the army and the clergy, far from the *haciendas* and the factories, from the Porfirian killing fields and the pompous centers of power and wealth, where Vasconcelos began constructing his idea of the nation."[35] The son of a middle-class customs agent, the child lived an Edenic and isolated existence. As he remembers, relatively peaceful border life was achieved by virtue of his father's Winchester and his mother's prayers that saved the family from their only physical peril: barbarous Apaches. The other border *bárbaros,* Yankees, could be outwitted at their own game. Upon hearing classmates in his Eagle Pass school assert that "Mexicans are a semi-civilized people," young "Joe" would remember that his family regarded Yankees as recently arrived to culture. While his teacher affirmed his civilized status inside the classroom ("But look at Joe. He's a Mexican, isn't he civilized?"), in the school yard he would defend his nation against calumny, deescalating combat by strategic threat.[36] These dangers to his nation notwithstanding, Piedras Negras was a sovereign Mexico that allowed provincial families like the Vasconcelos clan the luxury of criticizing the government while at the same time receiving State benefits. Thinking themselves morally superior to government barbarism, relishing the opportunity to pursue the culture that would assure their incorporation into civilized citizenship, the northern bourgeoisie not only imagined the nation, they also imagined it in their own exalted image.

For Vasconcelos that familial exaltation was also quite specifically gendered. Not only was he the son of his customs agent father, he was also the son of his adored and adoring mother. Her religious parables and moral fables gave him another vision of Mexico. His narration of that vision, as literary critic Sylvia Molloy points out, is at once "the story of the hero's quest for . . . a national revolutionary identity" and "no less the story of another quest, sexual in nature, conducted through an impassioned, at times disturbingly intimate bonding with the mother. . . ."[37] But if the Creole Ulysses's Oedipal journey is indeed remarkable (one only has to read his dripping drama of his mother's last few days—and nights—before she left him to his glory in the capital and returned to Piedras Negras),[38] the account of his sexualized political trajectory is all the more so. It is not only the mother whom the first-person text both eroticizes and then "mutes" by "projecting the erotic onto a higher plane." It is not only the nation, conflated with the mother, that becomes eroticized[39] and whose seductive characteristics (barbarism) must be muted. Nor, eventually, will it be only a wife, object of desire wrought object of derision (doubly betrayed through the hero's adultery and his "disgust" with her labor in childbirth), who must be muted, subsumed. Vasconcelos will also momentarily eroticize—only to deny the erotic power of—other women who were overtly linked to the national political project. Two cases exemplify women who participated in, and to different degrees protested, their own erasure of erotic agency. It's not hard to speculate that the sensuous piety of Gabriela Mistral's early poetry—treating unconsummated love and divine motherhood—would have enticed the writer of eroticized maternal paeans. Later Vasconcelos could be quite pleased with Mistral's literary production in Mexico. *Lecturas para mujeres* reads like something his mother, in her purest imagined state, might have delivered. And as he was drawn to Mistral he was as surely compelled by the aristocratic arts patron and journalist Antonieta Rivas Mercado, whose public writings during his presidential campaign are devotions evidencing a fervently chaste passion. This textual chastity will become ironic in the face of Rivas Mercado's private writings that gave the lie to her sublimated sexuality.

In addition to Molloy's analysis of Vasconcelos's (de)eroticized motherland, Licia Fiol-Matta's essay on the "spiritually maternal" Gabriela Mistral and Jean Franco's examination of Antonieta Rivas Mercado's "cuckolding" of an adulterer make indispensable reading.[40] Each study presents a different aspect of Vasconcelos's formulation that has been largely ignored by biographers concentrating on the public aspects of his nationalism. But the contributions of these critics—especially when read together—give us a better idea of how the psychology of public and private concerns intertwine to construct the (image of a) man who in turn had so much to do with constructing (the image of) a nation.

For readers of literary criticism unaware of the "open secret" of Mistral's lesbianism, Fiol-Matta's analysis of "Gender, Sexuality, and Nation in Gabriela Mistral" may surprise. Though Mistral's "masculine" appearance was often one of the first attributes her contemporary and mid-century critics mentioned—perhaps disregarding the fact that for women in men's worlds an unstable gender identity can sometimes be turned into an asset—her sexuality has been at best insinuated and at worst circumlocuted. That Mistral, mistress of her own image, might have done the insinuating and the circumlocution (points well made by Fiol-Matta) also suggests why such a muted but powerful "maternal" figure would attract Vasconcelos.

The reasons seem to lie with the Oedipal *political* journey Vasconcelos undertook. The idea of an erudite maternal schoolmarm, impassioned about elevating all Hispanoamérica, must have resonated with Vasconcelos's memory of his mother's tutelage. If his didactic mother served as surrogate Nation, how could the "Teacher of América" and self-styled "spiritual mother" (who had never given herself to the disgusting business of childbirth, but instead "adopted" the children of her continent) serve as any less? In asking Mistral to collect a treasury of reading for women he not only replicated the treasury his mother shared with him, he also ensured that future Mexican citizens would have a "mother" who, having conveniently placed the erotic on such a high plane as to render any sexuality invisible, was just like his own. If their class status encouraged the bourgeoisie to imagine the nation in their image, so too did their psychology.

Vasconcelos's eroticization and desexualization of Antonieta Rivas Mercado had less happy results. Rivas Mercado's public adulations of her presidential candidate gave meaning to his messianism while subsequent private writings and one very public act effected what cultural critic Jean Franco has called "the collapse of the dream of the hero."[41] Rivas Mercado's "passion" had a double edge. Her spirit belonged to Vasconcelos right up to the moment of their brief affair, and her heart, if not her body, belonged to the "probably homosexual" artist Manuel Rodríguez Lozano right up to the moment of her "cuckolding" suicide. With that ultimate act, Franco tells us, "she was to find a devastating way of interrupting the immortal hero's journey to fulfillment by displaying her own mortality."[42]

That was the end of her story, no matter how much the autobiographical Vasconcelos tried to extend the tale by textually reviving "Valeria" (Antonieta) in order to deny the damning power of her final narrative. While Franco maintains that the memoir's successive explanations of the suicide made an attempt to place final "interpretive power in Vasconcelos' hands," we might also read his excess of protestations as succeeding only to reveal his failure.

But failure at what? Certainly his disavowal of his need for "Valeria" shortly before her death contributed to her fatal decision, as did other straits Antonieta found herself in. His refusal to believe her announcement that she was about to kill herself, and his neglect to fully act on his suspicion that she might do so, surely made it easier for the writer to carry out her plan. But these are not the failures that his overworked rewriting of her suicide exposes. In his frenzy to have the last word, "to prove the deadly effects of women's and gay emancipation,"[43] we see a different failure: the failure of a "Founding Father" to recognize the humanity in himself and in his fellow citizens. It is Rivas Mercado's diary and death, and not Vasconcelos's memoirs, that rewrite history.

With public and private unshrouded, how can we not read her campaign eulogies in their fullest context? How might our understanding of the significance of *vasconcelismo* change as we regard Rivas Mercado's early Vasconcelos in the light of her later writings? What Franco calls the journalist's "Father of the nation, the supreme phallic power"—and Antonieta's conceptualization of that nation, or "the body/woman through which the hero passes"—transforms in Rivas Mercado's diary, amazingly copied down in Vasconcelos's memoirs: "'Today I have finished my account of Vasconcelos' campaign. I have reread it and found it good, only that it amuses me to think that my readers will believe me to be very much in love with Vasconcelos. . . .'"[44] Rivas Mercado's act and Franco's analysis send us back to print and visual expressions of nationalism that Vasconcelos fostered, so that we might search for other "interruptions" that mark the hero's (and thus the nation's) less-than-immortal heroism.

To understand another dramatic intervention in *vasconcelista* nation-building, we should return briefly to Vasconcelos's intellectual formation. His education in the north had not been limited to Euro-American inspiration; looking to German interpretations of Greek culture, for instance, he developed a taste for an "estética bárbara" that would later become a full-bloomed passion, informing a theory of life and culture of Dionysian excesses. An outward exuberance borrowed from this aesthetic would come to characterize his public heroisms and fuel his civilizing projects. But while Vasconcelos could rationalize passion for himself, anything faintly smacking of barbarism for the masses would be unacceptable. They were to be moved from their allegedly exotic, barbaric primitivism to a higher cultural plane.

The erotic economy Vasconcelos maintained in his personal relationships extended to his public life and shaped his paternalism as a spokesman for the

State. Antonieta Rivas Mercado could not have written a better scenario for the rationale that marked his ideology throughout the 1920s. Through her eyes the masses were not only a part of that feminized national body that the hero must traverse, but at the apogee of *indigenismo* those feminized masses were also allegorized in their most elemental state. They formed the allegedly submissive half of the marriage of two cultures: native peoples. Franco recounts Rivas Mercado's campaign vignette:

> Those masses were represented for her by an "ancient Indian woman" who approached Vasconcelos after his speech, threw herself at his feet, and, "embracing his knees, unconsciously repeated the gesture with which Thetis greeted the father of the Gods, and a single word filled her mouth and moistened her eyes, 'Father.' Father, who is strong, who knows everything, who guides and defends his child through life's turbulence, Father."[45]

Not until the consecration of "Tata" Cárdenas (or "Father," as native peoples dubbed the '30s revolutionary president) would Indians do the naming. Yet widespread characterization of Mexico as an indigenous nation—and widespread characterization of those potential citizens— began in the '20s with José Vasconcelos and Diego Rivera at the Ministry of Education. In addition to commissioning the murals, Vasconcelos traveled around the country with the artist, learning about the provinces and their native inhabitants in order to better instruct the unenlightened. Formulating a "mística de la educación," he become known as the "Decolonizer" and "Knight of the Literate."[46]

The ideological precepts of these two laurels are worth examination. The first title refers to Vasconcelos's belief that the role of Culture is to morally uplift the miserable while simultaneously freeing them from the conditions of colonialization. The second term can be seen as an ironic warning that the great "Decolonizer" would attempt to recolonize the masses by assimilating them into a nation of his particular invention, for he would never be able to appreciate the whole of *el pueblo mexicano* as sovereign citizens. His "potential Mexicans" were also "potential Barbarians," ready "to sack civilization in a trice."[47] Yet as Anderson observes about lettered communities' ideas regarding the incorporation of illiterate groups, "Half-way civilized was vastly better than barbarian."[48] In addition, liberal recolonizers could circumvent problems occasioned by imperfect assimilation by maintaining what Anderson calls their "cosmic optimism," which is what Vasconcelos's personal philosophy allowed him to achieve. Like the early nineteenth-century Colombian, Pedro Fermín de Vargas, who, as Anderson notes, advocated a plan to "hispanicize our Indians," Vasconcelos seemed to hope that "the Indian is ultimately redeemable," if not by literal "miscegenation with the whites," de Vargas-style, then by a figurative impregnation with *vasconcelista* programs in civilizing education.

What is clear about these projects that called for an elevation of the supposed inferior group is that their basic impulse was to eliminate "racial problems" by eliminating "races." Thus, de Vargas declared that "it would be very desirable that the Indians be extinguished,"[49] and Vasconcelos conceived a "raza cósmica" that, in practice if not in theory, would assimilate indigenous people right out of existence.[50] The Secretary's insistence on a "spiritual aristocracy" very quickly slipped into what he was really after: a material aristocracy. Whatever the agenda ostensibly outlined, whether it was the redistribution of private property for the Indians (de Vargas's plan) or the dissemination of public education for the masses (Vasconcelos's mission), the covert project, as Anderson so clearly sees with respect to the Colombian, was to annihilate undesirables by making them *"like everyone else."*

In realizing this goal, Vasconcelos's fabrication of the nation was almost entirely dependent on heavily symbolic rhetoric and overdetermined iconography. Whether rendered in print, aural, or visual terms, these idealizations exemplified the "best" of the barbarous or the heights that the civilized could attain. Such propaganda permitted the comfortable classes to remain comfortably distant from half-civilized citizens-in-the-making who could be assumed to be achieving at least halting progress toward the ideal.

Blanco characterizes the idealist's project like this:

> Vasconcelos wanted a muralism like that of the Renaissance, or even better, like the magnificent sets for Wagner's operas. The pride of the Race. Indians did not live in a country that devalued and inhibited them, on the contrary: public buildings, the covers of magazines, statues, concerts, all would be constructed in a liturgy of racial grandeur of the people that would offer them redemptive images. Quetzalcóatl and the glory of indigenous cultures would be wrested from archeological oblivion and shown to native peoples: "This is who you are."[51]

These liturgies of invented subjectivities became increasingly repellent to the people whom Vasconcelos most depended on to concretize his vision. The more he insisted on the idealization of women, Indians, and mestizos, the more the muralists separated themselves from *vasconcelismo*. Although he had mobilized Rivera's talent and enthusiasm to render intelligible the "sacred silent languages"[52] of Mexican culture and history, Vasconcelos would find himself maintaining "the opposite pole of the same *indigenismo*" that Rivera defended. At first there existed a friendly rivalry:

> Vasconcelos had traced a curious allegorical plan that Rivera did everything he could *not* to respect, painting little-idealized and hardly cosmic Indians all over the place. Vasconcelos would come in to the Ministry and see how his aesthetic-metaphysic

map of the country was filling up with these "ridiculous figures" ["monigotes"] and he'd say to Rivera, *"Ay, Dieguito, ¡indios, más indios!"* Though in the end he'd let Rivera do what he wanted.[53]

But Vasconcelos's incursion into the new "mass media" vividly illustrated the limits of friendship—and the parameters of ideological sovereignty. State patronage notwithstanding, Rivera and the other artists who were chosen to give concrete expression to official cosmology instead expressed their own visions of the nation. Eventually they covered the walls of almost every government building in the capital. As Rivera increasingly gravitated toward a social and economic view of the history of indigenous exploitation, Vasconcelos insisted evermore on his idealized vision of the noble savage as an icon of autonomous purity. A split was in the making; *vasconcelismo,* as any other ideology, was permeable. And nowhere was the Father of Decolonization's vulnerability more graphic than on the very walls of his Secretariat, used by Rivera to record his contempt for the turn the Secretary's politics had taken since the pair's original conception of the project. Immediately after leaving his post in 1924, disgraced by the very rhetoric that once made him so promising, Vasconcelos could see himself—thanks to Rivera's pedagogy—as others saw him. The muralist's fourth floor fresco shows a burlesqued Vasconcelos, his back to Mexico, his pen inked by the contents of a cuspidor. He is joined, as a recent (and thanks to his efforts, still popularly priced) SEP publication points out, by nine others "distant from the problems of the people." The final irony: Vasconcelos is seated "on the white elephant of his extraordinary projects, turning his back on the *cultural essences of the country.*"[54] The messianic minister, who had so perceptively anticipated the power of the icon to educate and socialize, could not have had a more mordant lesson about the mutability of that power.[55]

EMILIO *"EL INDIO"* FERNÁNDEZ (1904–1986): "I MAKE MOVIES TO MEXICANIZE THE MEXICANS"

Vasconcelos's dream of uplifting the masses and Rivera's desire to politicize them not only illustrated how parallel projects might literally share the same space, but also pointed to the ways in which other discursive practices began to complement and disturb hegemonic thinking. By the mid-1930s, a decade after the frescoes of the Secretariat of Public Education were completed, a more modern form of socializing iconography was in place: Church- and State-approved cinema. Claiming its legitimacy both from "high" culture (scripts based on great works) and an artistic intelligentsia (screenplays completed by great writers), the cinema was a porous amalgamation of ideas.

Myths of the nation and its citizens flowed in alternating currents between people and historical conditions, producing a cinema of didactic codes that borrowed from the vernacular of the muralists and the reinvigorated rhetoric of a *vasconcelista* nationalism.[56]

As the apotheosis of Vasconcelos shows how nationalist rhetoric might develop, another Great Man Story demonstrates how the cinema's discursive practices could become influenced. The biographies of the two men are strikingly alike: José Vasconcelos and Emilio Fernández grew up in the Coahuila desert, twenty-two years and seventy-five miles apart; both men formed a sense of the nation face-to-face with "Yankee imperialists" and indigenous peoples;[57] both apprenticed in the United States and then campaigned exhaustively for public education in Mexico; both idealized women, mestizos, and native peoples in order to assimilate them into the nation; both mythified and believed themselves the new messiahs of nationalism; and both, ultimately, were profoundly religious. Certainly the differences between Creole-descended Vasconcelos and half-Kickapoo Fernández are greater than this superficial sum of similarities, but with regard to their meaning as cultural icons, it is precisely the surface that determines their symbolic value. Coupled with the origins of their belief systems, it is Vasconcelos's and Fernández's self-aggrandizing heroic status that invested each man with extraordinary powers of influence by which he "Mexicanized the Mexicans."

By 1926, about two years after Vasconcelos found himself painted into a corner, a twenty-two-year-old Fernández was being prompted to learn about film so that he could help initiate a national cinema. According to a much-recounted and perhaps even apocryphal story, the exiled Adolfo de la Huerta—Vasconcelos's previous champion—was the first to suggest to *Indio* Fernández that film is the revolutionary tool *por excelencia*.[58] According to the director, the two compatriots found themselves in Los Angeles where the inspiring conversation took place. The former Interim Revolutionary President had resided there following his failed December 1923 rebellion against President Plutarco Elías Calles, and the future filmmaker had only just arrived from working in other U.S. towns as something of a migrant laborer.[59] The tale, as related by Fernández in interviews beginning in 1970,[60] bears repetition less for its truth value than for its character as an explanatory fiction. Telling a succession of interviewers of his alleged exploits became simply *El Indio*'s way of inventing new moral fables. Like his forty-one didactic film melodramas, his life stories bask in the kind of verisimilitude superior to some unimaginative narrative where facts muddle truth. If Emilio Fernández, putative Revolutionary soldier since the age of nine or ten (when he purportedly fled to the war after shooting his supposedly adulterous, Kickapoo mother's lover), had indeed talked with the man with whom he had apparently joined forces in that December uprising (that is, up to the point of his own chronology-defying capture and escape from prison), he might well have heard the following words, suitable for an autobiographical Fernández film if not entirely credible as history:

> . . . I found myself with Adolfo de la Huerta, who came to get me out of jail because they'd surprised me with arms and I wanted to rebel again . . . and only because I was exiled: I lasted nine years in exile, and he told me: "You're in the Mecca of movies and the cinema is stronger than a horse, stronger than a 30–30, than a Mauser, than a canon or an airplane. Learn cinema and then go to Mexico and make Mexican cinema like you've just seen."[61]

The film he'd just seen, he claimed in this 1985 interview, was about Mexico. "Looking at the screen I told myself," he said, that "yes, this is Mexico; this is the kind of cinema Mexico should make." One wonders what film he actually saw, or if he even saw one at that particular time, given the nature of the work he remembers: "It was an Eisenstein film." Though elsewhere he avers having seen the 1925 *Battleship Potemkin* when Eisenstein came to Los Angeles in 1930 (a film that had been praised by Diego Rivera during the muralist's 1927 visit to Eisenstein in the Soviet Union),[62] the movie he reputedly viewed in conjunction with Adolfo de la Huerta's motivational chat could not have been both by Eisenstein and about Mexico. But the fact that in 1926 the Soviet filmmaker had some five years before he would travel to Mexico to begin shooting the film Fernández seemed to be speaking of—if Fernández were indeed thinking of Sol Lesser's compilation of the footage Eisenstein shot in 1931 in Mexico[63]—is not as important as the fact that Fernández characteristically recast history in order to fashion scenarios that exceeded mere truth. Maturing as an extra in Hollywood during the dramatic '20s and '30s could have only added to a cinematic sensibility that understood life in terms of its artistic representations. Aging in Mexico at the end of a prolific career when the country was experiencing anything but a Golden Age of cinema might well have prompted a melodramatic memory that functioned as allegory, his embellished recollections designed to make a point. Though he invariably placed himself as the protagonist of encounters real and imagined, his stories made him larger than life while also entirely human. Emilio Fernández took inspiration from men and monuments ranging from Mexican Presidents Adolfo de la Huerta and Lázaro Cárdenas to foreign filmmakers Sergei Eisenstein and John Ford. His self-fashioning is a citizen-patriot narrative with a resounding musical score.

As an expert myth-maker, Fernández knew how to make use of what Benedict Anderson has described in an analogous context as the "non-arbitrariness of the sign." Anderson uses the expression in reference to linguistic "ideograms," defining them as "emanations of reality, not randomly fabricated representations of it."[64] Fernández's use of visual ideograms seems to take a cue from Vasconcelos's visual education project, and then moves a step beyond. While the filmmaker's symbols may be fabricated representations of reality—as Rivera's stylized figures are—Fernández nevertheless works to give his icons a stable, symbolic meaning. Though the muralist's panorama of figures may bear an unmistakable iconographic significance, there is a dynamic sense of mutability in Rivera's work. Fernández takes that dynamism and freezes it: Rivera's types become Fernández's stereotypes. This is particularly clear in the opening sequence of Fernández's 1947 *Río Escondido*, where the director redeploys symbols already invested with meaning. Two decades after the murals in the Education building were complete and had become part of a national lexicon of icons, *El Indio* reinscribed the images in Rivera's mural in the stairwell of the National Palace by using them to frame his didactically nationalistic film. A controlling voice-over further fixes the images with the significance Fernández assigns them. *Río Escondido* is just one of Fernández's films where the workings of ideograms (coded by Gabriel Figueroa's cinematography or novelist Mauricio Magdaleno's scripts) so clearly produce a meaningful symbolic system. More than any other director of the Mexican mid-century, Fernández can be characterized as an oratorical image-maker.

El Indio thus provides one of the best paradigms for comparative study. Yet his cinema has so long been sanctified as a unique entity that critics are reluctant to "place his name in the same sentence with those less distinguished."[65] Others, eager to stress the undeniable importance of Fernández, enthuse that his films "did not simply represent Mexican cinema, they *were* Mexican cinema."[66] Without denying the enormous importance of Fernández and his mainstay cinematographer Gabriel Figueroa, we have to be careful not to let these statements represent too expansive a meaning. While Fernández's signature *María Candelaria* (1943) won international respect and highest accolades at the Cannes film festival in 1946, for example, its romanticized Indians (Dolores del Río and Pedro Armendáriz without shoes) were an initial embarrassment in Mexico (Fig. i.2). It took an international taste for the primitive to recode the film's "genius" for Mexican audiences, and even then "prize-worthy" meant different things for different publics.[67] We can say that Fernández-Figueroa films "*were* Mexican cinema," but the statement gains accuracy in the context of a polyvocal celluloid nationalism.

"WOMEN," "PATRIOTS," AND MATILDE LANDETA (1910–1999)

Golden Age cinema was comprised of a host of films by many exceptional directors. Fernando de Fuentes, Julio Bracho, Luis Buñuel, Ismael Rodríguez, Alberto Gout, Alejandro Galindo, Roberto Gavaldón, and Juan Orol are

FIGURE i.2. Dolores del Río with beloved *marranito* in *María Candelaria*. Courtesy Cineteca Nacional.

among the most noted. Sequences from these directors' works have recently been excerpted into a scintillating new documentary about Mexican melodrama, Marcela Fernández Violante's *De cuerpo presente: Las espirales perpetuas del placer y poder* (Present in Body: The Perpetual Spirals of Pleasure and Power, 1997), that I discuss in my concluding chapter. After half a century the films of trailblazing women directors Matilde Landeta and Adela "Perlita" Sequeyro are gaining critical attention.[68] Like Emilio Fernández's cinema, these latter films sometimes earned prestige in a world market before they found their audience at home. Sometimes, as happened with Matilde Landeta's Golden Age trilogy—*Lola Casanova* (1948), *La Negra Angustias* (1949), and *Trotacalles* (Streetwalker; 1951)—they achieved national recognition when the political culture was more closely aligned with the themes of the films. During the International Year of the Woman in 1975, the United Nations Women's Conference held in Mexico City prompted the nation's film archives, housed at the Cineteca Nacional, to schedule a festival of international women directors. They unearthed *La Negra Angustias,* a film about a woman fighting in the Mexican Revolution, and rediscovered Matilde Landeta, a filmmaker who had ignited her own revolution (Fig. i.3). But while Landeta's importance as Mexico's first professionally trained woman director was widely celebrated, political exigencies took precedence over rigorous film scholarship. In some quarters Landeta's films were merely regarded as filling a potentially embarrassing gap in the Cineteca's programming of women directors.[69] In other arenas hagiography replaced balanced analysis. Only over the course of the last two decades have we seen critics and filmmakers beginning to regard Landeta's work in an increasingly comprehensive light.

By 1991, shortly before I met her and began a friendship that included an excavation of her treasured archive, the eighty-one-year-old Landeta demonstrated once more how her life and work might be read as a whole. Some six decades in the film industry behind her, she had just completed her fourth feature film, *Nocturno a Rosario* (1991). Employing stars from Patricia Reyes Spíndola to Ofelia Medina,[70] Landeta relates the story of Romantic poet Manuel Acuña's relationships with the aristocracy and working classes during the epoch of Mexico's occupation by the French. "This movie won't be a *taquillera*," she told me en route to a special screening outside Mexico City in 1992.[71] But "box office hit" wasn't her goal. Her film's portrait of a young, liberal, impoverished poet who became suicidally attracted to an older, conservative, elite woman is refreshingly different from blockbuster love.

The "love story" that motivates the making of this historical film is even more compelling. It is—as its director demonstrates in her role as an "extra," purposefully striding into the opening sequence of her film to invite us to review the past—an homage to cinema as historian. In her modern prologue to *Nocturno,* where Reyes Spíndola moves through a plaza in the historical

FIGURE i.3. One woman's Revolution: breaking up the men's club on the set of *Angustias*. Courtesy Matilde Landeta.

center to ask a public scribe stationed there to recall an Acuña poem, we're made to consider what still remains of the past and what links us to it. Long after this initial scene of writer and client cuts to the stately Landeta as a pedestrian on the square, long after she passes a doorway that sweeps open to reveal life in Mexico in the mid-nineteenth century, viewers might still find themselves considering the role of the scribe in relation to a filmmaker. In my case I wondered how a scribe with quite another history would transform to prose what she had learned about Landeta the summer the cineaste opened her home and heart to an outsider. How would Landeta survive her death in my memory, or in the remembrances of local or foreign scribes and documentarians who had tried to convey a sense of this filmmaker's extraordinary place in the making of Mexico?

Researching and writing this book across a dozen summers, interspersed by semesters with legions of thoughtful film students who interrogated critical methods with undaunted urgency, I have been concerned with these questions over time. A summer of shared public and private life with Landeta convinced me from the outset of my study that whatever understanding of her work we might achieve would be enhanced by reading the films in their historical context, and by appreciating the filmmaker herself as one aspect of that context. In this effort I have valued the work of contemporary scholars and filmmakers who have interviewed Landeta in print and on camera.

Thanks to the creative expositions born of these scholar-artists I have been able to flesh out my impressions of the director's circumstances and philosophies, while learning more about her films' histories and their organizing principles. To this effort I'm interested in contributing more detailed analyses than we have yet seen of two of her lesser-known films, *Lola Casanova* and *Trotacalles*. Though such an offering may seem to unbalance a book where other filmmakers are represented principally by a single film, my privileging this one filmmaker redresses the dearth of Landeta film criticism, and suggests how the complexities of a national project might be more fully comprehended if marginalized movies and their makers were unreservedly presented in order to reveal their occluded participation in the construction of a multivalent nation.

The work of filmmakers Marcela Fernández Violante (*Matilde Landeta,* 1992) and Patricia Díaz (*My Filmmaking, My Life,* 1992), as well as that of the film critic Julianne Burton-Carvajal ("Daughter of the Revolution: Matilde Soto Landeta"[72]), lend us particularly complex portraits of the artist. Finely crafted interviews from each of these three distinct sources rely on the intimacy Landeta nurtured in all her friend-biographers, but we feel her presence most intensely in these representations. In Fernández Violante's documentary we also enjoy the presence of those with whom Landeta worked: the pioneering editor Gloria Schoemann; Meche Barba, star of *Lola*

Casanova; director Carmen Toscano (*Memorias de un mexicano,* 1976); and the talented Elda Peralta, who was featured in both *La Negra Angustias* and *Trotacalles* (plus a host of other Golden Age films), and who grew to become a close friend of Landeta and a writer in her own right.[73] Díaz's documentary gives us views of other protagonists of Landeta's intimate circle, and includes an interview of cherished friend and colleague Marcela Fernández Violante. Julianne Burton-Carvajal's exquisite mosaic of Landeta's memories advances the testimonial genre and lets us hear in detail the voice of a resolute woman who, orphaned from her mother as a toddler and relinquished by her father into the care of her aristocratic maternal grandmother, decided to part from her conservative San Luis Potosí family to begin a career in cinema. The critic, having taped and faithfully edited hours of recorded reminiscences as might a filmmaker, leads us through Landeta's labyrinthine history. Of striking out with beloved brother Eduardo to join the movies in Mexico City, for instance, Landeta, through Burton-Carvajal, gives us this:

> . . . in 1930 Eduardo returned to Mexico City [from the States], full grown, strikingly handsome, accustomed to living on his own, and in search of a job. Our father owned a series of tobacco shops, tiny hole-in-the-wall places in downtown Mexico City. Eduardo rented one of these and began selling cigars. He lived in a rooftop room on Calle Uruguay not far from the Zócalo [the huge square in the city center]. . . . At nineteen, I had decided that the time had come for me to be independent of the family as well, so I rented an adjacent maid's room on the same rooftop as my brother. We had a little electric grill and lived on oatmeal, mostly. Since Eduardo did most of the cooking, I couldn't complain.[74]

Capturing her vivacity and pluck—we can hardly imagine a young Mexican woman of means and family giving up everything to live in a rooftop maid's room without appreciating her extraordinary mettle—these kinds of verbal images constitute a fine companion for the filmed biographies. Along with the documentaries, the collected memoirs allow us a privileged view of a filmmaker whose independent frame of mind inflected her cinema.

In particular, all three of these life stories chronicle Landeta's ideas about gender, demonstrating how her views were formed by her experiences. What fascinates me are the connections we can reasonably make between Landeta's own performances of gender roles and the dramatizations of gender that her protagonists stage. Documenting the filmmaker's most daring enactment, for example, Patricia Díaz gives her spectators a moment of docudrama as visual referent for Landeta's voice-over explanation about how she captured the attention of the exclusively male filmmakers' union in order to advance her case to become assistant director. Landeta's appearance at the studio dressed in clothing to make the (wo)man, her all-business suit, tie, hat, and requisite Mexican-national mustache in place, not only made for headlines in the guild, but also prefigured the filmmaker's attitude toward the cross-dressing *coronela* in *La Negra Angustias*. In the movie, in complete contrast with Francisco Rojas González's eponymous novel (1944), the Zapatista colonel's assumption of masculine accouterments—from pants to power—is as easily and as "naturally" accomplished as Landeta might have wished her own ascension to a position of power to have been (Fig. i.4). And when Angustias temporarily trades masculine garb for a high fem look (a permanent change in the novel, along with her "natural" refeminization), Landeta sees that bit of drag as performative and as empowering as the donning of men's clothing (Figs. i.5 and i.6). While her protagonist's enactment of the feminine serves to warn her of the dangers of a kind of male-fantasized femininity, Landeta's own purposefully perverse use of such a male fantasy served her to achieve power. Anatomy as destiny would drive neither Landeta's Angustias nor Landeta herself, but employing the popular Freudian dictate against itself would be a neat trick. Burton-Carvajal gives us the fullest expression of this sleight-of-hand that Landeta ever formally pronounced:

> I knew how hard it would be to convince 300 Mexican men that a woman should be promoted to assistant director. I felt like my whole career was riding on that meeting and thought out my strategy very carefully. As my letter of petition was being read to the assembled membership, I rose to stand before the group . . . [c]areful to adopt a very docile, feminine pose—hands clasped together, eyes downcast, head tilted to one side. . . . The discussion got pretty heated, as I knew it would, with some members hurling insults. This aroused the *quijotes*—[those courtly gentlemen]—who came galloping to my rescue. Ironically, members who had not initially been in favor of giving a position of authority to a woman ended up supporting me because they wanted to differentiate themselves from the loudmouth brutes. . . . I had taken a calculated risk by using "feminine wiles," and it worked. After eleven years in the business I finally earned the promotion that should have been conferred automatically after two or three.[75]

The great coup here, presaging part of what I will be discussing in my second and third chapters, is Matilde Landeta's ability to use and thus unmask both extremes of Mexico's melodramatic gender roles—mythic masculinity and fantastic femininity, roles she herself delighted in for their articulate use value—against the very system that perpetrated these exclusive positions in the first place. But before examining her strategies in more detail, let's look at the interplay between two "revolutionary" directors whose differently marked politics allow us to see the range of revolutions sparked throughout the rebuilding of Mexico.

FIGURE i.4. Independent production as means to power: the car she hocked to make her films. She kept the rifle. Courtesy Matilde Landeta.

FIGURE i.5. Masculine-garbed María Elena Marqués as La Negra and Elda Peralta as a quintessentially feminine Federalist wife. Courtesy Matilde Landeta.

FIGURE i.6. Phase or fatal flaw? La Negra's fleeting heterosexual fling requires high fem drag. Courtesy Matilde Landeta.

GENERALES OF THE POST-REVOLUTION:
MATILDE LANDETA AND EMILIO FERNÁNDEZ

Considering that the categorizations of "revolutionary" and "reactionary" are useful inasmuch as they reflect a historiography of film criticism, and considering that film's inevitable contradictions are what make it the interesting testimonial artifact that so many recent film revivals claim it to be, the first part of this book regards key films of both Emilio Fernández and Matilde Landeta as equally expressive—if differently motivated—examples of a common film tradition. Thinking about these two directors in tandem can remind us of the figuratively and almost literally intertextual world of filmmaking in 1940s Mexico. In sequences from their films we can see examples of eclectic cinematic forms and the effect of filmmakers working together. Not only did Fernández and Landeta share the same extraordinary editor,

FIGURE i.7. Managing "potential citizens": quinine queue in *María Candelaria*. Courtesy Cineteca Nacional.

Gloria Schoemann, not only did the two depend on many of the same production crew members, not only did they employ the same groups of renowned musicians to melodramatize their plots, but they worked with each other as director and assistant on a number of films. Landeta explained the ramifications of this to me graphically:

> Following *"Indio"* Fernández around in the Xochimilco mud of *María Candelaria* was reason enough to make me want to direct my own pictures. There he was, high and dry, shouting orders like some Revolutionary general, and there was I, the muck sucking up my shoes, trying to do my duty and keep my mouth shut. I knew I couldn't last long as the camp-follower kind of *soldadera;* I had to direct.[76]

Landeta's comments on the relative status of female and male filmmakers are analogous to the relative power of "revolutionary" female film protagonists. My first chapter examines how this limited power functions not only for mestiza civilizers, but for indigenous women and men supposedly lacking the requisite civilization for citizenship in a post-revolutionary nation. The goal of Fernández's political melodrama discussed here, *Río Escondido*, is to *strategically* enfranchise women and indigenous peoples in order to manage, if not reward, those "potential citizens."[77] Fernández's stylized representations of native peoples obscure the materiality of their lives, facilitating their symbolic appropriation into discursive nationalism instead of their enfranchisement in real terms (Fig. i.7). His romanticized portrayals of Mexico's judiciously incorporated mestizas become discursive icons of mediation between the nominally enfranchised indigenous population and the fully vested ruling elite.[78]

Examining '40s cinematic patriotism through the optic of '90s redeployments of Golden Age rhetoric, I analyze a 1990 retrospective film festival and museum exhibition of '80s indigenous Seri portraiture whose politicizing aim seems to parallel goals mainstream melodrama set a half-century ago. While regarding María Félix's civilizing role in the now canonical *Río Escondido*, Chapter One also looks at the person—and the "artifact"—that the diva has become. I find her at the opening of a retrospective Fernández/Félix film fête and art show where, like a character in one of her movies, she mediates between images of Seris and State-sponsored rhetoric about native peoples' assimilation into the fabric of national life.

Like all of my chapters this one was written in a time that I seek to preserve in order to maintain the political ambience of its present tense. Chapter One's "present" stretches from 1990 to 1992. Constructed in the pre-Zapatista era when relatively few were writing about the lack of legislative incorporation of indigenous people as first-class citizens,[79] the chapter stands as one more sign marking the distance that the Mexican government has yet to travel toward drafting equitable legislation for native peoples. As of this writing in late summer 2001, and on the literal heels of the frustrated March for Indigenous Dignity that the EZLN (Ejército Zapatista de Liberación Nacional) made to the capital in order to foster discussion about pro-indigenous reforms of the Constitution, the Zapatistas have curtailed dialogue with lawmakers until the political and cultural rights of indigenous peoples are appropriately recognized by the Constitution. Constitutional "reforms" approved by the Congress in April 2001 not only negate earlier accords, but as Subcomandante Marcos and the leaders of the EZLN proclaim, the changes negate the right of entire populations to participate as entitled subjects in civil society.[80]

Chapter Two, also written before the Zapatista uprising, investigates rhetoric about indigenous assimilation through a study of Landeta's 1948 *Lola Casanova*. Based on anthropologist and writer Francisco Rojas González's novel of the same name (1947), Landeta's ethnographic, historical melodrama is primordially concerned with national foundational myths. Setting her film in the colonial period, an epoch as much invested in the consolidation of power as was the post-revolutionary era, the filmmaker conceives citizenship in transcultural terms. Conforming to mainstream cinema's glorification of Mestizo Mexico, and at the same time critical of its rhetoric, she envisions a *mestizaje* wherein both indigenous and Creole peoples would transmute into new national subjects. In her imagined community there is also a place for traditional native peoples who resist totalizing assimilation and choose sovereignty over any kind of economic, political, or cultural mixing.[81] Unlike the portrait artist discussed in my first chapter whose "allegorical" renderings of Seri peoples divorce them from their environment, Landeta represents Seri peoples in their own milieu. Instead of images of disconnected peoples, she offers a view of their engagements with daily life. While her fictionalized ethnography combines myth and history—particularly in the person of Lola Casanova, a *criolla* whose narrative of captivity motivates the plot—her self-conscious use of the melodramatic mode enables spectators to sort fiction from fact. In a film where expressions of feminine excess are not divorced from expressions of feminine agency (in the same way that native peoples' agency constitutes part of their representation), Landeta proposes that melodrama's capacity to "say all" be employed to expose a less restricted view of the marginalized than that wrought by more stylized representations offered by filmmakers like Fernández.[82]

The third chapter moves our investigation of cinematic nation-building into the epoch of Mexico's industrialization and modernization. *Trotacalles* (Streetwalker; 1951) represents a challenge to mainstream melodramatic dogma about poor-but-honest-prostitutes-with-hearts-of-gold-who-rise-above-their-station-to-become-members-of-the-monied-classes. At the apex of *Unidad nacional*, the government's programmatic call for economic development at the expense of the working classes,[83] Landeta's project advocated a different unity: that "workers" of the lowest echelon bind together in sisterly solidarity. This chapter reads *Trotacalles* against the backdrop of *desarrollismo*, and decodes the film's aesthetics in order to reveal how it speaks to an alternative political reality. Another cycle of films popular in Mexico at the time offers useful comparison: Hollywood *film noir*. These tales of urban crime and corruption resonated with Mexico's eminently popular cabaret genre. But where post-depression, post-war Hollywood imagined pessimistic scenarios of the city after dark, with few exceptions the *cabareteras* offered promises of a glittering nightlife that would herald the dawn of a new capitalist day.[84] Their realism notwithstanding, the U.S. films stopped short of dismantling traditional hierarchies of "Otherness." While Landeta borrowed from *noir*'s realist impulses, she simultaneously eschewed the cycle's maintenance of conventional gender paradigms. Her Mexican melodramatic imagination, informed by her own rather melodramatic trajectory as a woman in an occupation dominated by men, sparked representations of women who neither succumbed to the margins of their own plots nor arose as spectacles of their own life stories.

Trotacalles resists both the rhetoric of national unity and women's alleged complicity in the birth of a new unified citizenry gestated in representations of the fancy bordellos and other hot night spots of the *cabareteras*. What I call the film's "allegory of human and commodity exchange values" functions to reveal the elite's seduction and betrayal of working classes who, under President Miguel Alemán, must "prostitute" themselves for their very survival. Landeta's characterizations of a wealthy banker and his wife, together with portrayals of an impoverished prostitute and her pimp, stage the political and economic melodrama of *alemanismo*'s greatest crimes. Yet while *Trotacalles* might draw direct lines connecting governmental abuse of the working poor with their mistreatment by the private sector, the film does not end with unrelieved pessimism. Cinematic pleasures to be savored in Landeta's melodrama include the realistic representation of pleasure itself. Even in hard times, the filmmaker seems to say, pleasure is not the exclusive domain of those who can afford its vanities.

HOME LIFE: THE NEOMELODRAMAS
OF ALLISON ANDERS (1954–)

The fourth chapter bridges a half-century and an international border to discuss Allison Anders's 1993 neomelodrama, *Mi vida loca*. Given the recent fascination with the 1940s (particularly as manifested in film retrospectives and art exhibitions[85]), given Los Angeles's status as the third largest Mexican metropolis in the world, given the city's efforts to manage—if not enfranchise—a citizenry of migrant souls in the face of anti-immigration laws, welfare and bankruptcy "reform," and urban rebellion, I detect the possibility of a new cycle of melodrama informed by Mexican Golden Age concerns and aesthetics. The chapter includes a reflection on the mechanics of gendered spectatorship in Mexamérica as specifically reimagined in an earlier Anders feature, *Gas Food Lodging* (1991), also forcefully connected to Mexican melodramas of the past. Focusing on *Mi vida loca* as an especially compelling example of this "neomelodramatic" trend, I return to the questions posed by the migrating image of the Tzotzil spiritual leader and his chroniclers: Who represents whom and to what ends? Who looks at representations and how do the represented gaze back at their observers? Whose narratives attempt to explain or contain such (meta)representations? In a society riven by class struggles, by ethnic conflicts, by gender trouble, what is at stake in all this looking?

Chapter Four's approach to these questions depends on a reordering of conventional hierarchies regarding subject/object relations. Departing from the kind of ethnographic melodrama Landeta employed in *Lola Casanova*, in *Mi vida loca* Anders extends the genre's capacity to witness and fictionalize by inviting—both literally and through her aesthetic choices—the objects of her study to participate as speaking subjects of their own narratives. I see Anders herself as a participant ethnographer, and discuss details of her decade spent living in the community she dramatizes on film. Without coming to the same conclusions as did a few of the film's contemporary, professional critics, I also ask "what a white girl is doing in a brown girls' film" and come up with answers that relate Anders's class affiliations and her communitarian spirit with a film that has refreshingly responded to these questions. As another "white girl" from a nearby barrio writing critically about a "white girl's/brown girls'" film, and as someone with longtime Latina/o friends who care very much about their on-screen representations, I engage as primary critics of the movie a community of spectators that *Mi vida loca* specifically addresses.

Since my completion of the chapter in 1996, these principal critics have grown to a wider audience as the film has gained increasing attention. In my courses at the University of New Mexico alone, I've screened the film to hundreds of students who have voiced unusual consensus about the movie: here was a complex film that merited the same amount of discussion as any canonical work. Though their responses to different elements of *Mi vida loca* have varied as much as their ages (spanning from seventeen to seventy-something, with an average age in the mid-twenties), what strikes me is that these very heterogeneous students have reported feeling passionately about the issues and art of the passionate *Mi vida loca*. Whether or not they personally relate to the movie, they become caught up in it, its democratic melodrama exciting their participation in much the way that so-called women's pictures of the Hollywood '40s spoke to viewers. In their encounters with the film, they have been both affectively aligned with popular press reviews that, like the movie, speak from the heart, and intellectually stimulated by academic criticism that, like the movie, reveals how the heart can speak.

While I refer to these articles in the chapter, film scholar E. Ann Kaplan's powerful *Looking for the Other: Feminism, Film, and the Imperial Gaze*, with its psychoanalytic examination of *Mi vida loca*, was published after I finished my analysis.[86] Rather than integrating her newer commentary into the body of my writing (though I couldn't resist engaging it here), I've decided to leave the piece in its original form to preserve my initial response. By this, I want to honor the influence of that primary "interpretive community"—my Latina friends and their teenage daughters—as well as sustain the impact of the historical conditions that urged me to write: the 1996 congressional discussions and eventual repeal of "welfare as we know it." Like Anders, having received life-sustaining food stamps in my own time, the kinship I felt with her and with the economically impoverished Chicana/o characters on the screen drew me intimately into a film that might have "distanced" others.[87] Though my own ethnicity and cultural capital might have distanced me as well, my persistent economic class and my continued community alliances have made for common cause that is stronger than that offered by many other educated white people whose class interests I don't share (say, those senators railing against welfare entitlements).

With Kaplan, however, whose work focuses on the intricacies of privilege and privation vis-à-vis gender, ethnicity, and "looking relations," I do share interests. I too come to *Mi vida loca* as a white feminist concerned about representing "race" and ethnicity in a practice, as she points out, that has been criticized for its lack of attention to these issues.[88] Yet because of the pervasive nature of white supremacy that Kaplan cautions whites not to forget, and "despite [our] feminist politics" or even my extended-familial ties or my class affiliations, I too "cannot avoid aspects of the oppressive white look" in my own "looking" at/for/with the "Others" represented in my book.[89] What we as white critics *can* do, Kaplan asserts, is to understand the "'subject/object' look . . . as mutual, as a process, a relation."[90] With respect to this mutuality, like Kaplan, I too welcome other perspectives on the conclusions I have drawn regarding others.

Meanwhile, in my own effort to look with an eye for others' looking, what I most clearly see is Allison Anders's respectful view of looking as relation. As I discuss in Chapter Four, her relations in the neighborhood she calls home are both affective and artistic. Her daughters integrated into the Latino neighborhood as "white *cholas*," while her family ethnicity metamorphosed through adoption and extension. Her script came into being as the direct result of all these intertwined relationships, while her camera recorded the relationships as if it were another member of the community. As I see it, Anders embodies the best of Kaplan's white hope.

Here's where the critic sees a somewhat different story. Though she appreciates Anders as a "Traveling Theorist," noting that Anders and other filmmakers like Julie Dash, Yvonne Rainer, and Claire Denis "'travel' within their own cultures, in the sense of moving out to imagine other identities, the struggles of other 'Others' . . . [in order to] construct new identities and produce new knowledge for spectators with their cameras," Kaplan ultimately seems to regard Anders as more of a visitor on a tourist visa than a migrating movie maker at home.[91] "Ethnographic" her film might be, but for Kaplan it lacks the kind of involvement the African American director Julie Dash has achieved with her *Daughters of the Dust* (1992):

> Unlike Dash's ethnographic project, Anders' hybrid film is distanced. In place of the passionate engagement of Dash's camera, Anders, perhaps as behooves an outsider, has her camera keep its distance. Indeed, Anders deliberately constructs her film as a series of little stories. . . .[92]

Without seeing documentation of any such camera work in her text, I am at a loss to understand the spatial distance of which Kaplan writes. My own close analysis of the film evidences a great deal of visual intimacy, which I interpret as characteristic of a filmmaker who functions as a *participant* ethnographer. And where Kaplan sees "little stories," I see "big" ones, our language curiously in dissonant rhyme, given my sighting of melodrama versus Kaplan's view of a "children's storybook." The movie, I write, is about "the big stuff: crazy lives, insane deaths, binding love, all stirred up." The movie, Kaplan writes, is about "girls and boys . . . who are forced by their circumstances to play adult male and female roles as they narrate their loves, hates and losses."[93] Here we seem to be relatively on the same page of the storybook, or hearing similar strains in the melodrama, however we may have sized up the narratives. But in the next measure, in the next paragraph, what we hear and see in relation to each other seems a reflection through an "acoustic mirror." For Kaplan the film is "emotionally flat." ("The structure, Brechtian style, distances the viewer and positions her to reflect on what she sees.") For me it's passionate. (The operatic structure and melodramatic style entice the viewer and position her to reflect on what she sees and feels.) Kaplan makes a case to explain why the filmmaker might have purposefully distanced herself. I make a case to explain how she's involved.

Spectatorship in action, then; our analyses say as much about the politics of looking as they do about the representations in the film. My reading of another white feminist critic also underscores the politics of difference within: not all white women look alike. While Kaplan has much to teach us about how psychoanalysis and politics function as a signifying system that can inspire us to "understand *the political process and the political success* of colonization," with regard to *Mi vida loca* she has yet to fully see how class and culture fit into that paradigm.[94] Her observations are distanced, leaving us, perhaps, a little emotionally flat:

> The closest the film gets to any sense of past Mexican culture is the little glimpse of the "old world" in the grandmother's house and clothes when Mousie stays with her for a short time. The only other moment figuring any "past" is when Giggles' mother, who takes care of Giggles' little girl when she is in jail, complains about the style and habits of Giggles' generation, recalling how different it was in her youth.[95]

The first part of the statement reflects the cultural bias we all have when looking for the other. As Kaplan so well understands in her groundbreaking and respectful book, it *is* hard to read someone else's history when we don't know the signs and don't know what to look for. I offer a detailed examination of the numerous signs of "past Mexican [and Chicana/o] culture" in Chapter Four in order to propose a wider view of history for readers to consider as part of that mutual looking relation that the critic urges. In that spirit I urge us all to look a little closer at the signs we *can* see in *Mi vida loca*. If the first part of

Kaplan's statement is only shortsighted, for example, the second part of her analysis suggests oversight. Here her interpretation is based on a misreading of the facts presented in the diegesis of the film. One of the many satisfying aspects of *Mi vida loca*'s emotional richness lies in the intimate relationship Giggles has with Rachel, her *sister-in-law* (to be possibly confused more as her friend than as her mother), with whom she bonds over *common* memories and *indulgent* complaints about the younger generation. However much Rachel clucks her tongue over the young women's differences of dress and politics of love (differences, Giggles reminds her, so like the ones that existed between the *pachuca* generation of their mothers and themselves), her disapproval is based on nostalgia for the past (promoted by a box of old photographs) and her motherly concern for the future of her considerably younger sister. Thus, far from sharing Kaplan's insistence on the film's "emotional flatness [that] suggests lack of any hope for a future, absence of any sense of history, or any notion of working toward change,"[96] my friends and I saw enormous hope in Giggles's pregnant *comadre* Rachel, who had found her way out of the gang and into a middle-class marriage with a Chicano cop who treated the barrio kids with respect.[97] For us this little detail made for a big story.

Finally, besides looking at any film as an autonomous creation, even a quick survey of the surrounding terrain can show how a movie works as a cultural commodity. In the face of mainstream cinema's dramatizations of the barrio as a war zone peopled with immigrants whom suburbanites should fear, I briefly align *Mi vida loca* with Chicano productions that envision barrio citizen residents as ideal audiences. In the face of the sociopolitical economy of post-rebellion L.A. that motivates *Mi vida loca* as well as my analysis of the moral universe it describes, I also examine the representation of violence. Since the Watts Riots in 1965, and especially since the Rebellion sparked by that infamous Koon, Wind, Powell, and Briseno decision in 1992, people have negotiated "getting along" with each other in a town marked by four "seasons": "fire, flood, earthquake, and riot." To melodramatize differently, to focus on the destruction violence wreaks rather than to celebrate the almost prurient voyeurism it attempts to arouse, is to propose new ways of imagining a community. This is what a white girl is doing in a brown girls' film. This is what we all, in our ever-shifting roles as natives and emigrants, tourists and resident aliens, can begin to imagine through our own looking relations.

NEOMELODRAMA IN MEXICO: THE MOVIES ACCORDING TO MARCELA FERNÁNDEZ VIOLANTE (1941–)

To differently imagine nation and citizen is also the project of the fourth filmmaker, whose riveting documentary about sound-era Mexican melodramas I analyze in my fifth, concluding chapter. Marcela Fernández Violante's articulation of multifaceted melodrama, *De cuerpo presente: Las espirales perpetuas del placer y poder* (Present in Body: The Perpetual Spirals of Pleasure and Power, 1997), dates back to her acclaimed feature on the late-1920s Mexican Cristero war, *De todos modos Juan te llamas* (Whatever You Do, You Lose; 1974), and her award-winning, pre-"Frida Mania" documentary, *Frida Kahlo* (1971). The filmmaker, one of the first women, and the only female survivor, to enter UNAM's film school in its early years (the National University's "CUEC," or Centro Universitario de Estudios Cinematográficos), is both heir to Matilde Landeta's extraordinary professional career and a one-woman vanguard of the new university-trained filmmakers.[98] In addition to formal film study and training in dramatic writing, her education encompasses the schooling in theater, music, and world literature that began in her parents' artistic home long before she inaugurated her university career. To date, she holds some forty national and international prizes for her work. In August 2000, in celebration of what she liked to think of as the "silver anniversary of my marriage with filmmaking," the Cineteca Nacional honored her in an *"Homenaje a Marcela Fernández Violante y Retrospectiva Fílmica."* In 2000–2001 she was at work on her newest film, *De piel de víbora* (From Snake Skin), produced by IMCINE (Instituto Mexicano de Cinematografía, the national production company). To judge from a carefully completed script that departs significantly from Patricia Rodríguez's 1998 novella of the same name, Fernández Violante has fashioned a smart woman's response to the increasing *impunidad* of a crime-ridden metropolis.[99]

As filmmaker, scriptwriter, professor, essayist, and union leader, Fernández Violante marshals what she calls her creative "ángeles y demonios" to make art that militates against "oppression, injustice, falsity, and everything that attenuates or corrupts the integrity and dignity to which all human beings have a right."[100] Her civic-minded films are both reminiscent of Landeta's work and representative of new concerns and empathetic strategies. From a wealth of movies she studies and archives in her own home (owing to the scarcity of films available for sustained screenings) the filmmaker has given life to innovative works that follow Landeta and constitute the crest of the second wave of Mexican women's filmic productions.

Like Allison Anders, Marcela Fernández Violante is interested in how violence operates in movies. For the prolific Mexican director of a quarter-century of Mexican cinema the violence featured in some seventy years of filmmaking has been naturalized by sheer force of repetition. One section of Chapter Five analyzes *De cuerpo presente* to illustrate how the documentary denaturalizes what commercial melodramas have regarded as the manifest destiny of movie violence. I demonstrate how the filmmaker uses these films' excesses excessively, showing her viewers by sheer force of satirical repetition that, however manifest, violence need not be destiny. Bloody revolution, represented in mainstream melodramas as wars between the sexes, might have incited citizens to become dutiful daughters and stalwart sons of the paternalistic State, or, as in Fernández Violante's new paradigm, women and men might have joined battles both to support *and* to upset the national family romance.

In this pellucid perversion of Mexican cinema's apparently static moral realm Fernández Violante succeeds in documenting Foucauldian "perpetual spirals of pleasure and power" that testify to the multifaceted ethics of even the most monolithic movies. Employing some of the same overblown filmic strategies to reveal her view of complexity as did the sardonic Luis Buñuel in his semi-serious, solidly satirical Mexican films, Fernández Violante melodramatizes filmmaking itself.[101] While Buñuel's intertextual tales referred somewhat slyly to the body of Mexican cinema, Fernández Violante's *De cuerpo presente* is that body incarnate, the film's very title an homage to the way a deceased person is referred to in a requiem mass. In her movie-about-movies, the award-winning director of seven fictional features and three documentaries personifies the product of seventy years of filmmaking and imagines that embodiment as a character in a morality (screen)play. Further in harmony with a Buñuelian world view, that representation of the regime of ethics is marked by constant interrogation of any high-ground claims to sacred legitimacy. There's nothing in her film claiming Mexico as "one nation under God" (an article of U.S. faith that some Mexicans, including President Vicente Fox, still long to nationalize). There's no casual representation of a Church and State alliance (implicit and explicit in mainstream films, the Mexican Constitution notwithstanding). Constructed as a critical allegory of the Christian mythos embodied in melodrama, there's not an unexamined *Ave Maria,* or an unconsidered cross, or a deity or a demon that escapes *De cuerpo presente*'s analysis of heavily laden signifiers of the secularized sacred. Instead, the laic requiem melodrama narrates a fable about new ways of envisioning morality and community: Mexico as a nation of manifold souls living under—and yet also testing, questioning, examining, and revolting against—the remnants of centuries-old divine right.

◩

In their own ways, all the arbiters of cultural citizenship I study here voice such concerns. In post-revolutionary and post-rebellion society, who wields moral authority to govern? By what means does power legitimate its might? How are citizens incorporated (or not)—and how do they figure themselves—into the national imagination? One hundred years of Mexamerican filmmakers have variously entertained these ideas. This book looks at four directors who found these issues central to their creations, and who crafted their films to address spectators and other movie makers engaged, however unevenly, in the drama of celluloid nationalism.

PART I

Post-Revolutionary Mexico

CHAPTER ONE

────────── ◨ ──────────

Re-Birth of a Nation:
On Mexican Movies,
Museums, and María Félix

Nation-building rhetoric of post-revolutionary Mexico is a symphony of patriotism, "our" indigenous heritage, and the sanctity of Mexican womanhood. Representations of the emergent state inform both elite and popular culture, from the novel to the ballad, but nationalism's voice resonates most powerfully in the vernacular of mass culture. Nation, race, and gender do not simply lie secluded in celluloid patriotism; in Mexican productions of the 1940s these discourses are absolutely central to film and its promotional apparatus. The so-called Golden Age of Mexican Nationalist cinema, emanating from a Golden Age of Mexican post-war regeneration, is renowned for its representations of legions of stylized Indians, their social conditions artfully explicated by teary-eyed *señoritas,* themselves variously inscribed as cultural mediators or idealized as Indian maidens. Deploying the conventions of melodrama, filmmakers like Emilio Fernández aestheticized the indigenous and fetishized the feminine in an attempt to gather all Mexicans under the banner of a unified national subject (Figs. 1.1 and 1.2).

The tensions between these "potential citizens" and the potent elite formed one of the uncontested premises of Mexican Golden Age cinema.[1] In Mexican political melodramas, the monumental staging of the promise of civilization and the threat of barbarism was rarely as directly represented as it was in the manifestos of destiny portrayed in Hollywood's contemporaneous films. Where all stripes of Hollywood's "cowboys and Indians" alternately civilized

FIGURE 1.1. The unified national subject: *María Candelaria*'s "colorful natives." Courtesy Cineteca Nacional.

FIGURE 1.2. Fernández's fetishized feminine: María Candelaria's face on another's nude form. Courtesy Cineteca Nacional.

and sacked each other and the land they lived upon, potential and powerful citizens alike often engaged in direct hand-to-hand combat without benefit of intervention—divine, feminine, or otherwise. The Mexican movie manifesto decreed a difference. Many 1940s films could have been launched as was the 1943 *Doña Bárbara:* a boatman powering civilization up-river into barbarous territory cannot even begin the journey without rhetorically asking his passenger, a lawyer named Santos Luzardo, "With whom do we travel? With God!"[2] But it was not only God and legal saints like Luzardo who mediated cinematic civilization and savagery. In a land where powerful politicos faced off barbarous masses, Mexican *caudillos* and Indians duked it out with the divine benediction of the feminine. From *la virgen María* to María Félix, female arbitration determined the process, if not always the outcome, of the filmic representation of Mexico's national project (Fig. 1.3).

In the 1990s high-stakes nation-building in Mexico reopened the debate on the meaning of civilization. Changes in the constitution, which had been virtually untouched since its drafting in 1917, began to legally enfranchise (but not necessarily empower) groups ranging from indigenous people to clerics. Concurrently, a centuries-old "potential citizenry" claimed the voice of its birthright. Challenging commemorations of "The Discovery of 1492," for instance, representatives from Mexico's many Indian communities addressed the quincentenary from an indigenous perspective. Celebrations of "Civilization" were recast as celebrations of civilizations' "500 Years of Resistance" to colonization. On the religious front, decades of enforced clerical silence on national politics, stemming from nineteenth-century edicts ensuring the separation of Church and State, ended with the political incorporation of the clergy. More and more, "civilization," as a polemic, has become disputed territory.

In addition to the interpretive struggles waged within national borders, extraterritorial space and the domain of foreign policy have also become sites for articulating the significance of civilization. In the early 1990s such debates informed and were informed by arguments for and against the Free Trade Agreement, which pitted proponents of the technological "civilization" of Mexico against trade protectionists who argued that so-called technological primitivism makes both ecological and economic sense. When Mexican citizens wage these kinds of battles transnationally, both from within Mexico and throughout the Diaspora, campaigns to civilize potential citizens become as complex as Vasconcelos's 1920s strategies were straightforward.

In response to these different interests' bids for the power to elucidate national priorities, the Mexican government contextualized the nation's glorious past and promising present in myriad new scenarios. A blitz of officially sponsored Mexican art exhibitions in the United States showcased the most strident of these representations. The enormously popular "Mexico: Splendors

FIGURE 1.3. Consecrated from on high: *La virgen María* (Félix) in *Río Escondido*. Courtesy Cineteca Nacional.

of Thirty Centuries," and its satellite exhibitions, exported a carefully framed national portrait intentionally designed to engender U.S. favor for the Free Trade pact.[3] Within Mexico the ruling elite's drives to save-and-civilize the natives took on a slightly different characteristic: art exhibitions were constructed to appeal to middle-class Mexicans who were wavering between possibilities for new civilization (Free Trade and big business) and old barbarism (protected production and small collectives).

While traditional displays like "Splendors" do bounce back to Mexico in the form of catalogues pyramided in department store windows,[4] other exhibitions of the national patrimony are part of the national product marketed within the nation. Removed from standard U.S. exhibiting practice, a new genre of what we might call national "art spectacles" is bringing the empowered elite and a "citizenry" evermore reaching its potential into direct contact. Paralleling the 1940s model of filmic feminine intervention between marginalized groups and the State (no better dramatized than by María Félix's rural schoolteacher in *Río Escondido*), is an astonishing new phenomenon (no better exemplified than by María Félix herself): flesh-and-blood "apparitions" of 1940s film stars and commentators who attempt to connect the contemporary Nation-State with a wide cross-section of its national subjects. These live performances use the authoritative space of the museum to unite film festivals, appearances of media stars, bandwagoning politicians, and social critics with fine art collections. Museum catalogues further promote the liaison; film scholars and art critics sanctify the union in public talks; journalists sensationalize the rest.

The reanimated rhetoric on salvation-through-civilization sparked by these multidisciplinary forums bears uncanny resemblance to Golden Age cinema's proselytizing of fifty years ago. The apotheosis of today's "endangered" indigenous peoples is now the stuff of museum exhibits much as it once informed the theses of Emilio Fernández's films.[5] Yet collections gathered anywhere from the National Museum of Anthropology in Mexico City to the Cultural Center in Tijuana seem to privilege the survival of "authentic" indigenous artifacts over the survival of "authentic" Indians. Museums' differentiation between Mexico's indigenous heritage (regarded as a valuable component of the national patrimony) and actual life in Mexico for indigenous people (seen as "inevitably bound for extinction") echoes old save-the-natives discourses that function on assimilation models.

Nowhere has this pattern been more forcefully borne out than in the exhibition-as-spectacle hybrid, exemplified most strikingly by film diva María Félix and cultural critic Carlos Monsiváis. Crowning a busy program at the Tijuana Cultural Center in the summer of 1990, Félix came to town—as she had done months before in other parts of the Republic, and as she would do months later on international television—to inaugurate French-Russian artist

Antoine Tzapoff's idealized portraiture of "fast-disappearing" northern indigenous peoples. Her mediation of the event—effected by her presence, a retrospective of her most nationalistic films, Monsiváis's homage to her career, her article in the exhibition catalogue, and a flood of interviews in Tijuana newspapers—illustrates how the 1940s rhetoric of Mexico's post-revolutionary nationalism and that of the country's more recent expressions of nationalism are inextricably bound together by old discourses on the nature of nation and civilization. However differently inscribed in new cultural practices, Mexico's official nation-building strategies continue to be dependent upon cultural arbiters, whose interventions between dominant and subordinated groups paradoxically serve to enthrone power structures while at the same time enshrining the powerless. It is one such arbiter, the Janus-faced Félix, Fernández's fetishized Mother of Indigenous Mexico, and alternately the State's fetishizer of the Indians, with whom this chapter now embarks.

PROTAGONISTS OF THE NATIONAL NARRATIVE

When María Félix first transfixed film audiences, she was twenty-nine years old, had two mediocre melodramas to her credit, and was starring in *Doña Bárbara*.[6] In the role that would transform her career, Félix was established as both a respected actress and an overdetermined icon. Félix—and her director, the fan magazines, and the critics—fashioned actress and icon almost literally from the same cloth. Doña María adopted Doña Bárbara's riding breeches, took on the fictional character's interest in witchcraft, and made herself over in the image of *La devoradora*, the devourer of men (Fig. 1.4). For her part, Doña Bárbara, soul of the untamed Venezuelan soil, became something of a naturalized Mexican citizen. As María Félix's Mexican face superimposed itself upon the waters of the Orinoco, that landscape—"farther away than the Cunaviche, farther than Meta, farther still than the Cinaruco, farther than forever"[7]—relocated just somewhat farther beyond the Prado Cinema in Mexico City. Venezuela's problems became Veracruz's solutions.

By 1943 Mexico was capturing the Spanish-speaking film market and nationalizing everything in the process. Mexico's Dolores del Río was no longer Hollywood's exotic Brazilian/"half-breed"/Gypsy/Polynesian; repatriated after twenty-seven films made "in the Mecca of movies," her roles in *Flor silvestre* (1943) and *María Candelaria* (1943)—the first a panegyric of the Revolution, the latter a romanticization of indigenous culture—assured her a place in the pantheon of national film heroes (Fig. 1.5). Others who had left Mexico in the 1920s returned. Filmmaker Emilio *"Indio"* Fernández, again, allegedly encouraged by his Los Angeles encounter with exiled president Adolfo de la Huerta—"Build our own cinema, Emilio . . . Mexican cinema"—went back to his homeland with

FIGURE 1.4. Félix as Doña Bárbara, "the devourer of men." Courtesy Cineteca Nacional.

FIGURE 1.5. Dolores del Río, 1933: Hollywood's exotic Brazilian. Score from *Flying Down to Rio*.

the realization "that it was possible to create a Mexican cinema, with our own actors and our own stories, without having to photograph *gringos* or *gringas* or to tell stories that had nothing to do with our people."[8]

During the presidencies of Manuel Ávila Camacho (1940–1946) and Miguel Alemán (1946–1952), films premiered in the capital at the astonishing rate of one per week. This boom represented a threefold increase over the number of movies produced in the 1930s. In contrast with the '30s productions, films of the '40s relied more heavily upon a star system illuminated by actresses and actors whose symbolic significance remained relatively stable. In addition to Félix's "woman without a soul" and Dolores del Río's "exotic *ejido* flower," Sara García played the eternal Mexican mother; Pedro Armendáriz, the stalwart leader of men; Jorge Negrete, romantic *hacendado;* Pedro Infante, working-class hero; Gloria Marín, classic sweetheart; Marga López, taxi-dancing prostitute; Cantinflas, tongue-tripping interloper; Andrea Palma, mysterious cabaret goddess. As the protagonists in these films varied only slightly, so were the plots equally predictable. Yet reworked themes and archetypal characters did nothing to prevent eager crowds from patronizing the cinema. In the wake of a revitalized allegiance to things Mexican—fostered in part by previous President Lázaro Cárdenas's (1934–1940) nationalization of the oil companies, programs in land redistribution, and experiments with "socialistic" education,[9] and in part by the national pride inspired by relative Mexican technological affluence during the presidencies of Ávila Camacho and Alemán—film audiences flocked to features on the Revolution, urbanization, pastoral life, national history, and Indian communities.

To a remarkable extent the entire apparatus of movie production and distribution was saturated with the rhetoric and the representations of nationalism. Supporting the cinema's ideological didacticism, the illustrated press teamed up with advertisers and film stars to promote goods that would enhance the image of Mexico as a nation among nations. *Negro y Blanco y Labores,* a popular movie-and-sewing magazine designed for women, employed María Félix's image to introduce a cosmetic line that assured the triumph of the actress and rewarded the "efforts of her able Mexican directors." The star of *El monje blanco* (The White Monk; 1945), her face composed behind her "Filma Cake compac," triumphed in her role as a most "natural and human"—but especially Mexican—protagonist (Figs. 1.6 and 1.7). The makeup, a "Creation of Hollywood," was heralded as yet another triumph "that also serves the stars of our National Cinema as well as the Mexican woman." Smoothed uniformly over the complexions of humanized movie actresses and glorified Mexican women, "Missuky Social Makeup" staged itself as the great equalizer. Félix was not the only national patrimony. Beautified by Missuky, stars *and* spectators alike were prepared to triumph in their roles as protagonists of the national narrative.[10]

56

FIGURE 1.6. María Félix nationalizes Hollywood. *Negro y Blanco*, December 1945.

FIGURE 1.7. Mapy Cortés exoticizes Mexico. *México al Día*, March 1943.

CELLULOID PATRIOTISM

In addition to creating consumers and endowing women with a sense of national purpose, Golden Age Cinema and its promotional appurtenances initiated a nostalgic remembrance of the past. Modernity, however desired, was to be pursued with a backward look. Post-revolutionary nation-formation meant taking in the Revolution, its aftermath, and the future as all of a piece. Emilio Fernández's *Río Escondido* encapsulated these time-frames as it moved María Félix through Mexico City's modern presidential palace to an outlaw's municipal palace in the desert. Impediments to national progress, thematized in the film, lay in the unsolved problems of "primitive" Mexico: lawlessness, illiteracy, disease, "spiritual poverty" and its material equivalent. In Fernández's resurrection of 1920s nationalism, self-empowered and self-serving political henchmen who would carve up the nation into personal fiefdoms were as uncivilized as the savage politicos whose greed had forced the Revolution. As Vasconcelos had proclaimed with his literacy campaigns in the 1920s, as President Lázaro Cárdenas had seconded with his education programs in the 1930s, and as Emilio Fernández affirmed with his sententious 1940s films, the flame of the sacred lamp of learning, aloft in a rural schoolteacher's hand, was the only fire with which the fire of the barbarous, incendiary torch of war could be fought. By 1947, with public faith in old civilizing strategies beginning to fade, Félix's mediating light was the beacon that Fernández used to illuminate the triumphs of the past as well as the path to progress.

As *Río Escondido*'s opening statement is superimposed over Leopoldo Méndez's engravings, spectators are presented with textual and iconographic reminders of Mexico's "bloody past" as well as the nation's march "toward a superior and more glorious future." The first of ten images foregrounds the ignited torch that Félix, on the express orders of her President, will extinguish. Subsequent engravings preview the story of *Río Escondido*. The print that most closely evokes the spirit of the film (which was originally entitled *The Rural School Teacher*) features the *maestra* with her young charges, gazing at a portrait of nineteenth-century President Benito Juárez, "who," as Félix will later intone to the village children, "was an Indian, just like you" (cover photograph). In Fernández's hands Méndez's depictions of the need for indigenous peoples' education become reminders of Diego Rivera's earlier monumental representations of the nation's struggle toward universal literacy. To further underscore this connection, Gabriel Figueroa's camera dramatically sweeps Rivera's national palace murals while the anthropomorphized voice of the Bell of Dolores (the symbol of Independence) majestically moves spectator and protagonist into the opening sequences of the film.[11]

We immediately begin to learn, as one engraving foreshadowed, just "how immense is the will" of the "little teacher." Amid Rivera's representations of the "triumphant and terrible" history of Mexican civilization, Rosaura (Félix) pauses with us on the palace staircase to contemplate those who went before her: armies of teachers who formed the backbone of the Mexican educational system and the mainstay of its supporting rhetoric. About to contend with the results of some of the same oppressions illustrated in the stairwell, Rosaura, who suffers from an incurable disease, seems to take sustenance from these reminders of her predecessors as she hurries to receive instructions about her special teaching appointment in the desert village of Río Escondido.

Rosaura's reflections prompt me to pause here and consider the triumphant and terrible history of those schoolteachers, who had proven to be both indispensable and problematic to administrations wanting to recuperate traditional models of a national family. Years of sending strong women off to reconstruct the post-revolutionary nation had taken their toll. The effort to "put to rights a world turned upside down by the Revolution," as Jean Franco has explained, called for a kind of institutionalized patriarchy, where "the broken family, the cult of violence, and the independent 'masculinized' woman [had] to be transformed into a new holy family in which women accede[d] voluntarily to their own subordination not to a biological father but to a paternal state."[12] As agents of social change, the teachers were ultimately antithetical to the long-term goals of this project; consequently their primary service to nation-building had to be carefully controlled. What is interesting is how this control was exercised through representation. With Fernández these historical teachers' inherent contradictions are resolved within the fictional person of Rosaura, whose days in the province are numbered. It is precisely the little teacher's terminal illness that allows her to board a north-bound train to fulfill her destiny. Rosaura can act outside the familial paradigm since her impending death assures her separation from and subordination to the paternal state she serves. As the martyred *maestra*, she will not disrupt the restoration of the post-revolutionary family. Her revolutionary actions will not be regarded as those of a "real" woman, wife, or mother, and her maternal ministrations will not be seen as revolutionary, but as a part of the great new melodrama, the Revolution.

Fernández mandates Rosaura's concession to the patriarchal nation from the first. Upon ascending those stairs in the national palace, she hurries to the office of none other than the Head of State, President Miguel Alemán. There Manuel Dondé (mistaken by some critics as Alemán himself[13]) outlines the nation's nationalist agenda to a feminized Félix. Gone are the breeches of the "devourer of men," replaced by the more ubiquitous black *rebozo* and concomitant feminine tears of sympathy for the country, the Indians, and the "good Mexicans" she must serve (Fig. 1.8). Fernández's choice of Félix—so

FIGURE 1.8. Female arbitration of the nationalist project: Félix about to receive her presidential mandate in *Río Escondido*. Courtesy Cineteca Nacional.

long identified as a "savage man-hater"—works especially well to underscore the transformation of the independent woman to dutiful charge of the state. When Félix trudges off on her journey to the Sonoran outpost, accompanied by a celestial choir, undulating Mexican flag, and images of Diego Rivera's murals, her apotheosis begins. In the course of the film she takes on the virginal role in the new holy family. "Adopting" three village children whose mother has been felled by smallpox, she restores Benito Juárez and a map of the Republic to their rightful places in the reconsecrated schoolhouse; she reempowers a weakened Church to support the Indians; she conquers evil incarnate in the body of a would-be rapist while she herself remains pure; and ultimately she dies of a heart condition, but not before hearing the President of Mexico's grateful benediction. In the final footage the celestial chorus renews audiences' spirits as the little teacher's hagiography is etched across her headstone.

Representation of native people in *Río Escondido* is no less orchestrated. From a filmmaker who is proud of his Kickapoo blood, but who insists on "the civilizing influence" of elite culture,[14] we are presented with "idealiza-

tions" of "some poor little Indians" who must be saved from barbarism, ignorance, despotic *caciques*, and wayward religious leadership.[15] *Río Escondido*
delivers in celluloid what its director promised in interviews: a vision of "the
indigenous person as the purest, most authentic, most beautiful [being], pos-
sessed with superior traits."[16] In Fernández's patriotic-pamphlet style the vil-
lagers' significance is coded as a kind of visual ideogram, a "non-arbitrary
sign,"[17] whose meaning, "truth," and "authenticity" are traced not to any reality of the Seri, Yaqui, Pima, or Papago groups of the Sonoran desert, but back
to indigenist discourses launched by Mexico City philosophers in the 1910s
and 1920s.

One congruence between Indian "truth" and reality did exist. Neither
Fernández's fictionalizations nor the real people he represented were legally
incorporated into the Mexican national fabric. In film and in fact, as far as the
government was concerned, indigenous people were discursive categories and
not legal entities. For example, as Rodolfo Stavenhagen points out, the writers of the 1917 Constitution acted "as if, with formal juridical structure, they
could erase a social reality that made them uncomfortable."[18] The Constitu-
tionalists superseded legislation—"Indian people do not even appear in any
part of the Constitution"—with the rhetoric and practice of a "politics of
assimilation."[19] Throughout the first half of the twentieth century this policy
was enforced by literacy programs legislated only for Spanish-speaking rural
populations. Indians were assimilated, at least on paper, into a mass of undifferentiated *campesinos,* or "country people." By disregarding sociolinguistic
differences between Indians and mestizos through the practice of all-inclusive
laws, those who would assimilate native peoples into the national culture suc-
ceeded, instead, in assuring their political disenfranchisement.

As "Indian" became increasingly synonymous with "unincorporated
national," devoid of any other legal status, the intent of the government's liberal paternalism became commensurately clear. Through representation or
rhetoric, Indian peoples' cultural, linguistic, and political sovereignty—and to
a certain extent, that of the rural schoolteachers sent to "Mexicanize the Mexicans"—was erased. Symbolic erasure was closely followed by what Stavenhagen calls the "political negation of the indigenous person," and the subsequent loss of "a legally recognized territorial base." While indigenous groups
did own part of their ancestral lands, Stavenhagen argues that their unlegis-
lated possession was responsible for some of the most egregious abuses of
indigenous territories.

Although Fernández never suggests that Río Escondido's indigenous
populations have a legal right to their land, he does rage against territorial
abuse as an example of moral injustice. While the evil municipal president
controls the amount of water available to the village Indians, at issue is his
unequal distribution of the resource, not his unjust possession of water rights.

That this *cacique* oversteps the boundaries of his "legal" ownership is only demonstrated when Rosaura fails to civilize him, to humanize him into respecting the Indians and permitting their moral development through education. In Río Escondido it is only the abuse of power—not its usurpation and accumulation—against which the little schoolteacher has been sent to fight. However much Fernández praised Cárdenas-style "socialism," *Río Escondido's* politics are more in accord with the liberal paternalism of the 1920s. It is a morally indignant Fernández, not a politically astute filmmaker, whose righteous rhetoric determines the actions—and their significance—of the women, Indians, and evil *caciques* who wage the national holy crusade.

MUSEUM CURIOSITIES

> The museum is the ceremonial throne of patrimony, the place where [the national treasure] is kept and celebrated, where the semiotic order—used by hegemonic groups to organize the museum—is reproduced. To enter a museum is not merely to enter a building and look at objects, but rather to enter into a ritualized system of social interaction.[20]

In September 1990, forty-two years after *Río Escondido* debuted in Mexico City, the film and its star made the trek to northern Mexico to bring "culture" to what many capital-dwellers have generally regarded as a cultural wasteland: that Yaqui/Yanqui/Mexican/U.S. border outpost called Tijuana.[21] Crowds wrapped around the monolithic globe-shaped museum in the Cultural Center to await the arrival of María Félix, whose official duty was to inaugurate the opening of Antoine Tzapoff's exhibit of indigenous portraiture. Félix, winner of that year's Presidential Prize for her service to the nation, was greeted with all the fanfare befitting the Indian princesses she portrays in several of Tzapoff's works. Aging film fans dressed to the nines, rivaled only by youthful transvestites in full Félix drag, ignored the ninety-degree heat to pay proper respect to the star. A Chicano cultural historian reminisced about his aunts' love affairs with Félix films. A Tijuana priest murmured (ir)reverently that if he couldn't have an audience with the goddess, he hoped at least to touch the hem of her garment. Interrupting the excited flow of devotees and art patrons filing into the museum, underemployed Indians and mestizos hawked Adams's Chiclets. Once inside, visitors were greeted by an enormous *Portrait of María Félix, Riding Amazon-Style upon a Rhinoceros*. Cameras, held aloft by the crowd, recorded what they could. Carlos Monsiváis, the nation's preeminent chronicler, added to the inaugural speeches. *La Doña* smiled and waved graciously. Tzapoff bowed his head in an attitude of prayer.

Patrons fawned over Félix as they shuffled through the exhibit in her wake. Shortly after the ribbon-cutting ceremony, strains of ex-husband Agustín Lara's "María Bonita" urged an elite minority toward the reception area and away from the paintings. The public stood gawking outside the cordoned-off area, craning to get a glance of that arched eyebrow. Between breathy dialogues about the actress's film career, one could hear serious students of art commenting on the "remarkable authenticity and overarching reality" of the portraits. Indeed, the Amazon Queen looked a lot like Félix in the final shot of *Enamorada* (Fernández's 1946 nationalization of *The Taming of the Shrew*), and the indigenous male figures bore an unmistakable resemblance to their creator, would-be Indian Antoine Tzapoff. In the unlikely event that spectators misinterpreted the meaning of such visual organizing myths, Fernando Gamboa's catalogue description clarified. In Tzapoff's work, "Man is converted into a hero, woman into an allegory, parallel to this magnificent and nostalgic world in extinction. Never, perhaps, has the preoccupation of ethnographic and ethnological exactitude resulted in more faithful representation in painting."[22]

This exaltation of Seri, Yaqui, Kickapoo, Pima, Tarahumara, and other northern indigenous people into male heroes or female allegories—in the images of Santa María and San Antoine—served to obliterate the cultural and economic context of these peoples and organize their symbolic extinction. Tzapoff's foregrounding of nostalgia matched museum curators' directives to funnel visitors quickly into the inner spaces of the ethnographic preserve and away from the waiting vendors hunched outside the great domed museum. In the uninterrupted amble of patrons passing before representations of "purity" and "authenticity" something was lost, underscored by the comment of a European tourist who wondered out loud why the Indians couldn't be encouraged to save themselves through judicious family planning, education and health programs, and, I suppose, morally uplifting events like the one we were attending.

The initial part of the question had merit: *why?* Why, indeed, are these groups disappearing? Local Tijuana newspapers, which might have engaged in thoughtful speculation, were merely awash with what Monsiváis, on the occasion of another Félix fête, called the "language of cinemaphilic fanaticism combined with official bread-and-circus cant."[23] Félix, icon of the dutiful daughter of the State, was deployed in these articles and in the accompanying catalogue of the exhibit to mediate the significance of the art work, the meaning of her film retrospective, and the fact of the fast-disappearing northern Indian groups. Distinctly absent from such pieces as the diva's contribution, "The Commerce of the Scalp," were questions about the reasons twentieth-century indigenous people might be disappearing. Save-the-natives rhetoric had the same feel as a Vasconcelos asking a Rivera to paint "Indians, more

Indians" on the walls of government buildings. In Tzapoff's hyperrealistic portraiture, as in Vasconcelos's desires for the same, what was required to be preserved was the nostalgic representation of Indian people. As Fernando Gamboa's essay ecstatically explains, "The painting of Tzapoff turns its back on the influence of postmodern art. It launches its effects of shadows within its frames [of] extreme realism, and proposes idealizations." Tzapoff's undeniably striking creations of "a world bound for extinction" do inspire great concern. But that concern is for what has gone unproposed in his paintings. His nostalgic idealizations promote a premature narrative closure and inhibit other proposals and the telling of different stories. In turning his back on the influences of postmodern possibility, Tzapoff turns away from the very heroes he would save. "Authentic" and "pure," his mythic Mexicans find safe ground only in the museum, the "ceremonial throne of the national patrimony."

On behalf of the exhibit's curators, writer Salvador Elizondo (son of *Río Escondido*'s producer of the same name) supports Tzapoff's reductive narrative with his resigned acceptance of "the inevitability" of Seri Indian extinction. Elizondo simultaneously asks that we "keep in mind . . . that the Seri tribe is presently reduced to less than 500 individuals" and subsequently that we appreciate *"the value of a scientific testimony of enormous importance."*[24] Elizondo's praise of Tzapoff's representations of "archetypes rather than individuals" contributes to the trend of "collecting natives" as so much scientific data, or so many museum pieces—a disturbing practice that ultimately suppresses the meaning of testimonies to the disappearance of indigenous people.

It is instructive to contrast the discourse of recognized native sons, lavishly catalogued with other artifacts of the museum, with that of the author(ity)less newspapers positioned outside the influential sphere of the Cultural Center. On the day the Tzapoff exhibit opened, an article without a byline appeared on the back page of *La Jornada,* in the space often reserved for Cristina Pacheco's politically provocative short stories.[25] The Mexico City daily, unlike the Tijuana press, which featured Félix's figure in "Amazon" garb, ran a photograph of an aging Seri woman who would have had no place in Tzapoff's "allegories of womanhood." The accompanying article, without making any claims for the kind of "extreme realism" that Tzapoff achieves, nevertheless begins to outline some of the very real forces threatening Seri sovereignty.

According to the boldface headline, the Seris "Reject Investors' Proposals." From the outset, readers are assured that this indigenous group will hang onto its ancestral lands, and that neither the Mexico City investor (Televisa's deceptively named Víctor Hugo O'Farrell) nor the United States's Gulf y Pacific Seafood Company will seize control of the fishing area that the Seris, perhaps prophesying the worst, have called "The Sacrifice." Thus, whether or not the dangers posed to the Seris by Oklahoma or Mexico City investors are borne out is not immediately at issue. What is of vital testimonial importance in view of the "inevitable" indigenous extinction is the documentation and publication of some of the ways that Indian lands—constitutionally unprotected, as Stavenhagen reminds us—are at risk. By writing the unwritten, *La Jornada* does not necessarily shore up the Seris's listing fishing industry, but it does interrupt the resigned fatalism provoked by nostalgic nationalism and discourages reductive "saving-of-the-natives" as artifact collection.

We can chart María Félix's carefully constructed rhetoric somewhere between elite and popular discourses of the new indigenism. Carlos Monsiváis observes that Mexican film divas often occupy that place "between the sword and the shawl" maintained "again and again between *la* beautiful *señorita* and the Long-Suffering Mexican Woman."[26] The space between a rock and a hard place, Octavio Paz had proclaimed by the end of the 1940s, is the place of nothingness, the domain of *la Chingada*.[27] As feminist scholarship has countered, that place is the site of Malintzin, of cultural mediation, and of zealously controlled discourse on gender and race.[28] Before Doña Bárbara, Félix is Doña Nobody; her "meaning" is manifested only as she takes on the significance of the characters she portrays. This transformative process legitimates Félix's persona and establishes her as a cultural mediator whose discourse will be controlled by the kind of roles she is permitted to play. When the actress, representing herself, comes to Tijuana to bear witness, her testimony is bounded and authenticated by audience identification of an extensive history of María as "*la* beautiful *señorita* and the Long-Suffering Mexican Woman." But can a woman tell her own story? Is Félix—film icon and art patron, self-fashioned and other-constructed—a reliable witness?[29]

In recent decades, in full view of the powerful testimonies that women are sharing—"masculinized," politicized women, the likes of whom fight in revolutions throughout Latin America—the control of women's stories is of increasing interest to those who would control nations. In the 1990s control of Félix's representation, as well as what that representation in turn represents, becomes an extension of the control exercised over Rosaura/María as the national evangelist first made her way into "uncivilized" Indian territory. In Tijuana the sinister implications of control are masked by the deftness of a postmodern turn of events: it is Carlos Monsiváis, in inimitable style, who steps in to tell María's tale, to frame her narrative, and to introduce *Río Escondido* to an audience just back from the Indian exhibit. The seriousness of the catalogue yields to the often tongue-in-cheek playfulness of Monsiváis's analysis, but the sometimes inseparable panegyric and parody combine to reinscribe Félix with the same aura of emblematic power and testimonial credibility endowed by movie presidents and real rulers alike.

How can I complain when chronicler and crowd are having such a swell time? But Monsiváis, master of ceremonies, is also the indisputable master of the narrative. The power of the image is the only story Félix controls. She takes her cues from his lines, cocks her head just so, leans attentively into his praise, *"surrounded by a wealth of adjectives in the manner of necklaces or votive lamps: beautiful, primordial, splendid devourer, cruel, dominant, lucid, exceptional."*[30] Monsiváis talks and the audience pays heed, paying homage to *la Doña* in bursts of applause as he pauses, breathless with adulation. He speaks in the same hushed tones he remembers a young fan using on another occasion, *"with the emphasis of someone who employs prayer to the saints: praising, adoring, admiring."* His narrative and his presentation testify to an ultimate truth in his written words: *In the religion of the cinema, to be a "goddess of the screen" is a literal burden. Each gaze cast upon María Félix scatters incense and myrrh, each comment is a prayer, each exclamation a laic rosary. Her essence does not lie in her* presentation *of self but rather in the* apparition *of her being, the renewing miracle of someone who has not given in to the demands of time.* . . . Before the microphone our presenter regards his apparition and continues reverently, *"She is, why avoid the word, a myth. And in her case, for once the term is justified in all senses of the word."*

Monsiváis, as expert in "mythography" as he claims Tzapoff to be, both mystifies and demystifies mythic creations. He can render genuine homage and reveal falsity at the same time; he is the first to point out how myth-making works. Yet however nimbly he positions himself (he has a way with words), whether constructing or deconstructing the myth, Monsiváis *has his way* with words. He honors, he adores, he analyzes: María is Mexico, María is the Virgin Incarnate, María is the Goddess of Desire.

At the end of the hour-long review of her film career, María arches her body in satisfied exhaustion, and speaks: "So much life recounted in such a short time. To tell the truth, I'm in pieces." Grateful and proud, the exquisite remnants of a woman allow an embrace. Renewed, she rises to salute her now-frenzied audience. At her side Antoine Tzapoff gazes mutely into the distance like one of the sanctified Indians in his portraits. Monsiváis joins them. María's triple incarnation of the State, the Church, and Mexican Womanhood reflects in the trinity embodied on the stage. Monsiváis as (official) storyteller, Tzapoff as (officially recognized) deifier of Indians, and Félix as (officially promoted) icon form a new kind of holy family. The audience—drenched by the kind of religious fervor such a manifestation brings about, sated by expressions of patriotism inspired by the national nature of the event, and moved by the erotic tension released in the Goddess's waving hand—can do nothing more than burst into spontaneous applause. And the ovation, as the chronicler himself put it, *was thunderous.*

Monsiváis's almost parodic staging of the making of María Félix can claim a place in the tradition of rhetorical fictions of twentieth-century Mexico, and within discursive practices beyond the border. In light of what *Van-*

ity Fair has called the "Mexico Mania" engendered by "Splendors of Thirty Centuries," novelist Edmund White interviewed the "Diva Mexicana" with the intent of explicating her exotic Mexicanness. White's article is remarkable not only in its treatment of María Félix as a kind of endangered species in the eyes of New York museum patrons, but also for the encouragement he obviously gives Félix to tell a particular story of her role in Mexico's national formation. First he remarks upon the actress's transformation from alabaster Creole to Queen of the Indians:

> When she was young, she told me, she was as pale as that white bird Stanislao Lepri painted to represent her. Now, almost as a tribute to Tzapoff's fascination with Indians, she has turned herself into a dark-skinned shaman, all high cheekbones and chiseled features, her dark-reddish hair swept back from the carved arrowhead her face has become.[31]

White next gets his "shaman" to describe the most curious element of her mythic construction. He gives us Félix as National Heroine, speaking about her receipt of the Presidential Prize for her Lifetime of Service to the Nation:

> I kept thinking of my film *Río Escondido*, in which I play a schoolteacher who visits the president to ask him for a favor for her students. My character crossed the great plaza, the Zócalo, just as I did; climbed the stairs of the presidential palace, just like me. But the president she met was fictional, whereas mine was real. And my character had come to ask for something, whereas I was invited to receive.[32]

With these unremarked inclusions of the *Doña's* proud statements, White succeeds in displaying what he called "the artifact Félix has made of herself." Yet I wonder once more if Félix's much-rehearsed testimony is the authentic curio that White would like to showcase. While the writer may have no more ulterior motive for grooming the Félix myth than the desire to tell a compelling story, his interview, like Monsiváis's compelling narrative, images Félix within a rhetoric of nostalgia—whether nationalistic or not—whose discursive power can negate whole populations, to say nothing of a woman who might attempt to testify on their behalf.

"PAÍS MUERTO/SOCIEDAD VIVA"

Sociopolitical conditions in Mexico have changed since the Tijuana, New York, and Los Angeles extravaganzas, but remarkably continuous threads persist in new permutations of old nationalist discourse. After late November 1991, when a repatriated Félix televised her triumphal return from Parisian to Mexican society, Mexican news media became adorned with the face of the septuagenarian actress and patron of the arts. In the first half of December that year, *la Doña* graced the covers of no fewer than six magazines, from weeklies offering pro-government "political commentary" to self-defined "antiestablishment" periodicals that depend upon the nearly nude to sell copy. However styled, Félix continued to be national news, and, as ever since her appearance as Doña Bárbara, her image was deployed to invigorate national pride. For a country, as critic Claudia Schaefer points out, that exported its artistic "Splendors of Thirty Centuries" in efforts to "define and legitimate its national identity," the "Splendor" of Félix in her home court made for a dazzling display of the new sovereign nationalism. "Whether we like it or not," explained my Mexico City cab driver en route to an interview with chronicler Monsiváis, "with *la Doña,* Mexico marches forward." He underscored his point with a nod of his head toward a freshly painted sign on the bricks of a warehouse, the only splendor in a working-class neighborhood. The script could be appreciated for blocks, white letters on a green and red field: "México Marcha Adelante." Satisfied with the textual documentation, the driver continued, "You see. And last week she started fixing up our historic downtown area."

Saving the *centro histórico* from development or dilapidation is indeed yet another of the actress's concerns. Forever aligned with centers of power, continually confused with history, María Félix, Monsiváis insisted that afternoon, *incarnates* the nation. Even, or perhaps especially, in the face of the crisis that he calls "dead nation/living society," Félix, "like the *Virgin de Guadalupe,* doesn't just represent Mexico; she is Mexico." Manifesting herself thirteen days short of that other virgin's feast, Félix miraculously appeared to millions of viewers during a marathon interview with Televisa's Verónica Castro. The actress's save-the-nation pieties were reminiscent of those she deployed with Tzapoff in their Tijuana restoration project. In both venues the seamlessness of Félix-as-México interceded "naturally" between people and State, binding and conflating *pueblo* with *gobierno,* masking, as Schaefer says in a parallel context, "the miseries behind the splendors."

Visual texts link the Tijuana splendors with Televisa's splendid display of the *doña.* The continuum here is transparent. What we were asked to save at the Cultural Center were images—images of Seri, Yaqui, Kickapoo, and Pima people, nationalized as citizens under the unifying portrait of Our Lady of the Rhinoceros. This same "allegory of woman" organizes our visual experience of Félix's Televisa interview (preserved on video and "available at Mexican supermarkets everywhere"), only this time the amazon does battle with those who would allow the *centro histórico* to teeter on the brink of extinction. In addition to the visual referent of Tzapoff's fantasy of Félix as native queen, and beyond the incarnation of the goddess herself (the cameras stage her seated in an ornately gilded chair before her immense Rhino portrait), the common denominator of the Tijuana and Televisa extravaganzas is the demand for the preservation of images of Mexico without much regard for what these symbols represent. Whatever Félix's intentions, whether she is an agent of nostalgic nationalism or merely, as Monsiváis asserted in our conversation, a "consequence" of nationalism run amok, the "[dead] Mexican nation marches forward" only on the strength of warehouse-mounted slogans, through national television evangelism, and by the efforts of museums to preserve the patrimony. However complicit we may be with these representations, surely we can begin to look to sources other than those populated by María Félix's various images for a "living Mexican society" that always and already "marches forward."

Since the quincentennial year the place of the *sociedad viva* is everywhere. Restoration of the nation's historic center has meant more than refurbishing old buildings. Hegemonic groups' organization of old orders in museums and beyond have yielded to the presence of new structures, evidenced in forms as diverse as constitutional amendments or indigenous articulations of the meaning of the millennium. The diffusion of these multivalent discourses has depended not only upon their showcasing through mass media and public spectacle, but upon the polyphonic response all of these events have engendered. With 1992's thoughtful conversations about nation and community in mind, I returned to Tijuana/San Diego to talk with some of the people who had attended the Tzapoff exhibit, and there I discovered visitors' new takes on what they had witnessed two years before.

"I still wear my marvelously cheap copies of Félix couture," one of my transvestite friends told me, "but since her failure to address national economic restoration in favor of local cosmetic gentrification, I've modified my look. Now I ground her light skirts with serious leather boots. You know, to kick up a little controversy, make my own statement." Working-class friends from the housing development where I had spent my Tijuana research summer expressed similar concerns. "I never thought of her as one of those *Chilangas* [here used derisively to describe someone from Mexico City] who didn't give a damn about anything outside the capital," a former neighbor said, "but now I'm not so sure. Fixing up the national *centro histórico* is great, but isn't Tijuana part of the nation? We could use a little fixing too." As spectators, museum patrons, and citizens begin to engage in direct dialogue with each other, obfuscating cultural mediations like María Félix's can be seen for what they are: exercises in monological nation-building.

Interventions in master narratives, as Néstor García Canclini's *Culturas híbridas* reminds us, can reorganize power relations. The idea that monological nationalism (or even a monologue about nationalism's stars) can be displaced has also been dramatized by Elena Poniatowska's interruptive *Todo México*.[33] Very much present as witness and listener, Poniatowska inserts herself into her interviews and literally interrupts the often nationalistic testimonies of "all Mexico." In the spirit of García Canclini's "strategies for entering and leaving modernity," I offer a snippet of Poniatowska's dialogue with María Félix, not to suggest a "solution" to the "problems" of nostalgic nationalism, but to indicate another discursive strategy that disrupts monologic mythmaking:

> FÉLIX: Look, Elenita . . . I'm thrilled with what I'm about to do: go out on the street, stroll through my city—each day it looks prettier. . . . Each day the progress of my nation is more notable. Each day things are better! And all because we've had such great leaders.
>
> PONIATOWSKA: Ah, come on! I wouldn't believe a word of what you're saying even if God Himself told me. Isn't that demagoguery? [34]

Demagoguery! The final, illuminating impertinence stuns. With these words, any residue of my own complacent fascination with the mythic María—arising from years of cinematic pleasure at Mexican movie revival houses, from Monsiváis's witty monologues, and from the thrill of seeing *la Doña* in the flesh—is now completely disturbed. Escaping rhetorical traps, Poniatowska's dialogic interventions encourage an active spectator response so very different from the unconsidered adulation elicited by Tzapoff's or Televisa's exhibitions. In talking back to the Divine Miss Mexico, Poniatowska interrupts, for a precious moment, any unconscious flows of patriots filing into Cultural Centers of Nationalism. If nations, the world's *centros históricos,* are truly to be saved, if women's voices are not to be used against their own efforts, might not a little unsettling dialogue be a good place to begin the interruption of homogeneous, nostalgic nationalism?

CHAPTER TWO

---------- ◪ ----------

Las de abajo:
Matilde Landeta's Mexican Revolution

On the threshold of mid-century industrialization, post-revolutionary Mexico produced discursive melodramas in which the characterization of the nation and the enfranchisement of its citizenry were at stake. From political platitudes to cinematic commonplaces Mestizo Mexico reigned supreme. The "civilization" of the Spaniard and the "fortitude" of the Indian would meld to wrench new triumphs from past tragedies, replacing lethargy with industry, overcoming primitivism with progress. Political melodramas staged by mainstream nationalists came to convey the idea that "Indians"—gloriously pure—nevertheless required civilizing, and that women—purely glorious—were the ones most suited to this nation-building task.

The recruitment of particularly female "architects . . . of the exaltation of [indigenous] Mexico" is strikingly evident in the shorthand of the country's dramatic advertising of its literacy crusades (Fig. 2.1). By 1945, for example, readers of *Negro y Blanco y Labores,* in the midst of articles about glamorous film stars and glamorous home economics for urban ladies and *"las que viven en el campo,"* were urged to find a "compatriot" and teach her to read and write. Adopting the *"mística educativa"* of José Vasconcelos to promote literacy and culture, campaign propaganda, christened "Que México Sepa" (Mexico Must Know), featured the image of a young indigenous woman imploringly handing a primer toward an unseen other. Though we might imagine the girl to be *offering* her services to someone else, the possibility is undermined by the fact of the ad's placement in a magazine designed for literate women. And given the graphics, *Negro y Blanco*'s ideal readers could not have failed to notice the

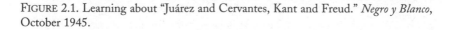

FIGURE 2.1. Learning about "Juárez and Cervantes, Kant and Freud." *Negro y Blanco*, October 1945.

position of the girl's book that nearly slides from the advertisement into their hands: the text's giant alphabet is oriented for the girl's uncomprehending gaze, not as instruction for another. Readers are clearly meant to interpret her wishes as they are meant to decipher the charged icons and text-laden rest of the ad. Melodramatic clarity facilitates the task. Just beyond the horizon of the girl's immediate environment, emphatically marked by palm trees and farm equipment, Modern Mexico awaits, sketched promisingly in an urban sky traced by ghostly images of planes, buildings, bridges, and electrical towers. Progress, it would seem, could only be painted by the efforts of a literacy teacher, here rendered in reduced but commanding stature in the lower left-hand corner of the page where the eye falls to read the crusade's triumphal denouement: "National Campaign against Illiteracy." Such a civilizing figure is urged to action by the dictates of copy that would have nation-builders employ the power of none other than "Juárez and Cervantes," joined, but of course, by "Kant and Freud," in order to realize the future:

> Mexico must know how to read and write; must find out that the world does not end in broken-down shacks, in miserable cornfields. Mexico must learn of other lands, of other worlds; must learn to read the works of the great writers. Must learn who Juárez and Cervantes were. Kant and Freud. When Mexico learns, the dreams of industrialization, of progress, of a luminous life shall become true. You are the architect in this vast plan of the exaltation of Mexico. Begin teaching a compatriot to read and write.

Within this national context and simultaneously critical of its practices, pioneering proto-feminist filmmaker Matilde Landeta directed a trilogy of groundbreaking works that addressed genre, gender, and ethnic politics. *Lola Casanova* (1948), in particular, illustrates the filmmaker's representations of women and indigenous peoples who alternately spoke for hegemony's "civilizing" projects and who voiced resistance to such totalization. Tracing the "melodramatic imagination" that fuels Landeta's projects is the task of this chapter.

PRELUDE

Using the past to make pronouncements about the present, Matilde Landeta's *Lola Casanova* invoked the kind of nostalgic ecstasy described by Roger Bartra, where "modern culture creates or invents its own paradise lost."[1] Landeta's cinematic adaptation of anthropologist Francisco Rojas González's prized novel was very much a part of a tradition of weighted melodramatic chronicles that, like so many other post-revolutionary works, attempted "to trace the outline of cohesive nationality . . . [and impose] order in a society convulsed by the abrupt arrival of the modern age and rocked by the contradictions of the new industrial lifestyle."[2] In Landeta's story of national unity a social order was proffered that would depend on both adherence to and revision of masculinist histories of the past. Arising from liberal approbations of a mestizo state, the filmmaker's proposed imposition of order required viewers to consider the role of Creole women in mediating citizenship for indigenous peoples. In a departure from male directors like Emilio Fernández, who deployed female protagonists merely to set up the conditions for a future mestizo nation, Landeta detailed a gender-balanced, if still ethnically uneven, *mestizaje* in the making. By this she envisioned "nation" and its legitimizing strategies in a new vocabulary that at once applied and criticized male lexicons while challenging and also reiterating hegemonic ideologies. A look at *Lola Casanova*'s introductory sequences will begin to unveil the workings of her cinematic rhetoric and sociopolitical vision.

The first shots, as both the screenplay and the images attest, give us a "panoramic view of Pozo Coyote," a clearly marked nineteenth-century desert town populated by purposeful "people of different types."[3] A voice-over confirms the visual documentation: "Here life is lived with the exaltation of work, which transforms all." And indeed, as industrious basket weavers construct objects of beauty and utility from materials at hand, skilled artisans unite "wood with shell" to shape handsome boxes that later will be filled with valued treasures. As Landeta's natural objects (in their most elemental state) are mined and then reconstructed in the form of marketable resources, so too are her humans (in their most organic purity) imaged as the natural resources that will produce the new laboring citizen of Mexico's burgeoning industrial economy (Fig. 2.2). Setting her action at the beginning of the twentieth century, Landeta characterizes her founding citizen/worker as a descendant of the "pure white race," but she embeds the seeds of the mestizo future not only in the detailing of her worker's tasks, tools, and trading goods, but in his "embrace [of] a Seri Indian woman." Children, as if anticipating the happy progeny of this new couple, frolic together in this scene, and yet as the screenplay insists, they are still "perfectly marked" by their individual racialized characteristics. But change is in the air. As Landeta's male narrator begins to relate in the opening sequences, there is "something like a breeze, like the breath of someone who watches and waits" for the right instant to "amalgamate everything." This vigilant someone stands ready to "mold a new man and with him create a new world and a new human destiny." Thus, viewers learn, the nation "prepares for the advent of the mestizo, priceless flowering of humanity on this continent."

While racial mixing takes time—first, "the old die as Seris"; next, "adults age giving up their Yori [Creole] culture"—it has a clearly satisfying outcome:

FIGURE 2.2. Emblems of an epoch: new laboring citizens of Mexico's burgeoning industrial economy. *Negro y Blanco*, October 1936.

"the young mature with attributes of both peoples." Proclaiming the right for Mexicans to enjoy this sort of dual cultural citizenship is an interesting proposition, and one that differs distinctly from the Vasconcelos/Fernández formula where indigenous peoples are meant to acculturate to the extent of losing their own culture. In Landeta's bicultural Pozo Coyote, "amalgamation" comes closer to transculturation than assimilation. As the final scenes testify, and as these first sequences preview, audiences are meant to take pride in the fact that the new citizen can not only "speak in Spanish," but also "think in Indian."

As Landeta will insist throughout *Lola Casanova*, thinking in Indian should not be practiced only by those raised in the idiom. Indigenous sensibility and world view have something to offer the mid-century Yori who is willing to learn about, and adopt, the attributes of both cultures. Like Landeta (and author Rojas González before her) viewers who took the time to consider the world described in the fictionalized documentary would themselves be more prepared to call for democratic enfranchisement for all citizens in the post-revolutionary national unity project. It was incumbent upon Landeta's contemporaries, face-to-face with the modern age, to recuperate the past in order to move forward. Since progress, as national literature and cinema had long maintained, was dependent on the nation coming to terms with its innate "national character," then that character, a unified self embodying an amalgam of traits inherited from its dual ancestry, had better be understood. For Landeta, "Speaking Spanish and Thinking in Indian"— or the inverse—ultimately meant thinking and speaking as a Mexican. In her articulation of national coherence, *mestizaje,* more than a social policy to incorporate or assimilate indigenous peoples, was the critical fulcrum upon which a bicultural national character balanced the past and the future in order to "mold a new man and with him create a new world and a new human destiny."

Like the indigenous Virgin of Guadalupe, like native Mexican Malintzin Tenepal, Lola Casanova represents the national character *por excelencia.*[4] A combination of myth and history, the figure of Lola Casanova as a third aspect of this holy female Trinity presides over both film and text from their beginnings. In his novel Rojas González alluded to the interwoven folkloric and factual dimensions of Casanova. He prefaced his text with a citation from Fortunato Hernández's 1902 study of the indigenous peoples of Sonora, quoting Hernández's oral sources that, "although they never personally met her," they could testify that Lola Casanova was a Sonoran woman taken captive by Seris in 1854.[5] Landeta situated her story even closer to history without allowing viewers to know or evaluate her sources. She proceeded with a written prologue simply affirming that the film was "aligned as closely as possible with the historic facts regarding what happened among the Seris between 1860 and 1904."[6] Her claim to the basis in truth from which *Lola Casanova* was launched immediately situated the narrative in the realm of expository documentary. Her audiences were about to witness the "true history" of the transculturation of indigenous Seri people. Since the elements of the Casanova story so incisively addressed the primary concern of Mexico's first half-century of revolution and reconstruction, Landeta was able to set up a correspondence between history and ideology. Lola's story, in Landeta's conception, thus became Mexico's story.

Mexico's national unity project emerged in the midst of the Revolution. In 1916 (one year before the Constitutional Convention and some four years before the end of armed conflict) Manuel Gamio invited the "revolucionarios mexicanos" to "gird themselves in the blacksmith's apron and grasp the farrier's hammer so that from the miraculous anvil they might forge a new nation wrought of the blending of bronze and iron."[7] In Landeta's hands the sounds of Gamio's anvils grew in crescendo from the exaltation of work that was to transform everything.

The opening sequences of *Lola Casanova* shift from the narrator's exaltation to the exaltation of the protagonist, She of the Baited Breath, whose monument to social transformation is the film's *raison d'être*. Observed seated against the neatly whitewashed walls of humble adobe, the Creole-gone-native sighs a refrain established by previous narration: civilization is a wondrous thing. A chiming of passing cow bells is enough to remind the storyteller that "Years ago our brothers and sisters would not have allowed those animals to live; they enjoyed raw meat more than milk made into cheese . . . we really are another people now." Extradiegetic music swells. Primal drum beats support celestial sopranos and take over as yet another narrative testimony. Men and women of bronze and iron bend to their work; the bells of dairy cows proclaim the dawn of a new civilization; milk rendered cheese announces the advent of a new people (Fig. 2.3).

By the 1940s this metaphoric, hyperbolic, and very musical language flowed easily into the discursive crucible from which smithies of the nation hammered out their new mestizo. The tools of these founders—like Gamio's and Landeta's "miraculous anvils"—were rhetorical strategies that sought to meld history with ideology, past with present, enfranchised citizen with potential Mexican. These strategies, by virtue of their grandiose aims and exaggerated gestures, became the post-revolutionary Mexican embodiment of melodrama. Like the melodramas born of the French Revolution, the Mexican manifestation of the genre responded to political and moral chaos by offering up "truth" in the clearest, and most melodious, terms.[8] Borne on the strains of national hymns, carried by municipal bands striking up its cadence in town square gazebos, resounding in symphonies in the Palace of Fine Arts, melodramatic patriotism became the background music of everyday life. On screen, that great democratic meeting place of popular and elite culture, music and drama combined to wring cosmic significance from common signifiers. Milk cows signaled the construction of an industrious new race. *Lola Casanova*—product of history and fable, anthropological fact and fancy, emblematic of an epoch and uniquely critical of its time—was in itself a cinematic aphorism significant beyond the sum of its parts. In the themes of its *melos* and in the images of its *drama*, we find a nation in the making.

Hace cerca de tres meses que está operando con éxito una industria moderna de gran importancia para los hogares de la ciudad de México. Organizada con capital mexicano, "Lechería Nacional", S. A., instaló en menos de un año y a un costo de varios millones de pesos, una planta rehidratadora de leche, la primera en su género en el país y un modelo entre todas las de su clase en el mundo entero.

La función de esta planta consiste en la rehidratación, por los métodos más modernos y mediante la observancia de la higiene más rigurosa, de leche previamente deshidratada por la fa-

Exterior del edificio de oficinas de "Lechería Nacional", S. A.

MEXICO
Moderno

ría Nacional", S. A., pronto re sultó insuficiente para satisface la demanda de los consumidore por lo que fué necesario trae equipos adicionales que duplica ron esa capacidad.

Como los equipos tanto par la rehidratación de la leche, co mo para su envasado no permite que las manos humanas entren e contacto con el producto, ést llega a la mesa de los consum dores inalterada y con su purez original. Los recipientes esteril zados y sellados se usan una so la vez y así la leche rehidrata da "Sello Azul" es tan buena servirse en la mesa, que no e necesario ni hervirla para mayo

Estas máquinas automáticas dan forma, esterilizan, impermeabili zan, llenan y sellan herméticamente los envases modernos e irrellenables de la leche rehidratada.

mosa industria Kraft de los Estados Unidos, exactamente igual en pureza y calidad que la que bajo ese nombre se consume en el vecino país y en muchas otras naciones civilizadas del globo.

La capacidad original de producción de la planta de "Leche-

En rampas automáticas, las cajas que contienen el producto son transportadas a la flota de camiones para su reparto inmediato.

Cada carga de los tanques rehi dratadores es celosamente anali zada en este laboratorio, par asegurarse de que tiene todo e alto valor nutritivo y la purez originales de la leche antes d ser deshidratada.

protección, porque no ha sido ex puesta a contaminaciones.

La planta de "Lechería Na cional", S. A., representa un notable adición al panorama in dustrial de México, y una nuev organización al servicio de lo hogares mexicanos.

FIGURE 2.3. Off screen, U.S. technology modernized the nation: movie magazine drama of the "National Dairy." *Negro y Blanco*, March 1947.

INTERLUDE: MELANCHOLIC MELODRAMA

"The melodramatic imagination," writes Peter Brooks, "needs both document and vision, and it is centrally concerned with the extrapolation from one to another."[9] Moving from "truth" to the "promulgation of truth," melodrama, as a rhetorical strategy, relies on excess, exaggeration, and a seemingly unending reiteration of its world view. Its history as a modern genre illuminates how it could become such an effective tool in Mexico's post-revolutionary forge. In Brooks's delineation of the genre's beginnings we find a useful parallel to the Mexican engagement of melodrama:

> The origins of melodrama can be accurately located within the context of the French Revolution and its aftermath. This is the epistemological moment which it illustrates and to which it contributes: the moment that symbolically, and really, marks the final liquidation of the traditional Sacred and its representative institutions. . . . Melodrama does not simply represent a "fall" from tragedy, but a response to the loss of a tragic vision. It comes into being in a world where the traditional imperatives of truth and ethics have been violently thrown into question, yet where the promulgation of truth and ethics, their instauration as a way of life, is of immediate, daily, political concern.[10]

The Mexican Revolution, like the French, "attempt[ed] to sacralize law itself," foregrounding "the Republic as the institution of morality." As in France, what emerged from this attempt was melodrama—the "principal mode," stresses Brooks, "for uncovering, demonstrating, and making operative the essential moral universe in a post-sacred era."

In Mexico melodramatic absolutes characterized the discourse on national morality. The making of the post-revolutionary *patria* required sweeping dogma, as if to confirm Mexicans in a universal Faith. Triumph should replace tragedy, industry should overcome idleness, and progress should win over primitivism. The material of daily life, raised to its fullest symbolic power from its modest station (wooden boxes or hunks of cheese wrought into sacred icons), would "document" truth of the past or illuminate the present in order to produce a vision of the future. Melodramatic rhetoric would "locate and . . . articulate" the morally righteous path to national unity. And in the most democratic way Mexican cinema would take over the job of the muralists to render, in a visual and aural vernacular, the terms of citizenship in this new nation.

The discourse of *mexicanidad* and the rhetorical strategies of melodrama thus became inextricably interlaced. From Manuel Gamio's *patria* to Octavio Paz's labyrinths of identity, the melodramatic imagination of the philosophers found expression in cinema. Here philosophical filmmakers dramatized the three greatest melodramas of all: original, sacred time (indigenous Mexico before the Spaniard); the fall from paradise (the Conquest and the birth of the first Mexican); the ordering of the nation-state (the Revolution).[11] However differently these melodramas were reenacted, at base there existed a sort of shared acknowledgment regarding the principal protagonist, Mexico.

Subject and object of a discourse that described and prescribed an ideal national character, Mexico and Mexicans were almost universally represented as the child of the two cultures that gave the nation life. The essence of *mexicanidad,* according to legions of cultural arbiters from essayists to filmmakers, issued in equal measure from Spanish and indigenous archetypal traits. What shaped the national character were notions made monuments. "Indians" lent the Mexican spirit the bravery of Cuauhtémoc and that of other *indios héroes;* Spaniards bequeathed the enterprising nature of Cortés and the *conquistadores.* The actual incorporation of real people—particularly indigenous people—into the formulation of the national subject was as weak as were public policies dealing with the marginalized. To the architects of Mexicanness, neither *"indios patarrajados"* nor *"gachupines afrancesados"* much mattered.[12] What was important was "history." Mexicans needed only to understand their roots. Thus the rhetoric of the paradigmatic national character's heritage was born, a discourse that effected the apotheosis of native peoples while redeeming the "nobility" of Spanish blood.[13] In a language that reduced all complexity to monumental types, advocates of national unity created a mythic mestizo whose parentage rivaled that of the Olympic gods.

If the heroic New Mestizo became known as the issue of fabled ancestry, his Other (and I do mean to discuss heroes, not heroines here) was nobody's child. The less glorified half of the myth of *mexicanidad,* if we follow the echoes of its most lauded articulator, dictated that the quotidian mestizo—the peasant, the *pelado,* the poor nonwhite—was literally and figuratively a son of a bitch, who traced his roots no further than *la Chingada* and *don Nadie.*[14] This Mexican, the protagonist of tearful songs and poetic lamentations, nursed the melancholy of the orphan whose rather common parents achieved sainthood upon death. Melodrama palpitated in every vibration of this mestizo's being, giving expression to a nostalgia and longing for a utopian past that he only imagined, but never lived.

Where melancholy was the content, melodrama was the form. In mid-century Mexico, as in post-revolutionary France, melodrama expressed its dualities "over and over in clear language, it rehearse[d] their conflicts and combats, it reenact[ed] the menace of evil and the eventual triumph of morality made operative and evident."[15] Where excess reigned, where exaggeration revealed all, where everything was always a question of life *and* death, melodrama held center stage. The cinema of the aptly named Golden Age was the best vehicle through which the melodramatic tensions of the nation and its subject could be displayed. Tied intimately to a government that patronized its efforts with lip service, while supporting the production of films economically through the Banco Nacional Cinematográfico,[16] the cinema documented, imagined, and orchestrated the excesses and exaggerations of its era. In post-revolutionary Mexico, melodrama, more than a mere genre, became the *primum mobile* of political and artistic expressions of the new national subject. We shall return to its excesses as Matilde Landeta deployed them after a brief discussion of Landeta's own story.

VOLUNTARY

Lola Casanova premiered to a world that took scant notice. *Películas Nacionales,* the major film distribution company, negotiated its debut—after a year under wraps—without fanfare. In a little-known theater on a Tuesday (never an opening night in those years), during the least propitious time of the year (Holy Week), and without so much as an "ad in the newspaper," Matilde Landeta saw her first directorial effort screened.[17] It was an easy way to bury a film, and it would have been an easy way to bury a filmmaker who had the temerity to fight her way into the exclusive men's club that was the Directors' Guild in those years (Fig. 2.4). But Landeta persevered. Her possessions in hock to finish a film that had suffered every director's nightmares, she made *Lola Casanova* with the express "disgust of the producers."[18] Yet it was not box-office failure that worried these producers; many reels shot during Mexico's Golden Age of movie making eventually would not amount to much. What seemed to bother them was that Landeta's project would be constitutionally unable to attract big loans up front that they could divert to their own uses. "They were accustomed to making films that gave them access to huge loan funds," Landeta explained; "they inflated the budgets of [whatever] film they produced, took salaries as producers, and it didn't matter to them what movie they made."[19] Finally Landeta had little choice but to produce her own films in order to direct. Consequently, she and her brother, film actor Eduardo Landeta, founded their own production company. Although she had both talent and skill—she worked her way through the industry as a "script girl," assistant director, and scriptwriter—Landeta's marginal status as a woman, and not the quality of her work, would determine the kind of support she could expect. Producers knew they were dealing with someone whom the directors' union only grudgingly admitted to their ranks (women were not even permitted to rise to the position of assistant director until Landeta herself forced the issue[20]), and they realized how little they could expect to siphon from the interloper's bare-bones budget. This woman's film was simply not worth their interest.

Landeta recovered quickly from their indifference. She completed her second film, *La Negra Angustias,* the following year. Eduardo Landeta introduced

FIGURE 2.4. Landeta, in trademark pants unusual for the times, seated between *Angustias* author Rojas González and protagonist María Elena Marqués, flanked in turn by Andrés Serra Rojas of the National Film Bank. Courtesy Matilde Landeta.

her to the Monterrey theater owner who would premiere this radical adaptation of Francisco Rojas González's novel about a *Coronela* in the Revolution. The film recuperated its expenses rapidly, and Landeta was ready for the next step. Her screenplay, *Tribunal de menores,* decried the socially reprehensible boys' reform system. It would eventually earn her an Ariel award, but she found no support as the director of her script. She turned instead to a third project dealing with a female protagonist. *Trotacalles* (1951) is the story of women's economic degradation in a men's club society. In her contestation of that society, Landeta's melodrama showed how membership had its privilege. National dreams of triumph over tragedy, industry over idleness, and progress over primitivism were enjoyed solely by a few good men. By the 1950s, with three films, dozens of scripts, and guild card in hand, Landeta had won a precarious place among the few. The heroics of this achievement resembled nothing so much as those of her fiercely determined heroines. Landeta's melodramas—both her professional life and her movies—gave testimony to women's engaged participation in constructing a nation.[21] In her cinema, triumph, industry, and progress were no longer the sole prerogatives of the male protagonists of Mexican modernity.

RITORNELLO: NATIONAL
MELODRAMAS' FEMININE CHORUS

By the mid-1930s and into the early 1950s communicants of Mexican nationalism lifted their eyes unto altars that were cinema's silver screens. Their devotion to a pantheon of gods and goddesses assured the almost holy status of an industry committed to reproducing the myths of a paradisiacal national past in order to conceive fantastic visions of the future. Poised between Revolution and Industrialization, nationalist cinema created a Golden Age of hero worship, where the recounted exploits of many a Mexican Ulysses brought honor and pride to the homeland.

The heroines featured in national quests tended, like the Queen of Heaven Herself, to intercede between the divine and mere mortals by negotiating citizenship for the unincorporated masses. These hordes of "potential Mexicans" were represented on the screen as generic Indians, peasants, and urban poor.[22] Scores of film goddesses "Mexicanized" the masses in patriotic melodramas where citizenship—and a place at the right hand of Our Father, the State—could be conferred upon those who truly believed in the trinity of national values: triumph, industry, and progress. The watchwords of the nation became cinema's bromides. The Revolution, reenacted in countless films, saw its eventual triumph during the reconstruction period that lasted in cinematic representation through the early 1950s. Filmic portrayals of the industrious new nation were couched in the lofty terms of an "exaltation of work." Progress was measured in terms of "race." Progenitors of the new *raza cósmica* would forge "a new man and with him a new world and new destiny," unifying a nation and constructing its subjects.

Key in this formation were cinema's female mediators. Their glamorous images elevated them from the masses, even as their less glorious representations of citizenship returned them to the rank and file of nationalism's foot soldiers. Film diva María Félix, for example, hallowed equally in fan magazines and the national press, required respect and a distant veneration.[23] This "Byzantine Virgin" combined with her opposite aspects—*La Devoradora, La Diosa Arrodillada, Doña Diabla*—to inspire a kind of fear of the divine, rendering her manifestations of Holy María, Mother of Mexico, all the more personal.[24] Spectators were on intimate terms with this María, transformed from shrew to *soldadera* in Emilio Fernández's *Enamorada* (1946; Fig. 2.5), made savior of savages in his *Río Escondido* (1947), and featured as the future of indigenous Mexico in his *Maclovia* (1948). Rivaled only by Dolores del Río, the indigenous Virgin of Xochimilco (Fernández's 1943 *María Candelaria*), and emulated by many other actresses, the accessible María was the prototype of a pantheon of film goddesses used by male filmmakers like Fernández to incorporate viewers into the new national family.

FIGURE 2.5. Félix: from shrew to *soldadera* in *Enamorada*. Courtesy Cineteca Nacional.

Landeta's heroines, female heads of their own new families, mediate citizenship from a distinctly different perspective. Where Fernández's women gain discursive power vis-à-vis men—their status derives from their relationships to stalwart *padres de familia* or to the paternalistic head of the Republic himself—Landeta's protagonists, distanced from divinity and men, act to confer power upon themselves. Lola Casanova, a positive kind of nineteenth-century Malinche figure, denies victimization at the hands of her indigenous captors to become an active member of her new community. "La Negra" Angustias Farrera, *Coronela* of the Revolution, is amazingly able to punish men for their abuse of power. Considerably less powerful, yet still psychically strong, Azalea, *Trotacalles*'s mid-century urban streetwalker, maintains a certain kind of power by exercising her moral authority. Though feminine expression of power is neither easily won nor comfortably maintained (like their director, the protagonists inhabit a world of gender inequality), Landeta's female characters do react to male initiative, but these influential mediators also initiate actions of their own.

The traditional representation of feminine agency in post-revolutionary Mexican film presented a different story. This was cinema with a mission: to return the distaff to its rightful place and thus reconstruct the broken national family.[25] "Feminizing" the woman who had been excessively "masculinized" by her participation in the war or by her dominion at home in the absence of a man was the task of mainstream melodrama, a cinematic mode made for creating, and subsequently managing, excess. Within its terms, within its ability to "locate, express, and impose basic ethical and psychic truths,"[26] filmmakers found the perfect means to rationalize and to emotionalize the rhetoric of woman's return to the domestic sphere. One could leave the theater secure in the knowledge that it simply "felt right" that the protagonist was tamed in the end (María in *Enamorada*), that it was infinitely sad, but oh-so-understandable, that she died a virgin martyr (Dolores in *María Candelaria*, María in *Río Escondido*), and that it was God's Will for the Good of the Country that endless other heroines returned to hearth and home or ascended to heaven to join the Holy Revolutionary Family.

Where mainstream melodrama contrived and controlled displays of feminine excess in alignment with male mythologies of the heroic national subject, Landeta pointedly "betrayed" male mythmaking and used the power of melodrama to create a new female citizen.[27] Excess, with Landeta, is still rendered in mythic proportions, but the exploits of her heroines serve to expose the mythic nature of the genre. When Meche Barba, as Lola Casanova (and not Pedro Armendáriz, as some Mexican Moses), guides her people to the Promised Land, Landeta disturbs what conventional cinema claimed immutable. Gender expectations challenged, it is a short leap for spectators to confront the naturalizing strategy of the genre. Landeta invites us to reflect. If the task of melodrama is to rehearse "basic ethical and psychic truths," and if her works represent truths that are different from those of mainstream movies—yet fundamental and moral within another frame of reference—might the genre itself not be more subject to discursive laws than to some notion of absolutes? Can viewers, asks Landeta, trust the melodramatic mode to help make sense of the world?

In an intriguing confusion of significant moves, Landeta seems to be questioning the genre itself. At key junctures in her cinema, melodramatic sequences are often self-reflective; a kind of wry wit is at work. This is especially evident when the director plays with spectators' assumptions about gender. Angustias Farrera, Colonel of the Revolution and Avenger of Wronged Women, orders castration as punishment for a cocksure countryside rapist. In the name of the women whom he has violated, and for all the cinematic heroines seduced and abandoned since the 1932 *Santa*, Angustias stands tall for justice. Such a stance in conventional melodrama would call for an appropriately stirring score: somber tones, serious cadences. Landeta alerts our attention to both the genre and its gender politics by literally changing the score. She uses *melos* against *drama* to indict cinema's often unchallenged male violence against women. As the camera holds on a pensive Angustias framed against spiky maguey and shown towering over her revolutionaries in repose (bringing to mind, though Landeta elevates the female figure, the musician-soldiers in Fernando Leal's 1921 painting, *Zapatistas at Rest*), the considerably less cocky rapist screams off-camera to the gentle strains of a trio praising a woman's sweetest qualities. The beautiful melody is punctuated with his cries of pain (the fruit of a rapist's own violence), and the murmurings of Angustias's pleasure (the product of a woman's revenge).

It is in the production and management of this kind of excess—the reversal of popular clichés—where Landeta's melodrama clearly articulates its truths. *La Negra Angustias* exemplifies this most overtly. Feminists have taken particular note of its protagonist's exceptional status as a *leader* of men at a time when women soldiers were lauded principally for *following* their men. Yet *La Negra Angustias* pushes reversal even further. Rather than acceding to Rojas González's original designs, in which Angustias, like *Enamorada*'s virago, is tamed and feminized in the end, Landeta plots the triumph of the Revolution through the agency of a woman. With the filmmaker it is Angustias's battlefield *¡Vivas!*, not her resigned diaper-washing songs imagined by the novelist, that score the final melodramatic building of a nation. Ultimately, this "betrayal" of the award-winning writer's text is the reversal that not only reveals the artifice of his melodrama, but alerts our attention to the discursive strategies of the often melodramatic chroniclers of Mexican nationalism (Fig. 2.6).[28]

TUTTI: MELODRAMATIC *MESTIZAJE*

The multiple treacheries of *Lola Casanova*—both Rojas González's ethnographic novel and Landeta's fictionalized documentary—are as much a response to their time as they are a product of it. Evoking the polemics of nation-formation, these works negotiate between the State's rhetoric of national unity as expressed in mythological terms and the ethnographer/documentarian's proposals for social cohesion as revealed through (an attempt at) scientific study. As politically invested melodrama the film performs this balancing act vividly, marking it and its progenitor as distinct from either the strictly romantic or wholly indigenist works of mid-century Mexico.[29]

In the film version of *Lola Casanova* fact and fantasy meet in a display of contradictions. Landeta articulates the tensions of the period through the heightened language of melodrama, her syntax punctuated with elaborate reversals and betrayals. At moments her apotheosis of the mestizo echoes the integrationist rhetoric of the early post-revolutionary governments. Her Seris and Creoles are as cosmic as any race imagined by Vasconcelos. In these

FRANCISCO ROJAS GONZALEZ

LOLA CASANOVA

NOVELA

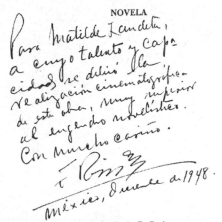

E. D. I. A. P. S. A.
Edición y Distribución Ibero Americana de Publicaciones, S. A.
MEXICO, D. F.
1 9 4 7

FIGURE 2.6. With the production of *La Negra Angustias*, Rojas González acknowledged the "superiority" of the film over his novel. Courtesy Matilde Landeta.

instances her allegorical mestizos emerge from the melodious orchestration of two cultures: indigenous instruments play sophisticated symphonies while Seri characters (imports from the National Ballet) execute modern dance steps on Sonoran sands. In other sequences Landeta deliberately breaks faith with her own allegorical strategies by portraying individualized characters whose self-expressions are unique to their circumstances. Her representation of a Seri women's council, for instance, counters the stereotypes of passive "Indian maidens" offered all too frequently in conventional cinema.

By shifting the terms of truth-telling in her melodrama, as well as by suggesting that there are truths other than the stock-in-trade that spectators are accustomed to, Landeta asks us to consider the axioms of melodramatic post-revolutionary rhetoric. Viewing the film in the context of its contemporaneous criticism underscores its contradictory tensions. We can see that for one guardian of ethnographic fidelity, for example, the professional dancers undermine the authenticity of the film. Nonetheless this same historian seems well pleased with other "accurate" documentation, and suggests that the film be shown in the company of an anthropologist who would distinguish fact from fiction.[30] Representing the romantic perspective, another reviewer felt that the dancers "translated the reality of Seri civilization" into a language comprehensible to cosmopolitan audiences.[31] In the film the tension indicated by these disparate responses is sustained by two interlocking plots that pit myth against history, raising questions regarding both registers.

The first (and most allegorical) plot concerns Lola, the only daughter of a widowed Creole (Fig. 2.7). She lives in relative luxury until her father loses an investment cargo in a shipwreck off their northern Mexican coast. In order to salvage her father's fortune, including the house he gambled away in desperation, Lola decides she can do nothing but marry the poker player who now holds the deed. This cardsharp is an evil Spanish *cacique* who has long terrorized the region's indigenous population for his own gain. En route to her wedding, she is attacked in her carriage by avenging Seris. The father dies,

FIGURE 2.7. Meche Barba's Lola Casanova before enlightenment. Courtesy Matilde Landeta.

the Spaniard runs away to be killed another day, and Lola is taken captive. Her initial resistance to captivity breaks down as she comes to appreciate, participate in, and eventually help cultivate Seri civilization.

In the second plot Isabela Corona, as Seri leader Tórtola Parda (Brown Turtledove), propels much of the action. Although peppered with "inaccuracies" or romantic "translations" of Seri life and customs, here ethnographic specificity subordinates allegory. Tórtola Parda calls a meeting of the people to choose a new male leader after the Spaniard's slaying of the previous chieftain (Fig. 2.8); Landeta details hunting and fishing techniques. The Seris begin their trek to the place where the young chief Coyote Iguana (Armando Silvestre) will direct their attack against the Spanish; Landeta documents the group's changing attitude toward old age and death. Lola Casanova introduces western medicine to the Seris; Landeta describes Tórtola Parda's healing practices. Even as we are drawn into the narrative—Lola and Coyote Iguana fall in love, opposed by Tórtola—Landeta maintains a focus on the specific and particular qualities that make Seris Seri, not merely undifferentiated "Mexican Indians."

Thus, far from preempting a thesis, *Lola Casanova*'s ethnographic melodrama takes great pains to sustain a left-leaning post-revolutionary ideology

FIGURE 2.8. Isabela Corona's Tórtola Parda wielding influence in *Lola Casanova*. Courtesy Matilde Landeta.

of national unity. Unique to Landeta's filmmaking is the manner in which the women and indigenous characters promote or resist the great social cohesion project. For these civilizers, themselves on the margins of national citizenship, *mestizaje* is either the desired result of the union of diverse peoples, or something to be avoided altogether. In contrast, the *mestizofilia* beating in the breasts of post-revolutionary intellectuals manifested itself solely in an excess of allegorical rhetoric.[32] Integration of "Indians" may have been one of the mainstays of its discourse (evidenced, again, everywhere from the cinema to the government-sponsored murals), but "Indian" was conceived of primarily in negative terms vis-à-vis Creole culture. "Indian," decreed endless essays, novels, films, and speeches on the national character, was simply everything "civilization" was not: primitive, passive, fatalistic, enigmatic, existing outside of time. At the same time, "Indian" might also be rendered in historical specificity, portrayed in pre-Columbian grandeur and reflecting upon the Edenic past. In this way hegemonic discourses could incorporate indigenous peoples into the national creation myth without worrying about their enfranchisement into the fabric of national life.

At first glance *Lola Casanova*'s allegorical fictions appear to follow similar rhetorical strategies. Lola, a Creole Malinche, betrays her Spanish ancestry in favor of regaining paradise lost. But nature will out; the force of her "white beauty" melds with the "nerve" of Coyote Iguana, and a new epoch is formed with the birth of their child (Fig. 2.9). Since she now has this child, shall we say Mexico, to care for, Lola makes tracks back to the margins of civilization. She finds traders willing to exchange their goods for the pearls Coyote Iguana gathers from the sea. Bringing the merchandise to the pueblo, she arouses consumer desire. It is relatively simple for her, and for the women eager to enjoy material comfort, to convince Coyote Iguana that commerce with the Yoris is better than war. Seris, dressed in the impeccable white cottons of the working peasant, then journey to Guaymas to establish trade. It would seem that the post-revolutionary banners of triumph, industry, and progress were never raised higher.

Working here within the discourse of the institutionalized Revolution, Landeta nevertheless offers a shift in the paradigm. Reversing the notion of women's return to their rightful place as refeminized helpmeets, she empowers Lola by granting her sovereignty over her new family. Indicative of the ethnocentric paternalism of the epoch, however, the Creole gains her position of authority at the expense of indigenous suffering. Coyote Iguana must die so that Lola can take his place. By the same token, Lola the Creole must metamorphose. It is only as a mestiza that she will wield power. The idea that transculturation must proceed in both directions—that not only indigenous peoples but Creoles as well must undergo profound change—was something that the post-revolutionary ruling elite hardly imagined. However allegorical

FIGURE 2.9. The Creole Malinche betraying her Spanish ancestry in favor of paradise lost. Courtesy Matilde Landeta.

and romantic her vision of Lola Casanova, Landeta's proposal that Creole culture consider its own position was quite radical for its time.

Spurred, perhaps, by her own difficulties as a woman working in a male-dominated sphere, her filmic radicalism finds its greatest expression through the reversal of gender hierarchies. These reversals, in turn, encourage us to think about ethnic parity. When Lola wrests the narration from the anthropological voice-over that initiates the film, we are surprised, in the context of mainstream melodrama and Rojas González's text, that a woman is actually telling her own story. When we realize that she is addressing the young indigenous leader of the Seris, effecting a transfer of power, our surprise turns to curiosity. If a marginalized female citizen is suddenly a speaking subject, why not the marginalized Seri?

Enter Tórtola Parda. Mainstream melodrama would inevitably cast her as the evil woman, congenitally and irredeemably bad. Though this stereotype occasionally threatens to manifest itself in Isabela Corona's character, Landeta proposes a much more complex scenario. By "betraying" transculturating Seris, Tórtola Parda becomes the leader of traditionalists who will continue to live apart from Creole culture (Fig. 2.10). In Landeta's lexicon this clearly is unfortunate; cultural cohesion is the optimum. But as her Seris disappear into their different sunsets we have a very good idea, thanks to the filmmaker's careful documentation, of what kind of mixed tragedies and triumphs await them. If Lola Casanova, mother of a new civilization, ultimately moves into the realm of allegory, Tórtola Parda, guardian of the "old" civilization, comes to represent the reality of Mexico's unenfranchised indigenous communities. In the dialogue between the Lolas and the Tórtolas we hear echoes of nationalist rhetoric and witness examples of resistance to such a totalizing project.

FINALE

Matilde Landeta's importance as a filmmaker must be appreciated against the backdrop of her times, the climax of Mexican nationalism, when an anxious and nostalgic nation lived a discursive revolution on the threshold of industrialization. Melodrama, a genre of monumentalization, was the perfect medium by which the politics of the past could themselves be monumentalized in order to legitimate the politics of the future. The aggrandizement of the meaning of

FIGURE 2.10. Traditionalist Tórtola about to "betray" transculturating Seris. Courtesy Matilde Landeta.

the Revolution permitted the national conversation to embrace a variety of visions about the success or failure of Revolutionary ideals without calling the notion of national identity itself into question. One thing seemed immutable to the communicants of nationalism. Mexico was a nation among nations, and Mexicans citizens among citizens. That marginal groups—women without voting rights, non-Spanish speaking indigenous minorities, the urban poor— did not seem to participate in the conversation, much less in the search for national identity, only conferred upon them the status of "potential Mexicans."

Within this scheme and simultaneously in opposition to it rests the national project imagined by Matilde Landeta. Her films present us with protagonists who rehearse a unique search for national identity. Far from being potential Mexicans, her feminine and indigenous figures become citizens of the first order, founders of the nation and prototypes of both a sovereign and a transculturated *mestizaje.*

Landeta struggles to liberate her protagonists from the "Cage of Melancholy" where the myth of the national character resides. Her cinema negotiates the space between allegory and reality, sometimes contributing to the imprisonment of her characters, but more often freeing them from the logic of institutionalized revolution. Indeed, the range of her melodrama describes the most fruitful potential of that oxymoronic post-revolutionary State. We might say that her characters exist in a kind of "ecstatic melancholy" that enables them both to recuperate a mythic and Edenic past and to begin to envision a new future composed of something more.

CHAPTER THREE

---- ◪ ----

Pimps, Prostitutes, and Politicos: Matilde Landeta's Trotacalles *and the Regime of Miguel Alemán*

When Luis Spota, aspiring young journalist and pulp fiction novelist, approached filmmaker Matilde Landeta with an idea for a money-maker that would capitalize on the "fallen woman" film that was becoming the rage in Golden Age cinema, he encountered a stalwart woman experienced in reworking male-authored texts. By 1949 the thirty-nine-year-old director had already adapted two of Francisco Rojas González's national prize-winning novels, changing them considerably.[1] Her *Lola Casanova* (1948) extended the novelist's vision of the transculturation of indigenous Seri peoples. *La Negra Angustias* (1949) challenged Rojas González's idea that a leader of the Revolution would end up trapped as an abused mother living in urban despair instead of leading her nation into the battles of twentieth-century patriotism. *Trotacalles* (Streetwalker; 1951), the third part of the triptych depicting women's struggle to forge—and survive in—the new Mexico, subverted Spota's original designs, based on his lurid *Vagabunda* (1950), as well as his desires to cash in on his novel as a purely commercial film script (Fig. 3.1). "I told him I'd collaborate on a screenplay and direct the picture only if I could construct my own thesis," Landeta explains, emphasizing that she "wanted no part in making some story about a good girl who takes herself off to the brothel just so she can support her old dad."[2]

Indeed, though she suffered her own hardships as the only professional working woman filmmaker in the 1940s,[3] Landeta refused to play the good

FIGURE 3.1. Streetwalking: "A problem that nobody talks about, but all know." Isabela Corona, Miroslava, Elda Peralta, and Ernesto Alonso. Courtesy Matilde Landeta.

girl who would prostitute her talents simply to support patriarchal ideologies. Where she saw Mexican cinema—or in the event, novelists—"erecting models of female submissiveness and humility," she worked to unseat ubiquitous images of "abject *mujercitas mexicanas*" by producing her own complex characterizations of quotidian female heroism.[4] Without sanctifying these protagonists, Landeta managed to laud their successes and comprehend their failures within the context of specific sociopolitical structures. Working at the zenith of discursive patriotism, when national melodramas apotheosized the past and glorified the present, Landeta combined melodrama with social realism to comment lucidly on her nation's history and her contemporary society.

Her project did not pass unremarked. As early as 1944 the popular film magazine *México Cinema* took her part against a Directors' Guild that unjustly refused her promotion as assistant director: "Matilde Landeta, one of the most competent workers in the Mexican film industry, was dispossessed of a position as assistant director simply because she is a woman."[5] When she eventually won her stripes, she was praised for her work with the most notable directors of the day, including Fernando de Fuentes, Emilio Fernández, and Julio Bracho. By 1948 the press heralded her success as a full-fledged director. Banner headlines declared: "Finally She Triumphs!"; "How the Mexican Woman Works"; "A Woman at the Megaphone"; "Adventures of a Woman"; "Matilde Landeta, or, The Triumph of the Mexican Woman in Cinema."[6] As these titles suggest, the reviews articulated great pride in the fact that a woman had finally penetrated the male filmmaking establishment. Yet even beyond recounting stories of her tribulations and triumphs as a woman in men's society, the press engaged the specific details of her films. *Lola Casanova*, for instance, was noted for its realism. Thanks to Landeta, the "Indians in Churubusco [Motion Picture Studio]" were real for once, "human Indians . . . with all their virtues and defects intact."[7] While the "Anguish of [Making] *La Negra Angustias*" was outlined, so too was the nature of its narrative: "Landeta's depiction of a female revolutionary colonel is faithful to the hidden history of our nation."[8] With the release of *Trotacalles* even the international press acclaimed the work of one of the "few female directors of our Spanish language films."[9]

One of the most descriptive reviews of *Trotacalles* cited the filmmaker in a bold, five-column headline, "Let's Not Idealize Public Women," in approbation of her project "to remove the veil from the clichéd theme of prostitution."[10] The piece briefly contrasted *Trotacalles*'s politics with those of Emilio Fernández's *Las abandonadas* (1944), citing Landeta's view that Fernández's narrative of an abandoned wife-turned-prostitute is at best "half realistic and half romantic."[11] The fact that a woman would prostitute herself even to support her son irritates Landeta, especially when the abnegating mother ends up fostering her unrecognized offspring's career so that he can escape his class, become a brilliant lawyer, and defend wayward women much like his mother.

As the review begins to document, Landeta's concerns focused on women with fewer redemptive possibilities, whom she "traced with shades of realism." In turn, I am interested in tracing Landeta's realist aesthetic through an analysis of *Trotacalles* in its sociopolitical moment. Working out this chapter, I was intrigued by a number of issues that are addressed in the first section of my investigation: How had discursive post-revolutionary nationalism changed with industrialization and modernization? What effects did this ideology of the ruling elite have on the cinema of dance halls and prostitutes? How did Landeta "construct her own thesis" and contest the regime's romanticism? How did other cinematic themes and aesthetics affect her sensibility?

I found a link between these concerns and the conflicting practices of a post-war Hollywood cycle of dark cinema widely viewed in Mexico at the time. Mexico's cabaret genre resonated with U.S. *film noir*, particularly as it dealt with crime and corruption in the metropolis. But where the rhetoric of Mexican industrialization and modernization urged ultimate optimism in the nation's potentially bleak urban melodramas, Hollywood *noirs* were largely unrelieved embodiments of disillusionment from beginning to end. Against the tide of Mexican *noir*-ish romanticism that promoted the new capitalist values, Landeta took inspiration from Hollywood *noir*'s realist impulses in her effort to uncloak the workings of the prostitution genre, thus exposing the unredemptive poverty of the institution.

As I aim to show in the second part of the close analysis of *Trotacalles*, Landeta's clear-sighted representation of women's struggles departed from Hollywood influences when she refused to reproduce their hierarchies of "otherness." If *noir* acted as *agent provocateur* toward the status quo, it did so by challenging class conceits, or by dismantling gender paradigms, only to restore them. Landeta's alternative enriches both Mexican melodrama and the *noir* ethic. *Trotacalles* interrogates nationalist optimism commonly represented by cinematic metaphors of the supposedly luxurious lives of "public women." The film questions class attitudes and gender norms, examining the rhetoric of progress and the discourse of alleged feminine compliance with the dictates of modernity, by offering a realistic view of "private women" instead of a spectacle of their "public" lives.

I: *". . . Y LA REVOLUCIÓN MEXICANA SE BAJÓ*
    DEL CABALLO PARA SUBIRSE AL CÁDILLAC . . ."

The final image of Matilde Landeta's *Negra Angustias* perfectly describes the last triumphal moments of the Mexican Revolution, that epoch of radical reconstruction under President Lázaro Cárdenas (1934–1940), when *¡Viva la Revolución!* translated to a plethora of post-revolutionary projects from the socialization of education to the nationalization of petroleum. Yet even as the triumphant *coronela* Angustias shouted her *¡Vivas!* astride a hoof-pounding war horse, Landeta's contemporary spectators might well have motored away from the theaters (and the specter of the 1910s) into the dazzling lights but grim realities of late-1940s capitalism.

Two years later, with the release of *Trotacalles*, spectators' cinematic experiences might have been more congruent with their times. From its initial images of a shiny Cadillac barreling down the impoverished Plaza de las Vizcaínas, the film speaks forthrightly to economic inequalities brought about by the so-called development policies of Miguel Alemán's presidency (1946–1952). Landeta's unflinching look at *alemanismo* and the institutionalization of revolutionary practices concretizes and expands the popular expression that by the mid-1940s the Mexican Revolution "had climbed off its horse to step into its Cadillac."[12] In *Trotacalles*, unlike in other cinematic (or rhetorical) vehicles in which images of luxury cars offered a democratic fantasy of wealth and prosperity for all, the Cadillac is clearly marked as the property of the elite. Where the strategies of *alemanismo* depended on obfuscation in order to seduce and (re)produce a working class that would form the backbone of the new capitalist State, Landeta's contrapuntal filmmaking relied upon the clarity of social realism to detail the workings of sociopolitical seduction itself.

In brief, *Trotacalles* tells the story of two working-class sisters and their relations to men. Having been seduced and abandoned by the same man before the narrative begins, María (Elda Peralta) and Elena (Miroslava Stern) are seen employing two different means of survival: María, with the street name Azalea, has become a prostitute; Elena lives a loveless marriage with wealthy banker Faustino Irigoyen (Miguel Ángel Férriz). Pimped by Rudy (Ernesto Alonso), María/Azalea walks the shabby Plaza de las Vizcaínas. Disguised as the refined "Rodolfo," this same man plays the gigolo in the classy nightclub district, where a predatory Elena (who frequents the famous Cabaret Ciro with husband Faustino) also makes easy prey.

". . . ibas a los burdeles con [los que] llegan a ministros de la Defensa . . . y los veías en calzoncillos. . . ."

Years before he approached Landeta with his idea "to go with the current of the times and make a prostitute picture," Luis Spota spent some fourteen months as a journalist with presidential candidate Miguel Alemán on his nation-wide campaign tour. The writer's official capacity was to act as liaison between President Manuel Ávila Camacho's chosen successor (and his future cabinet ministers) and the press. In this role Spota had to have been familiar with Alemán's *Programa de Gobierno* (published in September 1945), which anticipated the essential elements of the *alemanista* project with astounding accuracy.[13] Spota's unofficial duties made him aware of yet other aspects of governance, as he confided in a 1980 interview:

> A political columnist has to have a great memory bank, a splendid archive, an infinitely great number of friends of all statures. . . . I remember the old generals . . . whom I met in the time of don Manuel Ávila Camacho. . . . Those young *tenientitos*—and I'm talking about military men—well, after a while they become Ministers of Defense, and there you are on a first-name basis with them because you've known them from the past. Alemán's tour, where I was close to these guys, was my great experience—fourteen months of a political tour on board a train— you'd go to the brothels with these fellows and you'd see them in their drawers. These men became political personages, distinguished university professors, great saints of the UNAM [the national university] and the Polytechnic, and you would have met them in their underwear, in a bordello.[14]

Prostitution and politics made cozy bedfellows in this decadent decade, where the *programa de gobierno* was dedicated to producing the greatest profit for the fewest number at the expense of those who were the most hard-pressed. While the pleasure principle motivated myriad desires among the ruling powers, *alemanista* rhetoric camouflaged these drives in a carefully articulated program of national development *(desarrollismo)*. The benefits and moral high ground of capitalism would unify the country; industrialization and private enterprise would fortify it; economic partnership with the powerful neighbor to the north would assure its future growth. The sanctity of presidential authority in all realms—governing the attitudes and behaviors of the army, the PRI (the newly realigned ruling party), the opposition parties, the unions, the entrepreneurs, and the laboring classes—would ensure peace and stability, *orden y progreso*, in the modern nation.[15]

Building this program from the bottom up first necessitated, as Carlos Monsiváis points out, "the forging of a new, submissive, sport-loving, alcohol-imbibing, working class, friend of order and fiesta, foe of communism."[16] The new citizen of this class, whose "marginal" autonomy would express itself "in the business of night life, in styles of living that mimed bourgeois ostentation, and in the admiration of the corrupt," represents the ideal *"santa"* whom those "sainted" elites would worship in their unholy bordellos. ("I presume those brothels were of good quality," Spota's startled interviewer interjected at the conclusion of the writer's story, proving that bourgeois fastidiousness still holds a place in the social imagination. He ventured no further when his informant explained that the illustrious fornicators very democratically patronized those places "wherever they happened to end up."[17]) With *alemanismo*, whatever the venue and whoever the participants, real or metaphorical denizens of the night, wrapped in (faux) furs and dangling (faux) gems, admiring this wayward entrepreneur or that corrupt official, were meant to covet more luxury for themselves and to inspire desire in others. A libidinous public, lusting after the spoils of a post-war economy, was both co-optable and consolable. Desire became a requirement of modernity and a badge of good citizenship.

The second task of the ruling elite, according to Monsiváis, was "to forge new types of public functionaries and impresarios who . . . would subscribe to the most successful North American model, separating themselves from the cares of ideology, manifesting a lack of those moralistic scruples that offend the logic of growth."[18] If the working classes had to prostitute themselves, so (to very different effect) did those who managed their labor, controlled the means of production, and owned the resources and revenues of the nation's patrimony. The edict of *unidad nacional* demanded everyone's cheerful cooperation in the business of nation-building. It rewarded its faithful with democratic inclusion in the simulacrum of a harmonious society reflected in song, cinema, and sententious speechifying. Monsiváis's recapitulation of the decade's dogma is irresistibly articulate:

> Nothing of "national plurality" or "cultural diversity." *Mexico is one,* and workers
> and bourgeoisie, *campesinos* and middle classes, Catholics and atheists shall form

a single spirit that detests the Nazis, admires the national cinema, recognizes the qualities of North American progress, confesses to romanticism upon hearing *boleros,* and loves poverty if it is suitably picturesque.[19]

Nowhere was this formula so neatly (or pleasurably) advanced as in the *cabaretera,* or dance hall picture, of the second half of the decade. If for obvious reasons the brothels or even the nightclubs were not entirely inclusive spaces, their cinematic representations most certainly were (Fig. 3.2).[20] Anyone could visit the exclusive Ciro or the Waikikí, take in the routine delights of the Club Verde or Salón México, or taste forbidden fruits at the House of Ruth.[21] Cinematic slumming could lead anyone anywhere and still rehearse the logic of developmental capitalism. *Rumberas,* torch singers, dime-a-dance *ficheras,* and conga line chorus girls, regardless of their station in life, were glamorous, fallen women with hearts of gold whose saintliness could overpower any adversity, even penury and death. Desire, configured in these films with all the signifiers of melodramatic *desarrollismo* (from enormous white telephones to those big black Cadillacs), was quenchable, if only one tried hard enough. Poor-but-heroic *ficheras* could find satisfaction in displacement. On the strength of her "dancing" in *Salón México* (Dancehall "México"; 1948),

FIGURE 3.2. Club Ciro habitué Rodolfo/Rudy as suave society man and pimp. Courtesy Marcela Fernández Violante.

for instance, Marga López's character puts her little sister through private school so the young woman can marry—whom else, but a wealthy war hero from the Mexican air force. Earnest *rumberas'* desires for both sensuality and saintliness could also be met. Ninón Sevilla's sexuality and maternal instincts serve and save a nation through song, dance, *and* motherhood; she rescues an abandoned infant citizen from a trash can between hot musical numbers in *Víctimas del pecado* (Victims of Sin; 1950).[22]

In stark contrast to these hegemonic visions of desires incited and ful-filled, Landeta's *Trotacalles* chronicles the resistance of those whose lives represented the antithesis of the national spirit: those recalcitrant few who refused to "hope for the best" in the face of reliable evidence that the exercise of desire in a categorically unjust society is a futile enterprise. Indeed, desire in *Trotacalles* is reduced to its lowest common denominator: the survival instinct. The enterprising individual is either the one who stays alive by virtue of her own wits, or the one who uses others to frustrate all desire but his own. Nothing of *"Mexico is one"*; Landeta's Mexico lives the class struggle that the rhetoric of *alemanismo* and its cinematic counterparts refused to acknowledge.

". . . yo había escrito mi argumento en un neorrealismo absoluto. . . ."

Class conflict, understood particularly in conjunction with gender inequality, deeply informs the filmmaker's work. Inspired by Luis Buñuel, by Italian neo-realism, by Hollywood *film noir,* and by her own lived experiences in Mexico City, Landeta made movies (directing four and co-directing fourteen), worked script continuity (seventy-five films), and wrote a score of screenplays with a method and a purpose. Working on her *Tribunal de menores* in the late 1940s, for example (a script that eventually earned her an Ariel for the film retitled *El camino de la vida* [Life's Road; 1956]), she formulated ideas by liv-ing a kind of "absolute neorealism." She described herself sitting below her apartment "talking endlessly with the band of abandoned kids who slept on the sidewalk, sharing bread and milk, discussing street life."[23] *El camino de la vida* is marked by these moments, as it is by Luis Buñuel's *Los olvidados* (The Damned; 1950) and Vittorio De Sica's *Ladri di biciclette* (Bicycle Thieves; 1948). *Trotacalles,* as a chronicle of post-war urban despair situated in a cine-matic climate of optimism, reflects class and gender struggles that Landeta not only observed first hand, but that she watched develop in somewhat par-allel circumstances in Hollywood *film noir.*

Regarding *Trotacalles* in the *chiaroscuro* light of *noir* is not to claim the film as some kind of Mexican example of the *noir* cycle. Yet such a perspec-tive does offer a way to think about the thematic and aesthetic concerns of films that challenged the epoch's conservative politics of representation. Given the post-World War II era's discourses of development,[24] given the

United States's role in constructing such paradigms, given Mexico's relations with the U.S. vis-à-vis economic expansion, and given hegemonic cinema's collusion with governmental rhetorics of progress, *noir*'s anti-Hollywood strategies are worth examining.

Though early theory in France and the United States split regarding *film noir*'s ultimate significance, there now exists a loose consensus that these films marked a "critical and subversive view of American culture."[25] If conservatives and progressives initially attached different meanings to *noir*'s "otherness," most agreed that its dark visions commented on an underside of U.S. culture not generally represented in Hollywood's more characteristic movies. Springing from gangster films and emerging from the so-called hard-boiled detective fiction of writers like Dashiell Hammett, Raymond Chandler, James M. Cain, and Cornell Woolrich, this post-war cycle of films particularly addressed the problems of returning war veterans whose reintegration into domestic life was tougher than optimism-in-the-face-of-gloom films (in the vein of the 1945 *The Pride of the Marines*) predicted. Whether *noir* films shared characteristic visual aesthetics (such as the much-noted *chiaroscuro* lighting of works like *Touch of Evil*, 1958), whether they sympathized with criminals or shady detectives (*Double Indemnity*, 1944; *The Big Sleep*, 1946), whether they pitted *femmes fatales* and fate against luckless, anxious males (*Detour;* 1945), or indulged their darkest whims in melodramatic excess (*Laura;* 1944), together these works constructed a sort of "obverse of the American Dream."[26] They replaced the "solid American values" pictures with films revealing the sordid concerns of a "criminal element," whose "otherness" resided in their extralegality and consequent distance from the social compact of homogeneity.

Parallel claims might be made for the group of Mexican urban dramas of dancers, prostitutes, and fallen women that challenge the indomitable spirit of the other prominent genres of the period: family melodramas, *comedias rancheras,* epics of the Revolution and the glorious Aztec past, or the poor-but-happy barrio sagas. Films like *Salón México, Víctimas del pecado, Aventurera* (1949), *La diosa arrodillada* (The Kneeling Goddess; 1947), *Crepúsculo* (Twilight; 1944), and *Distinto amanecer* (A Different Dawn; 1943) are imbued with *noir*'s darkest moments, both aesthetically and thematically, but ultimately they refuse to give up the "solid Mexican values" of national optimism (Figs. 3.3 and 3.4). Cities may be claustrophobic spaces of danger and desire, ringed by a darkness not dispelled by neon and jazz, women may entice and entrap, sin and perdition may threaten, but in the end melodrama redeems waywardness, offers hope, proposes a "different dawn." Spectator tears wash away the sins of the world. *Bless us, Father, for we have sinned; Mexico is One.* In the combined State-and-Church religion of the cinema, communicants receive their daily "*Bread:* the infrastructure of social services" and

Figure 3.3. *Salón México*: one of Mexican *noir*'s darkest moments. Courtesy Agrasánchez Film Archive.

"*Circus:* the certainty of belonging to a steamy, agitated collective, whose idols are exact projections of the soul of the people."[27]

Where these Mexican films engaged viewer complicity by their melodramatic appeals to cinematically enfranchised citizens, Hollywood *noir* elicited identification with netherworld desire by appealing to spectators' disenfranchisement from the civic body. Addressing anxieties brought on by the war,[28] fears of a recurrence of an economic depression,[29] and the terrifying notion of women and other aliens,[30] *noir* deployed some of the supposedly least reputable types to dictate the terms of the narrative. Like confessing picaresque characters from Moll Flanders to Pascual Duarte, good guys gone bad (the criminals) and bad guys going good (the private eyes) argued their cases in voice-over narrations that couldn't help but secure spectator sympathy.[31] The seaminess of their dreadful desires was significantly mitigated by the face of their humanity. Spectators could feel a certain kinship, a certain there-but-for-the-grace-of-God-go-I, with those whom conventional cinema categorically punished or hid somewhere just off-screen. Even when these figures lost

FIGURE 3.4. National optimism in Mexican *noir*: *Distinto amanecer*'s Pedro Armendáriz and Andrea Palma. Courtesy Agrasánchez Film Archive.

narrative control, when their unreliability as confessing criminals or confused private eyes became fully evident,[32] viewers were still meant to identify with the protagonists. While spectators might have hesitated to fully embrace wrongdoing, they may still have found a sense of relief with a cinema that dared represent what the monochromatic mainstream did not: America's "Other" characters in all their soiled hues.

Filling the screen with images of the underrepresented is not, of course, a necessarily progressive act. However "realistic" *noir* films might have been, however inclusive of the "Other," they ultimately rehearsed Hollywood's rankings of race, class, gender, and sexual orientation. Individual films sometimes broke with these strictures, but for the most part the *noir* world praised and vilified its own according to conventional mores. *Film noir*'s coding of "fallen women," "poor white trash," "sinister Orientals," "shiftless Hispanics," "villainous homosexuals," and assorted other "Others" amounted to as much negative typing as most cinematic practices of the time. We have only to recall one of the first examples of the cycle, *The Maltese Falcon* (John Huston; 1941), to remember just how bad everybody was, save the quintessential American male, Humphrey Bogart as Hammett-and-Huston's Sam Spade. As the

United States prepared anxiously for war during the film's production, evil in its diegesis is incarnated in the foreign, the deviant, the overindulged, and in Freud's "dark continent" of the enigmatic feminine.[33] With the exception of Spade's alter-ego secretary ("You're a good man, Effie"), *Falcon* characters in search of the fetishized, foreign, Maltese "dingus" vie with each other for oddness. The triple-passported homosexual Joel Cairo's (Peter Lorre) gardenia perfume hangs as heavy in the film as do the oversized pistols that the effeminate "gunsel," Wilmer (Elisha Cook, Jr.), is barely able to heft.

With the war underway and *noir* in full swing, evil became domesticated in the *femme fatale*, who, in contrast to conventional Hollywood heroines, was intelligent and complicated. If they were too smart for their own, or anyone else's, good, the decisive Barbara Stanwycks, Rita Hayworths, and Lauren Bacalls could still be regarded with awed respect. Even in films like the ones Florence Jacobowitz calls "male melodramas," movies like Fritz Lang's *The Woman in the Window* (1944) or his *Scarlet Street* (1945), at first the "force of evil" resides in the delectable favors an initially powerful woman offers an initially submissive man. In these Lang films, for example, Joan Bennett's confident character offers Edward G. Robinson's meek one a measure of intelligent passion that he enjoys up to the point of his almost-unconscious transmutation as a murderer or an accomplice to murder. Though Robinson is no Bogart here (nor is he the tough-minded Robinson of *Little Caesar* [1930] or the legal-minded Robinson of *Double Indemnity*), in the end this male protagonist's desires for escape from castrating domesticity—and his deep-seated anxieties in achieving them—sadistically dominate both films and both "deadly" female characters. Even in his masochism (his drives toward suicide) he typifies what Deborah Thomas sees as "the divided protagonist of *film noir* [who] projects deviant aspects of himself on to the genre's main representation of 'otherness,' yet [who] is caught between such deviance and his privileged [male] status (embodied in his point of view which defines the *film noir* world)."[34]

By the end of the war, *film noir*'s "essential male-centredness" locates its protagonists' fears in anxieties stemming from their ambivalence about returning to post-war civilization and domestication after the relative freedom (their "license to kill"; their unrestrained sexuality) that overseas existence afforded.[35] In addition to films like *Laura* (where veteran-turned-detective Dana Andrews can hardly tolerate a "dame" walking him by a furniture store), even vehicles like *Gilda* (1946) that take place outside the United States underscore the central worry for expatriate men. How will they move from buddy-love and the politics of foreign, homosocial space—as Glenn Ford's "Johnny" must disengage himself from his Nazi-loving, German-Argentine pal in order to embrace a good (because she's so bad) American girl (Spanish American Margarita Carmen Cansino [Rita Hayworth])—in order to go home? Here the hero's task is to allay his fears by displacing them on to the woman, whose otherness—an unbound, exotic sexuality evidenced in provocative nightclub acts—must be tamed and literally domesticated by her return with her (anti)hero to the United States. That such reentry to some U.S. suburb or some alien-filled city in the States will not be easily achieved for either female or male protagonist is suggested in the film's unbelievably happy ending, but this notion is not as important as *film noir*'s premise that when Johnny does come marching home it will be Gilda's lot to keep him there. Though this type of *femme fatale* might reincarnate as a Mildred Pierce (Joan Crawford) in the eponymous 1945 film (a woman who sacrifices herself over a hot stove, and then sacrifices other women and girls over a series of both real and metaphorical stoves in her chain restaurants), or appear reborn as the "redemptive woman" (Joan Bennett in Lang's *Secret Beyond the Door;* 1948), the women of *film noir* will never really be the main focus of the cycle's concerns. These Hollywood films, "from whose vantage point blacks, women, and immigrants, among others—and not white male Americans—are strange," are also "fundamentally about men with women used as decoys in a strategy of denial."[36]

Nevertheless, *noir* male figures debated hegemonic Hollywood's insistence on "America" as a homogeneous home on the range, and the cycle's errant men fairly begged to be read as nonconformists. Audiences were meant to admire the verve of *Double Indemnity*'s crooked insurance salesman (even if entrepreneurship did lead to mayhem, the swindler was still sweet Fred Mac-Murray). *Laura*'s deliciously bitchy homosexual villain evinced quite compelling style (even if his stylish excess resulted in murder, how could we not be somehow drawn to Clifton Webb's wit?). Not only did these films engage viewer identification by giving their variously shady male characters narrative control, but they encouraged spectators to question conventional cinematic truths by showing us the dark side of our heroes and their milieu. *Films noirs* looked at poverty, hopelessness, greed, graft, and corruption and asked victims, perpetrators, and private eyes to speak their piece. "America" might be more grittily complex than Hollywood mainstream imagined.

Complexity notwithstanding, as an oppositional strategy the genre's distortion or elaboration of Hollywood's images went only so far. Sympathy for *noir*'s "Others," including deviant male characters, was either chipped away overtly—the Hays Production Code ordained the punishment or death of the wayward—or, more insidiously, destroyed by subtle cinematic maneuvering. Traditional pecking orders were reaffirmed by plots that exoticized the marginal out of believable existence, by techniques of framing and editing that fetishized them, or by aesthetics and themes that naturalized "normal" masculinity, heterosexuality, and "whiteness" to the exclusion of any other vision. On this level they offered only slightly more resistance to hegemonic cinema than did Mexican exemplars of criminality. With particular regard to gender representations, if not to other concerns, Matilde Landeta found little to inspire her in Hollywood *noir;* instead, the most likely influence on this aspect of her work was the tough *"neorrealismo absoluto"* that she lived as a woman filmmaker in a male-dominated world.

II: *"A SUS PIES, SEÑORA. . . ."*

While allegories of the class struggle may well be imagined through multi-gendered metaphors, the largest percentage of institutionalized prostitution is nonetheless gender-specific, regarded by convention as "women's work." If *Trotacalles* asks viewers to attend to the realities and not the fictions of *alemanismo,* it does so by looking expressly at impoverished women's roles in the working class. Traditional hierarchies are profoundly disturbed because here prostitution is not mere metaphor; women are not exotic, unknowable beings, fetishized by the glamorous close-up (upon which Golden Age cinema seems to rest); poverty is not picturesque, and social spaces have more dimensions than a conga line.

From her first establishing shots of the murky Plaza de las Vizcaínas (recognizable as one of Mexico City's impoverished commercial sex districts), Landeta makes it clear that the bright lights of some posh cabaret won't bedazzle her spectators into believing that life for prostitutes is anything other than bleak. Her focus on the cheaply shod feet of the streetwalkers during the title credits immediately underscores this thesis. High heels and legs—privileged icons of glamorous female sexuality—are here unsensational, rendered in close-up shots that give testimony to the strain they must bear. Their task is to propel bodies (streetwalkers must literally walk) or provide them stationary support (tired bodies may incline against walls and still be considered on duty). Only when these high-heeled legs are met—and then are masked from our view—by speculative male footwear, does Landeta suggest that their third role is to provoke desire. As the camera backs away, we glean this knowledge with remarkably little voyeuristic complicity.

Indeed, any pleasure spectators might have derived from the traffic in women is immediately circumvented. As the credits fade and the narrative begins, our involvement with those female legs is solicited in a different way. Landeta invites us to follow the footsteps of one pair into a doorway while prefiguring doom in the form of a careening Cadillac moving toward the camera. As the high heels later exit the door they had previously passed through, a medium shot introduces us to the silhouette of our protagonist whom we'll come to know as "Azalea" (her working name) or "María" (her given name). In these first sequences she steps off the curb, moves into the path of the speeding car, and is instantly thrown down on the asphalt. A close-up inside the car affords a view of frantically braking male feet, which rush out of the auto to investigate the gravity of the accident. In front of the Cadillac, Azalea's legs extend in dangerous proximity to the wheels. But she has been neither spiritually nor physically crushed. Refusing driver Faustino Irigoyen's help to rise, she kneels in search of the scattered contents of her handbag. A crowd gathers, and Ruth (Isabela Corona), a "worn and tubercular prostitute,"[37] articulates what we have been shown so graphically: "Despicable louts! Just because you're rich you think you can run us down!" Azalea shouts that the "bum" should learn to drive, Ruth issues other insults, while a calm Faustino offers "my card, if there's anything I can do for you." Ruth wonders if the "old idiot" won't immediately contribute "just enough for a pair of stockings" since Azalea's are now ruined, even if her legs—indispensable tools of her trade—are miraculously unscathed. Yet Azalea balks at Ruth's suggestion; she wants nothing from this man. Faustino's white-gloved hands extract his wallet while his wife, Elena (Miroslava at her most vampish), looks on. Pulling out two hundred pesos, he tosses them arrogantly out the window of his departing car. It is Ruth who stoops to gather them from the pavement.

Trotacalles is thus situated in an economy of male commodification of women and female strategies for survival. Landeta examines institutionalized prostitution as suffered by Azalea and Ruth, and comments on more individual entrepreneurship as practiced by Elena and Faustino. That Azalea and Elena are somehow connected beyond this link is an idea established by countershots of the pair at the scene of the accident as they recognize one another with complete astonishment. When María visits Elena to return Faustino's money we learn that the two women are sisters, and an aspect of Landeta's thesis becomes yet clearer: All women are sisters; women should bond together for mutual support and affection; betraying one's sister is to treat her worse than might the most abusive man.

To begin to elaborate this point, Landeta lines up the sisters in parallel environments. Moving away from the tawdry street scene, she introduces us to Cabaret Ciro, a classy nightclub much in the style of those featured in 1940s *cabaretera* films. Ambient music and illuminated interiors contribute to a relaxed atmosphere and contrast markedly with the deep shadows of the Plaza de las Vizcaínas. But even here, where wealth seems to defy poverty in every softly lit corner, Landeta reminds us that all might be a dream. A sultry chanteuse sings "En dulce sueño" and spectators, at least, are encouraged to see through the artifice of the club's dreamy glamour.

For two of the characters, however, the "sweet dream" of romance seems a siren song. Elena (ignored by her husband, who is intent on his money-making schemes with the United States ambassador) extracts a cigarette in search of an attentive male to supply her a light, and, as a close-up of her eyes gazing upon a likely candidate suggests, perhaps something more. She is obliged by Rodolfo (played by Ernesto Alonso as a man on the make), who murmurs that he "has long been awaiting her," just as one of Faustino's business companions recognizes him and makes introductions. Acknowledging the formal introduction of "our famous banker don Faustino Irigoyen" and his wife, Rodolfo chooses the most submissive—and in this context, the most provocative—of formulaic Mexican expressions of greeting. He kisses her hand, gazes into her eyes, and proclaims himself "at your feet, Señora." Here Landeta's rhyme with the downtrodden feet of the title sequence strikes a discordant note even in the midst of this gay opulence.

The connection to prostitution becomes even more explicit as Rodolfo escorts Elena to the dance floor. We recognize Cabaret Ciro as the inversion of the Plaza de las Vizcaínas's impoverished *fichera* cabarets, where prostitutes *qua* taxi dancers charge clients for a quick cha-cha. At Ciro, the role of *fichera* falls to the elegant gigolo who doesn't dispense dance tickets to a string of anonymous partners, but uses other ways to charm (and ultimately charge) one female into a long and intricate "dance" that will last the length of the film. Once he takes her in his arms, Rodolfo feigns surprise that Faustino is Elena's husband, not her father, as he tells her he had previously imagined. His deliberate misreading strategically attempts to compliment Elena's youth, beauty, and possible class status, but it achieves something more. It becomes the cornerstone of the eventual revelation that Elena has very calculatingly deployed her charms to land a husband precisely as Rodolfo is using his to seduce her. Elena, counterpart to the *noir*-ish male gigolo, is the *femme fatale* who has clearly married Faustino for his money. For an increasingly unmasked Rodolfo, Elena's choice only increases her attractiveness. The dancers are well matched.

A judicious camera gives equal screen time to medium close-ups of the couple's circling faces; female and male participate in both spatial and linguistic registers with force. Elena boldly wonders if her civil state would "affect the fruit of another's garden," which Rodolfo obviously covets. He replies that "in this case the fruit is the most exquisite that I have ever seen." Thinly elliptical word play continues as Elena challenges Rodolfo's ability to surreptitiously pluck the highest of the fruit, and he responds that the trick lies in "knowing how to do it!" One merely "lowers the branch and cuts the fruit without the gardener ever becoming aware." Yet his proposition is not such a simple matter, for Landeta's protagonist will later reveal to Rodolfo that it was she who sought to savor the fruits of his tree.

This exchange, framed by Faustino's neglect of Elena and his passionate conversation with the ambassador, offsets spectators' complete condemnation of Elena as *femme fatale*. If she looks for attention beyond the condescension of a preoccupied husband who does little more than treat his *nenita,* his "little child," or his "beautiful, bored wife," to a ride in a speeding car and a drink at a fancy club, viewers understand that, like filmic *femmes fatales* before her, her construction of her own pleasure confronts a social order that denies women agency. And when Rodolfo begins to propose just how he would lower that branch and snip (castrate?) its fruit, Landeta enlarges the possibilities of *noir's femme fatale* by further prompting spectator desire for Elena's agency.

"Are you romantic?" Rodolfo asks her, intent upon finding a way past her defenses. "No," she responds, employing a rarely used conjugation, "Among us women there are those who can't afford to give ourselves that luxury." Her *"habemos mujeres"* construction calls attention to itself as much as the exaggerated bird plumage (ostrich feathers with a two-foot wing span) that is affixed to her hair; *rara avis* she might be, but she is also part of the species of "practical women" who can't afford the luxury of romance. In this she is not so different from her sisters, the streetwalkers, whose "practicality" also rules out romance. Elena's hard-nosed attitude affords her houses in Las Lomas, Cuernavaca, and Acapulco—worlds away from the dreary hotel room Azalea must occupy—but her commodification leads her toward truly lamentable psychic death. When Rodolfo takes advantage of Elena's practicality by pressing a key to a Reforma apartment into her hand, Landeta asks us to feel her indignation. "Whom do you take me for?" Elena asks a now-shadowed Rodolfo, whose back is positioned toward the camera. His leer is unmistakable as he turns and speaks: "For a 'practical' . . . and very beautiful woman, who knows what she wants."

Rodolfo's characterization of Elena is double-edged. While he treats the banker's wife as an expensive call girl, he recognizes her desire for power and presence, thus affirming this *mujer fatal's* bid to shape her own destiny. At the same time the fact that women's self-determination is circumscribed by a hegemonic male economy is not lost on Landeta. In this film women attached to men have little choice but to prostitute themselves in some way. Desire, whatever women's fantasies might elect, is, and must necessarily be, "practical." In Mexico of the mid-century, marrying for money (or worse, bestowing sexual favors for love or money) represented the height of female transgression. But as one critic has noted in a parallel context about *femmes fatales* in Hollywood *noir:*

> . . . in a forties world of male privilege, where a woman's best chance of acquiring status [or *surviving,* in Landeta's *noir* world] frequently lay most securely in submission to a socially privileged male, [her] manipulation of the system works against the injustices of the legitimizing process in the very act of its apparent affirmation.[38]

Elena's manipulation of an unjust system is classic. We learn that she was a bank employee who managed the only possible wage increase available to those in her position: she married the boss. Her sister was reduced to more drastic measures: prostitution was the only route available to the seduced and abandoned María. By referring to a labor market segmentation system here, and by commenting on María and Elena's choices within that framework, Landeta reveals a world that clearly questions the legitimacy of the social order and women's participation in that system. Herein *Trotacalles* resonates with the thematic sensibilities of the most trenchant Hollywood *films noirs,* where social misfits and outcasts from "black widows" to licentious insurance men magnify the fissures in the social edifice by their overt "affirmation" of (and their covert contempt for) the status quo.

What differs from Hollywood's formula in Landeta's paradigm is her democratic enfranchisement of *noir*'s "Others" as articulate agents who challenge the social order. María/Azalea, an unusual amalgamation of Mexico's forever-dichotomized virgin/whore figures, is as present with her desires, however modest, as her sister. No *femme fatale,* no salty prostitute with a heart of gold, Azalea is the prototype of what latter-day feminists have called the "sex worker." Her "practicality," her desire to survive, not only renders her outlook unromantic, it also makes it hard for Landeta or her spectators to romanticize her. Azalea's life circumstances may well reach melodramatic proportions—poverty has a tendency to be writ large—but her varied responses to strife save her from being cast in too romantic a light. In Azalea, Landeta unites *noir*'s realism with melodrama's emphatic descriptions in order to animate a usually passive subject to speak against social injustice.

The story of that injustice is narrated by editing decisions and thematic parallels that ultimately link the two sisters, and women in general, with each other and against male exploitation. Yet unlike *La Negra Angustias,* where this same theme is elaborated, there is no triumphant rallying cry at the film's end. Rather than a call to arms, *Trotacalles* is a cautionary tale. In response to the unrealistic optimism (and commensurate bad advice) of male directors' *cabaretera* films, Landeta blends *noir*'s pessimism with melodrama's *tristeza de la vida* to warn viewers of dangers that can be avoided only if social structures are disturbed.

It is hardly surprising, then, that marriage as a potentially exploitive institution should come under scrutiny. Landeta juxtaposes matrimony directly with prostitution not to dichotomize the pair, but to underline similarities inherent in both institutions. As the two sisters are paralleled, so too are their situations. It turns out that Rodolfo, the same suave man looking to sell his own sexual favors to Elena, is none other than Rudy, the crass character bent on marketing Azalea to other men. As Azalea's pimp and principal consort, and as Elena's purchased, extramarital conquest, Rudy/Rodolfo serves as common denominator by which the institution of marriage itself can be finally reckoned. By Landeta's calculations such unions are problematic at best. Rudy's commonlaw liaison with Azalea has about the same moral value as Elena's "legitimate" relationship with Faustino or her illicit affair with Rodolfo. And marriage, as part of a market economy, fares no better with respect to the other couples in the film. Faustino dispatches Elena to play cards "and lose a few pesos" with the ambassador's bored wife, who seems to enjoy no intimacies outside of gossip about other women's affairs. She does not even appear at Cabaret Ciro with her husband. Presumably, the ambassador will welcome her into his arms when his business deal with Faustino is concluded. A less obedient society woman, about whom Faustino reads in the newspaper, sacrifices her marriage, fortune, and good name when she is seen in the company of a poor-but-handsome soccer player. Her divorce seems just reward to Faustino, who uses the story to let his wife know that when a woman ceases to be of marketable value, she should immediately be released from the marriage contract and lose all benefits previously accruing to her.

Landeta questions the apparent moral legitimacy of marriage by staging happy domesticity (the society page over morning coffee, no less) in contradictory terms. The brilliantly lit, luxurious interiors of the Irigoyen kitchen contrast with the dark forces of Faustino's greed and Elena's desire. Impending doom is prefigured not only by Faustino's admonishing Elena via the newspaper article, but by his other seemingly casual remarks that raise the stakes of the breakfast conversation. Elena's fatal flaw, like that of other beleaguered *noir* figures, is to disregard Faustino's danger warnings. Spectators familiar with *noir*'s deadly pessimism suspect the worst: the banker knows about his wife's indiscretions and will punish her summarily.

Intercut with these brightly illuminated scenes are the *noir*-inflected sequences of Azalea's home life. A glaring light fixture casts deep shadows in the dingy room she shares with Rudy in the less-than-angelic Hotel del Ángel. Here desire and greed are reduced to base proportions. Azalea seems resigned to her life, hoping only that Rudy will remain "her man" and perhaps love her a little in the process. Rudy exhibits little inclination to do so; his desire is that Azalea support him and finance his "business" dealings with wealthy women. When her earnings decline as a result of her auto accident or her tending an increasingly ailing Ruth, her "indiscretions" reap a beating from Rudy. Domesticity, here or in ostensibly more pleasant surroundings, is categorically dangerous for women.

Trotacalles's focus on one of Mexico's most sacred institutions details an "obverse of the *[Mexican]* dream" in a notably different fashion than that in which Hollywood *noir* constructed its visions. Where male anxiety about women's participation in the social order propelled Hollywood narratives— Deborah Thomas theorizes that both the *femme fatale* and the "redemptive," domestic woman represented a threat to post-war male integrity[39]—Landeta's story is powered by her female characters' articulations of desire and dread regarding unions with *hommes fatales*. Where Hollywood *noir* heroes traded in a social economy that valued male-to-male relations above all else, *Trotacalles* describes a value system that both prizes female solidarity and admits (some) women's desire to be joined with men.

This bid for communitarian existence is best enacted in scenes where women together articulate their hopes and disappointments. Viewers are offered sequences of Azalea and Ruth and other women detailing their life stories as prostitutes. We see the consequence of those lives in Ruth's terminal illness as she coughs her lifeblood into a handkerchief while she struggles to deliver the moral message of the film. Embracing a death that will release her from a short lifetime of degradation, Ruth's deathbed speech is an exhortation to her companions and the audience to "build homes, raise children, and be useful for something or someone" (Fig. 3.5). Significantly, the difficulty in achieving that heavily melodramatized proposition is highlighted by *noir*-influenced representations of grinding adversity. The instant Ruth closes her weary eyes the *mariachis* accompanying her on her last journey cease. It

FIGURE 3.5. A streetwalker's final cough: "Build homes, raise children, and be useful for something or someone." Courtesy Marcela Fernández Violante.

seems that these sad street musicians' services were being paid for by the minute, and finishing their lament would require more *plañidera* funds than Ruth's companions could muster. Similarly, spectator investment in the pathos of the scene must be cut short. If Landeta's viewers are to follow Azalea's story clear-sightedly, if that "veil from the clichéd theme of prostitution" is to be removed, emotional responses must be budgeted.[40]

The wealth of female friendship and women's desire for heterosexual companionship (rendered in that melodramatic decree to "build a family") are here pitted against women's material poverty and their all-too-reasonable dread of male exploitation (expressed by *noir*'s realism). Sentimentality and romanticism simply have no space to expand in this tough woman's weepie, where ultimately survival itself is too expensive. Azalea, as María, is continually unable to warn her sister Elena of the dangers of existence in a world of men. Elena, perhaps overly cognizant that her status is precarious, tries to separate herself from her sister: "We're neither sisters nor equals," she protests to María when the latter tries to explain that the conditions of their estrangement stemmed from the seduction and abandonment of María by Jorge, one of Elena's previous suitors. Though viewers might regard Elena's harsh words as just cause to vilify her as the "bad" sister, the women's dialogue paints a nasty enough portrait of the double-dealing Jorge to make spectators question anew the legitimacy of the heterosexual pair bond. A subsequent scene underscores the perfidious nature of the Irigoyen marriage, suggesting that the *femme fatale* is not as fatal or as powerful as she would like to be. Faustino patronizes her, explaining that "a man my age marries a little chicken like you only to show her off. . . . After all, what else is she good for?"

Yet Faustino's exhibition of Elena eventually does more than "console an old . . . rich man," as he first explained. Not only does Elena keep the ambassador's wife happy at cards so that the diplomat can attend to Faustino's business propositions, but Elena's presence at Faustino's side undoubtedly attests to a virility that helps the aging banker to eventually secure the deal. Bringing home an expensive bracelet as a trophy, Faustino rewards his wife for services rendered: "You don't have to thank me," he tells her. "What's forty thousand pesos if it gives you pleasure? I just want you to realize the advantages you've got with a husband like me. Besides, you've earned the bracelet; it's your share of the deal I struck with the ambassador."

Faustino thus pimps Elena much as Rudy does her sister. Accepting this as her due, Elena misses seeing a trap that her husband has set to test her allegiance. He tells her that while he must travel to New York to "double his deal on the stock exchange" (and indeed, he invites his wife to accompany him), he will in any case leave a half million dollars' worth of diamond mine shares in her safekeeping. Not recognizing the double-dealing clues, nor the ironic significance of diamond mine shares, nor her role in the commodity exchange,

Elena begins to visualize the possibilities of life with Rodolfo, whom she now loves even though she knows him to be penniless. As Faustino hatches his plot, so does a considerably weakened *femme fatale* initiate hers. Viewers accustomed to *noir* outcomes anticipate that the antiheroine and her consort are headed for trouble.

Trouble has been presaged throughout the film by a series of bleak contrasts to the Irigoyens' wealth, glamour, and domesticity. Unlike the more mainstream cabaret films, *Trotacalles*'s *noir* sensibility affords a view of the working poor who are not redeemed at the film's end. Instead, their lives symbolize the moral poverty of the loveless unions of the rich, and indicate the depths to which the degraded will fall. It is noteworthy that the privileged site of difference in the film's comparisons of affluence and indigence is the place of compromised sexuality: throughout *Trotacalles*, the bedroom stands as a monument to failed fidelity.

Azalea and Rudy's hotel room, far from giving the couple a fixed address, functions as the marker of fleeting *amor pasajero*. In the place of transient love and ever-changing bodies, the prostitute and her pimp lead a de-eroticized life that underscores the mechanized, loveless character of their profession. Like those unsensational legs of the film's initial sequences, the bodies in this hotel room undress and prepare to sleep with one another without exciting the least bit of voyeuristic pleasure for themselves or their spectators. The most that we are invited to hope for is that Rudy will curtail his impulses to violence. Yet given this atmosphere and these circumstances, even this spectator desire is unmet (Fig. 3.6).

To rouse the appetites of another woman, the debonair Rodolfo creates a facsimile of luxury in the exclusive Reforma apartment he borrows from a friend. No less transitory than his hotel room, the apartment nevertheless aspires to bourgeois stability with its clean modern lines and tastefully appointed *mise-en-scène*. Above all, it resembles a stage, set to frame and facilitate Rodolfo's seduction and fleecing of the banker's wife. Here Landeta closely criticizes those "white telephone" melodramas that present such opulence as reality. Rodolfo may appear as stylish as Arturo de Córdoba's classy adulterer in *La diosa arrodillada*, but unlike director Roberto Gavaldón's exercise in extravagance, Landeta's decisively edited film permits us to see through Rudy's pretenses. She counterposes the elegant apartment with his bare-bones hotel room, Elena's grand bedroom, and Ruth's simple one, thus encouraging viewers to evaluate these highly significant private spaces in the context of a class analysis of a wider social order. That we do so with a measure of reluctance to fully condemn Rodolfo and Elena's actions is a tribute to Landeta's complex characterizations. Viewers may object to the adulterers' extramarital relationship, be outraged by Rudy's abuse and Elena's betrayal of María/Azalea, yet still be somewhat compelled to desire the couple's success versus the

FIGURE 3.6. María/Azalea's and Rodolfo/Rudy's pain-wrought relationship. Courtesy Marcela Fernández Violante.

triumph of a deceitful husband. Beyond stimulating our dreams of social equality, Landeta implicates her spectators in the realm of romantic desire, seducing us with erotically charged scenes where fully dressed lovers hint at a sexuality too explosive to uncover. We recognize the folly of our multiple identifications only when the scene shifts and *noir* replaces melodrama to electrifying effect.

We are again in a darkened street. Behind the wheel of Faustino's car, Elena appears as if about to drive herself to destruction. Leaving the working-class cabaret where she and Rodolfo have met to finalize escape plans, she heads for home for the last time in the Cadillac. María, now aware of her lover's and her sister's mutual desires for love and money and each other, appears in the nick of time at the Irigoyen driveway to try to prevent Rudy's desertion and Elena's demise. She argues with Elena, en route to retrieve her hastily packed bags, stolen (fake) stock, and (forged) passport, that Rudy is not only *her* man, but moreover a dangerous risk for Elena. "Don't be blind, Elena," she implores. "Don't sacrifice all the hard work it's taken you to get [where you are]. . . . He's not worth the trouble, not for a woman like you. . . ."

Still angry about purportedly losing former boyfriend Jorge to María, Elena prods her sister to desperation: "Rodolfo's worth something to *you?*" Determined to save her sister at any cost, María pulls out all the melodramatic stops, using her degradation to prevent Elena—and all the cinematically trained Elenas in the audience—from repeating her own mistakes. "What am *I* worth? Who am *I?* Whatever man pays attention to me, however miserable he might be, does me a favor. But you! Think what you could lose!" That María values survival above all else and that she would sacrifice herself in this display of rhetorical masochism for the benefit of her sister is finally the disturbing power of *Trotacalles*. An alternately love-struck and cynical Elena claims that with Rodolfo she knows love, desire, and their complete satisfaction; yet she would leave him before he could abandon her. She thereby presents herself once more as a practical woman who "knows how to conduct her own life." The tragedy here is located not so much in Elena's merciless view of heterosexual romance—after all, what man in this film has proven himself worthy of a woman's love?—nor does it simply reside in María's deplorable self-regard. In Landeta's lights true tragedy lies in the estrangement of women as sisters, which is occasioned not only by individual men, but by the corrupt institutions that support men's livelihoods against the best interests of women. Even though Elena condemns María as a streetwalker, even though María retorts that she became a prostitute "out of hunger and not vice," Landeta does not blame either of the victims of this androcentric order. In the end, the filmmaker's darkest circle of hell is ringed by women's profound alienation from each other.

This is borne out painfully in the last sequences. María's final "What will become of you, little sister?" is as despairing a comment as Landeta's portrayal of what eventually happens to María/Azalea herself. Discovering Rudy in front of the Reforma apartment, María begs him not to leave Mexico with her sister. His response is to hit her and abuse her with cruel epithets. María offers herself in sacrificial exchange for Elena's life: "Kill me if you want, but don't hurt Elena." They struggle, entangled. María threatens Rudy with exposure and scandal. He is enraged at this escalation of the stakes. If María's greatest fear is loss of sisterhood, Rudy's terror is being expelled from the very society he holds in both awe and contempt. We see him extract a knife and plunge it into María in an attempt to silence her betrayal of the confidence game that describes his entire identity as a man in a male-determined, class-bound social order. María falls to the ground, still protesting, "She's my sister!" as Elena herself makes an entrance in a speeding taxi.

The grief prophesied at the outset occurs with this second slamming of brakes and Elena's terrified face seeing her sister fallen and her lover on the run. For Landeta, the tragedy is rooted more in Elena's reactions than in María's fatal wounding. (Rudy's shooting by a passing policeman is even less significant; at this point his death functions as the just reward of the Mexican equivalent of a Hollywood Production Code punishment.) *Noir* despair is concretized here in Elena's alienation. Unlike fantastical melodramas where redemption assures the dying and their reunited loved ones a better world in the beyond, *Trotacalles* offers nothing beyond promises of hell. Elena rides away from the scene in her taxi (echoing and deepening the meaning of her first departure in the opening sequence) without comforting her dying sister, and Landeta's final images mirror the utter hopelessness of her callous act. In true *noir* fashion the unrepentant sister and wife returns home only to be turned away at her gate by a smug husband who has, as he explains, learned a thing or two from cinema. "I used that old movie trick," he tells her, "where the deceived husband surprises his wife . . . and it worked! You fell for it like an idiot. That stock was just so much valueless paper!"

Only at this juncture does Elena begin to realize that what has plummeted is her stock as a wife. It is her marriage that now exists only as valueless paper, and Faustino will make short shrift of that. Having met her taxi at the curb in front of his house, he pays off the driver as casually as he paid off María after running over her in his car, whisks Elena's luggage into the courtyard, and stands talking to her as if over breakfast. "I've known all along what you've been up to, Elena. . . . I just don't understand why you've returned here alone. I'd arranged to have you arrested at the airport. . . . Did your Romeo stand you up? I never would have believed it, with the sum of money he thought you had. . . . Well! Let that be a lesson to you."

The real lesson, as Elena is about to learn, is that Faustino is leaving her, quite literally, in the street. He enacts the figurative phrase *"dejarle a alguien en la calle"* (to leave someone penniless) by closing the gate with her bags inside and locking her out on the sidewalk. "What are you going to do now?" he wonders with some sadistic innocence. He walks into the garden only to return a second later to collect "the coat you've got on that's also mine" and leave her weeping at the gate. *Trotacalles's* theme music amplifies as she walks down the street to find other means of survival.

"¡Qué buen crimen! ¡A buena hora llegamos pa' verlo!"

Trotacalles's dark realism leaves spectators with a very clear idea about just what survival for Elena will entail. Her journey—from lower-middle-class secretary, to wealthy banker's wife, and (suggested by the film's finale) to *prostituta ambulante*—has been detailed with a great deal less sentimentality than that deployed by the lachrymose rags-to-riches films of the decade. Landeta's forthright narrative makes spectators attend with heart *and* mind to the story of seduction and betrayal. She even comments on those misinformed, spectacle-loving, depoliticized cinephiles, who simply "love a good story," in the person of the cabby, who drives Elena to meet Rudy, only to have her witness the gigolo's fatal wounding of her sister and his own gruesome death. The driver delights in the show: "What a great crime!" he exclaims, "We got here just in time to see it!"

If the middle classes, like the taxi driver, could be entertained by sleight-of-hand crime dramas, both cinematic and real, the politics and practices of *desarrollismo* stood a chance of survival. The trick of "The Cult of Progress" was to move citizens from revolution to capitalism, enticing them with visions of "society" fabricated by the mirage of materiality.[41] The self-made man was not only possible; he was a figure to emulate. With him believers would "applaud the launching of the national project, venerate the Good Families and the Best Society, not notice capitalist depredation, nor regard (repressed) workers' and *campesinos'* struggles, outbreaks of student rebellion, scarcity, or impoverishment."[42]

But the "great crime" of *alemanismo* centered not on the credulous masses, however unsavory their (government-cultivated) tastes. As Landeta suggests with Faustino Irigoyen, the criminals of the epoch were those impresarios who worked hand-in-hand with *la mano dura* of the regime to squeeze the country's resources for the benefit of the elite. Indeed, since Alemán consolidated his power into an authoritarianism by "co-opting . . . 'disciplining' . . . 'institutionalizing' . . . [and] repressing" every political voice in the nation from the PRI to trade unions, he looked to private entrepreneurs to advance his capitalistic goals. His very cabinet, as historian Tzvi Medin reveals, ". . . reflected the implicit logic of his national project, [and] came to legitimize the symbiosis between the national bourgeoisie and the ruling group of elites."[43] This mutual dependency, based on common aims, made for a remarkable roster of cabinet members. A prominent industrial magnate became Secretary of Economy while another headed Agriculture. A leading economist and big-business lawyer was named Secretary of Housing, and still another industrialist took charge of Mexican Petroleum. "And to top off these illustrative examples," an astounded Medin underscores, "we should remember that as president of the Bank of Mexico, Alemán named no one less than Carlos Novoa, who previously acted as president of the private Bankers Association."[44]

¡A buena hora llegamos para ver el crimen! While she doesn't detail his business dealings, Landeta has given us enough information to classify Irigoyen with the powerful Bankers Association that in 1947 "anticipated" a major peso devaluation and therefore precipitated the subsequent financial crisis of 1947 and 1948, when financiers' massive pesos-for-dollars exchange depleted federal dollar and gold reserves.[45] That Faustino has amassed wealth at a time when only the privileged had capital, that he deals with a U.S. economy instead of investing in Mexico, and that he evidences an eye for the exchange

value of all his commodities, including and especially his wife, symbolically places his character in the center of corruption that Landeta decried. As an analogy, the evils of pandering male companions of prostitutes compare graphically with the baseness of bankers like Faustino, for whom the commodification and marketing of the nation itself signify nothing more than business as usual. At a time when the very "corruption, lying, stealing, and appropriation of government funds that created a new bourgeoisie was assuring economic inequality," and at a time when this inequality threatened Mexico's survival and its integrity as a sovereign nation, as Daniel Cosío Villegas argued at the peak of the 1947–1948 crisis, the country was on the verge of losing its identity to its rich and powerful northern neighbor. Mexico, pimped, in effect, by its ruling elite, was on the road to "submitting" itself to the United States for "money, technical advice, direction regarding culture and art, and political guidance. . . ." Survival was so threatened that the nation was nearly driven to adopt "an entire system of values foreign to our history" and even "to effect the sacrifice of nationhood, and worse, the security of those who have labored to shape their own destiny."[46] It is remarkable how Cosío Villegas's catalogue of this potential loss of national selfhood is echoed by the class and gender inequalities delineated in *Trotacalles*.

Nevertheless, Landeta's bleak vision is not entirely unrelieved. Although corruption lurks on the fringes of her Club Verde, the working-class cabaret she compares to the ritzy Cabaret Ciro, the workers and most of the patrons are neither condemned nor romanticized. Given the national economic crisis, which fell proportionately harder on women than men, and harder on dark-skinned Mexicans of both sexes, the Club Verde represents a space of semi-viable employment and enjoyment for the dancers and musicians gathered there. It is particularly noteworthy that in these scenes the director's desire for realism has been achieved in near observational documentary style: long takes in full shots with a remarkably unobtrusive camera record a community in the grip of its pleasures. After a half-dozen women perform a circle dance, parading for themselves as much as for their audience, they invite the club's patrons to join them. The atmosphere is bright, as are all aspects of the *mise-en-scène*. Unlike Hollywood *noir*, where dank working-class bars, populated by shadowy, dark "Others," represent quintessential danger zones, the well-illuminated Club Verde appears democratically welcoming. Patrons, dancers, and musicians—some of whom literally represented themselves, as Landeta explained—portray a range of ethnicities and working-class people who historically frequented the dance hall.[47]

The Club Verde itself also existed in reality.[48] Its clientele included the railroad workers whom the film represents in a drunken brakeman who forces himself on Azalea. Sizing up the worker's vulnerability in one scene, Rudy decides to take advantage of the golden opportunity inebriation offers to relieve the *ferrocarrilero* of his week's salary. It is possible that the rolling of the so specifically identified worker can be linked to the late-1940s turmoil and corruption within the railroad workers' union, precipitated by the devaluation of the peso. The internal nature of the struggle could well be symbolized in Landeta's staging of the violence wreaked upon a worker by his corrupt union boss. Where union leaders deployed gunmen within the union to enrich their own coffers and maintain control, Landeta shows Rudy enacting his own disdain for a less well-heeled member of the working class. His robbery of the railroad worker parallels the union's maltreatment of its own. Once their internal problems were settled, they used the conflict as an excuse to help management reduce workers' salaries, slash their benefits, cut 12,000 jobs, and create 500 new sinecures for "workers whom we trust."[49]

If the "trustworthy" numbered so few in just one union, the figures that accounted for the "faithful" rich during Alemán's presidency were even lower. The wealthy, much favored by the government, were in effect "subsidized by the poor," and they nurtured "formulaic and hypocritical sentiments about the life of the poor that found their way into the cinema in general and the nightclub picture in particular, crystallizing a manichean view of poverty, codifying poor people's behavior, and reiterating the supposed 'natural laws' that mandated that the poor *owed* the rich submission. . . ."[50] *Trotacalles*, with its insistence on a significantly bleaker reality, denaturalizes the laws of *alemanismo* and its rhetorical sidekick, the *cabaretera* film, to suggest that indebtedness is much more purposefully imposed. Ultimately, Landeta's *noir*-ish paradigm of pimp, prostitute, and politico sheds light on the very depths that the bright, almost criminally optimistic discourses of *alemanismo* sought to obscure.

PART II

◩

Fin de Siglo *Mexamérica*

CHAPTER FOUR

Neomelodrama as Participatory Ethnography: Allison Anders's Mi vida loca

> Mexican popular culture is premised on the perennial confusion
> between life and melodrama, and the corresponding illusion that
> suffering, to be more authentic, must be shared publicly.
> —Carlos Monsiváis, "Mythologies"

The Free Trade, anti-immigrant, welfare reform years have brought suffering—and its expressive apparatus, neomelodrama—into full public view. The Mexican-U.S. border zone, where high drama is the stuff of daily existence, has provided the setting for a recent spate of family romances that intricately "confuse life and melodrama." Allison Anders's *Gas Food Lodging* (1991) and *Mi vida loca* (1993), together with films such as John Sayles's *Lone Star* (1996), Gregory Nava's *Mi familia* (1995), María Novaro's *El jardín del Edén* (1993), and Alfonso Arau's *Como agua para chocolate* (1992), share a debt to classic Mexican melodrama, where the blurring of fiction and fact has initiated decades of (happily) suffering spectators into life's moral mysteries.[1]

These neomelodramas, articulating moral codes of their own, alternately pay homage to and critique the traditional practices of the genre. *Lone Star*, for example, rewrites melodrama's incest taboo as codified more than half a century ago in Arcady Boytler's *La mujer del puerto* (1933). *Mi familia*, a sort of updated *Una familia de tantas* (Alejandro Galindo; 1948), takes its cues from a plethora of family sagas, adding magical realism to the mix. *Como agua para chocolate*'s magically real melodrama reconfigures Mexican epics of the Revolution, evoking the unconventional gender paradigms of Emilio Fernández's *Enamorada* (1946) and Matilde Landeta's *La Negra Angustias* (1949). *El jardín del Edén* reconsiders the melodramatized region of the border, moving purposefully away from the militarized depictions vividly envisioned by Alejandro Galindo's *Espaldas mojadas* (Wet Backs; 1953) and its successors. Defying the characterization of border-as-brothel in the manner of Alberto Gout's *Aventurera* (1949), *El jardín*'s realistically Edenic Tijuana itself becomes a protagonist in a new polyethnic, multicultural morality play.

In both *Gas Food Lodging* and *Mi vida loca*, Allison Anders confronts the realities of border dwellers' lives with an ethics and aesthetics that derive—and depart—from the ecstatic agonies of Mexican Golden Age cinema. Her work resonates with and rewrites rural and urban family melodramas, as well as darker melodramas of gangster and dance hall milieux. *Gas Food Lodging*'s interethnic love story is as freighted with familial anxiety as have been scores of romances depicting cross-class or mixed-"race" marriages since Fernández's *Flor silvestre* (Wild Flower; 1943). The Mexican nightclub and its smooth male operators featured in *cabaretera* films like Fernández's *Salón México* (Dancehall "México"; 1948) and Landeta's *Trotacalles* (1951) reappear transformed in (and by) Chicano/a contexts in *Mi vida loca*.

Anders's purposeful confusions of life and melodrama are also intimately linked to her own experiences. A single mother with a firsthand knowledge of the welfare system, she fashions her narratives of poor and working-class women's struggles and dreams with particular insight. Her images in *Gas Food Lodging* of a white teen from rural New Mexico sniffling in the dark as she watches an Anders reconstruction of a 1940s Mexican weepy aptly mirror the filmmaker's position and sensibilities, and anticipate her translation of melodrama's strategies into new social spaces like the Los Angeles Latino gang culture represented in *Mi vida loca*. Anders is a kind of participant ethnographer, in cultural critic James Clifford's sense, trying to figure out how to relate to her "subjects" and convey their (fictionalized) stories to her various potential audiences without losing a lot in the translation.[2] This chapter explores the translating ethnographer embodied in the neomelodramatist and attempts to read her translations in their own (trans)cultural contexts.

Turning, then, to the Echo Park district of Los Angeles where *Mi vida loca* is set—and where Anders lived for a decade—we can briefly consider how the film interacts with mainstream dramas about inner-city gangs, as well as how it relates to more independent features that deal with the grim realities confronted by today's youth. In opposition to monochromatic gangxploitation films like *Colors* (1988), for instance, where blurred medium shots with punishing docudrama lighting amalgamate the "hood" into a faceless mass, Anders humanizes her narrative from the first-person title to the film's closing credits, where she dedicates the film to her deceased "homegirl" and friend, Nica Rogers. While *Colors*'s cop protagonists see Los Angeles as a "war zone" that they "have the right to militarize," *Mi vida loca*'s intimate portraits of individuals within communities humanize the media-embattled barrios. The thin blue line that *Colors* defends with its criminalizing cameras mounted inside the "safety" of police cars elicits different sympathies, congruent with the expressly voyeuristic invitation the movie's publicity extends to its idealized spectators: "Two cops! Two gangs! One hell of a war! Director Dennis Hopper brings you as close as you can get to the violence on the streets of L.A. and still walk away." In contrast to *Colors*'s rationalization of the biggest LAPD paramilitary sweeps since 1965,[3] and against the corporate news media's rendition of people's outrage at police brutality in 1992,[4] *Mi vida loca* rejects the distancing aesthetics of the heli-cam in favor of intimate camera work that encourages viewers to see the neighborhood through the eyes of those who live there.

Mi vida loca's terms of enunciation and address share more common ground with Chicano productions that imagine very differently located spectators, who neither lust for gratuitous violence nor are much invested in walking away from what well may be home. Gang members in *American Me* (1992), for example, are not the disembodied rioters of docudrama, inarticulately looting the K-Mart and wielding the spoils of war. Edward James Olmos reveals the human face and wrenching personal stories of boys and men who participate in gang life on the streets and in prison. His examination of masculine subjectivity is unparalleled by mainstream films that purport to discuss Chicano identity.[5] But while both *American Me* and *Mi vida loca* respectfully chronicle *locos'* American lives from behind the lines, their narrative styles and ideal spectators are ultimately distinct. Olmos's *Scared Straight!* approach is a warning to young men to get out or stay out of gangs because they lead only to psychical or physical annihilation. Anders's melodrama, focusing on the ramifications of violence, including the violence of poverty, addresses those whom Chicana and Latina critics see *American Me* as almost literally erasing: young Chicanas whose "girl gangs" function as life-support systems.[6]

Like *American Me*, *Mi vida loca* also speaks to spectators whose lives intertwine with gang members. After attending a screening in Albuquerque only to hear the comments of a group of privileged white spectators who "really didn't see the point" (but proceeded nonetheless to pontificate about the film's moral meaning), I knew I needed a viewing context that addressed my primary community affiliations. So I went home to L.A. and my Highland Park-Lincoln Heights barrio, four miles northeast of Echo Park, to watch the video with longtime Chicana friends, whose age, like mine, aligned us more with Anders's own forty-something perspective than with that of her protagonist teens. Viewing and discussing *Mi vida loca* with my homegirls was a gratifying experience in community spectatorship for this resident alien white girl from Cheech and Chong's *Up in Smoke* neighborhood, since the politics of representation and reception engaged all of the women in the room. But we gave serious attention to the constitutional power inequities of that engagement, puzzling out critic Rosa Linda Fregoso's query: what *does* happen "when you wrap a white girl's story in brown girls' drapes"?[7] Answers that expanded and challenged Fregoso's perspectives on the film were suggested by our conversations that afternoon and during subsequent trips home. Buttressed by interviews with other teens from the area, they are incorporated into what follows.

Before considering the politics of participant ethnographic melodrama, let's look at some participant ethnographic criticism, the homegirls' take on *Mi vida loca*'s drama in three acts: "Sad Girls, ¿Y qué?"; "Don't Let No One Get You Down"; and "Suavecito," the name of the truck that metaphorically powers the entire melodrama. Esperanza, my guide to Mexican melodrama ever since our matinees at neighborhood Spanish-language cinemas, offered this summary of the first act: "Two girls meet, grow up, fall in (platonic) love, express their sublimated sexual desire through the same male lover, conceive and bear his children, and act out their love for each other in the only acceptable way: under the guise of obviously fake hatred. In some ways this is your typical Hollywood plot, only with girls."[8] However apt this interpretation, we'll find it—and Anders's script—hotly contested in the discursive turf wars that critics and journalists have been waging over this film.

While Mona's (Angel Aviles) and Maribel's (Seidy Lopez) story in Act I has inspired fierce debate in academic and journalistic circles, Act II's protagonist, Giggles (Marlo Marron), who struggles to find work after serving an undeserved prison sentence, has been greeted with a curious silence. Elena, my friend Esperanza's twenty-year-old niece, explained the lack of attention this way: "[Critics] either didn't even notice what was going on with a woman trying to get a job when that's almost impossible, or else they did see and it made 'em nervous that Chicanas are gonna take over business like we're supposedly taking over L.A." As we move along in the analysis we'll consider the critical silences Giggles faces on a number of fronts.

In response to the third segment, my friend Mónica talked desire, resignation, and revenge. Anders's story of a womanizer's (Jesse Borrego) conquest and betrayal of Alicia, La Blue Eyes, a dreamily romantic college girl (Magali Alvarado), *"es la historia de la vida"* about "men who love us and leave us." But Anders does not "seduce and abandon" her viewers as El Durán ensnares the gullible Alicia. The filmmaker's melodramatic imagination, tempered by humor, is not bound by traditional Mexican cinematic strategies but is in dialogue with them. Her spectators are afforded distance from the cinematic lure of melodrama, so long thought to trap women in a disempowering denial of the mechanics of representation.[9] Mónica clearly articulated Anders's rewriting of Mexican popular culture's representation and reception strategies: "She kills off the beautiful bastard and then plays a jig at his funeral! I stopped crying about *cabrón* men and had myself a serious laugh."

With its public rendering of suffering *and* its mocking of life's perfidy, *Mi vida loca*'s confusion between life and melodrama invites fully engaged spectatorship. The self-aware viewing positions to be enjoyed in the film are foreseen in *Gas Food Lodging*, when Anders has her protagonist, a teen called "Shade" (Fairuza Balk), imagine herself a character in the "Elvia Rivero" melodramas she has been weeping over (Fig. 4.1). In a gesture reminiscent of *The Purple Rose of Cairo* (Woody Allen; 1985),[10] where Mia Farrow's movie-entranced character is embraced by the matinee idol who has stepped off the screen in order to return her gazing adoration, Anders's Shade (also the viewers' shadow) reflects on the possibilities of a desiring, sentient viewer. It is a distanced Shade, dryly narrating the image of herself overcome with emotion, who attests to Anders's gratifying reworking of spectatorship theory. When the teen extends the interior space of the Sunn Cinema to comment on what happens when "reality" and "fantasy" meld outside the theater, we are invited

FIGURE 4.1. Melodramas to weep for: Nina Belanger as "Elvia Rivero." *Gas Food Lodging* frame enlargement.

to unite affect and intellect in order to establish a comfortable distance from that (allegedly) desire-destroying cinematic snare with which classic melodrama (theoretically) entraps unsuspecting viewers.

It's revealing to explore how the filmmaker accomplishes this. Tropical rhythms issuing from a bar, together with muted neon lighting and other signifiers of sordid sophistication, link *Gas Food Lodging* to the stylistics of 1940s cinema and anticipate Anders's translations in *Mi vida loca*. The impossibly long hood of a Cadillac—a standard feature of gangster movies on both sides of the border, as well as a marker of the Mexican dance hall picture—inserts itself as a reminder of nefarious wealth. The car pauses in front of the rundown bar, identifying an intermediate space between the "reality" of Laramie, a fictitious town in New Mexico, and the "fantasy" of movie melodrama. Shade's voice-over, functioning as our Elvia Rivero figure, narrates a love story from this in-between place while we watch a dead-ringer for Shade move into the neon-lit frame with her girlish pigtails swaying to a Latin beat. "My mom used to say that the easiest place to meet a guy was a bar," Shade confides. We smile knowingly; Shade is no future denizen of the low life. Elvia Rivero (Nina Belanger) has convinced her that she needs to find a man—"for my mother, so we can do all the dumb normal stuff families do."

Messages, in Anders's films, are intentionally mixed. The confusion of life and melodrama, she clearly understands, is what we've come to the cinema to enjoy and unravel. Like Mexican Golden Age audiences, we "are not seeking to 'dream,' but to learn skills, to lose inhibitions. . . ." In experiencing neomelodrama, we're prepared "to suffer and be consoled in style"[11] only if we can also celebrate and be amused by life's vicissitudes. We can thus indulge without risk in Shade's naiveté. Although the suave customer stepping out for a cigarette conveys the sense of danger and excitement ever present in the *cabaretera*, we know we're "really" in Anders's safe hands. When Shade announces that "One night I saw him—the one I'd been looking for," we're relieved that we know something more than our protagonist. Her Marlboro Man is no prettily disguised pimp in the manner of melodrama's characteristically evil Romeos, but a former friend of Shade's mother. We can afford to find pleasure in Shade's assessment that "It was like he'd walked straight out of an Elvia Rivero movie," because the man with "the clothes of a Teamster and boots from Spain" is a figure in Shade's melodrama, not Anders's. When Shade's dreaminess juxtaposes her alter ego and the silent smoker in a few frames of black and white Elvia Rivero-esque fantasy, the filmmaker inspires our understanding of the melodramatic mode and the possibilities of a desiring spectatorship for both women and men, since the constructed nature of cinematic fiction becomes as overt to Shade as it is to her spectators (Figs. 4.2 and 4.3).

FIGURE 4.2. Fabulous fake: a moment from an "Elvia Rivero" movie. *Gas Food Lodging* frame enlargement.

FIGURE 4.3. "Elvia Rivero" bit player as Fairuza Balk's desiring Shade in *Gas Food Lodging*. *Gas Food Lodging* frame enlargement.

Mi vida loca sustains the desiring, self-aware subjectivities proposed in Anders's earlier film, while maintaining dialogic continuity with the "mythologies" of Mexican melodrama.[12] Anders leaves behind the "rural innocence" of Laramie—which teases reality with its fictional status and its stagey look of a western ghost town[13]—for what we might call the "urban innocence" of a hyperreal Los Angeles.

I will return to a fuller discussion of border mythologies in the following sections, and further explore varied notions of innocence, but here I am most interested in prefacing how the filmmaker explodes the myth of "innocent" representations in cinema. *Mi vida loca* not only addresses the constructed nature of fiction, but self-reflexively regards the fabricated nature of filmic representations of reality. Ethnography, for the neomelodramatist, is consequently best understood in adjectival form: "ethnographic" proceeds toward a description of reality without ever arriving at the "truth." Participant ethnographic melodrama, involving not only the filmmaker but those whom anthropology used to call "native informants" and whom we now know to be participant ethnographers themselves, proceeds toward truth even more ponderously. On one hand, participants have their own ideas regarding their ethnographic self-fashioning.[14] On the other hand, melodrama exacts its own homage to (metaphors of) truth. If suffering and joy's often contradictory claims to authenticity do require a public forum, what more lucid arbiter than self-aware neomelodrama to weigh these claims and disclose the ramifications of their being staked in the first place?

A brief look at neomelodrama's historical antecedents suggests why Anders might choose this genre as an instrument for social change. Based on Peter Brooks's account of the birth of melodrama as a post-sacral genre arising from the French Revolution's production of a new, secular political ethics, we can posit a similar trajectory vis-à-vis the Mexican Revolution and the truth claims of its cultural productions. Mexican melodrama, from which Anders's and others' neomelodramas are nurtured, parallels French revolutionary rhetoric "where the word is called upon to make present and impose a new society, to legislate the regime of virtue . . . [within] a new world, a new chronology, a new religion, a new morality. . . ." Melodramas composed after the French Revolution—like those of post-revolutionary Mexico, including, in both instances, the diatribes of political orations—stage "incessant struggle[s] against enemies, without and within, branded as villains, suborners of morality, who must be confronted and expunged, over and over, to assure the triumph of virtue."[15] Anders's new, Mexamerican melodrama is conceived at a time when truth and ethics are again on trial for a Latino community. *Mi vida loca* responds to the media and police-incited moral panic of the late 1980s and early 1990s in Los Angeles, where outbreaks of white middle-class fear of impoverished youth of color resulted in spectacular police repression and concomitant civil disobedience. Anders's contemporary staging of a new morality that redresses the injustices of the "old regime" is also tied to another filmic representation of an earlier moral panic: the World War II era of radio, newspaper, and police-induced violence against young Mexican and Mexican American men recalled in Luis Valdez's *Zoot Suit* (1981). In the analysis that follows, I hope to show how Anders's deliberate confusions of life and melodrama draw upon the "revolutionary" ethics and aesthetics of neomelodrama's remote historical antecedents in order to describe a very different moral universe from the ones that feed contemporary panics.

GETTING ALONG IN ECHO PARK

Allison Anders is on intimate terms with cultural syncretism. As a fifteen-year-old in 1969, she made a painful cross-country journey from her Kentucky birthplace, through Florida, then Arizona, fleeing rural poverty, gang rape, and a gun-wielding stepfather, before settling in working-class Los Angeles.[16] To follow the outlines of her biography is to understand something about the formation of young women's romantic imagination in difficult, dramatic circumstances. Like thousands of girls in the rebellious '60s, she fell in love with Paul McCartney. Paul spoke to her from the Beyond, she thought (this during the days when the musician was rumored dead). His voice convinced her that she was his beloved, which was enough to convince others that she needed institutionalization. ("In retrospect," writes critic Ruby Rich, "not the worst trait for a future screenwriter and filmmaker" who would eventually pen *Paul is Dead*, along with a host of other award-winning scripts she would direct.[17]) After treatment in a mental hospital, a more concrete love affair took her to England. Pregnant, she returned to L.A. and Los Angeles Valley Junior College to study, wait tables, and make ends meet with welfare. She had a second daughter and fell in love once more, this time with the movies. In 1984 impassioned determination put her on the *Paris, Texas* set of her favorite director, Wim Wenders. From there, it was a relatively short jump to film school at UCLA and the rest of her creative life.[18]

When she moved to Echo Park in 1986, she "just basically decided that we were really going to get into the neighborhood."[19] But as she told me in an interview, it was her daughter Devon who made the easiest connections: "She bonded with the neighborhood immediately. Now she speaks perfect conversational Spanish."[20] In the Echo, Anders became the mother of culturally blended children, "white *cholas*," who form a small part of "a whole faction of an unknown subculture in Los Angeles."[21] Devon's primary community constituted a vibrant group her filmmaking mother had never seen on screen. Devon spent the eve of her sixteenth birthday with the Chicana friends from the neighborhood with whom she grew up. Anders remembered observing, "You've known these girls since you were eight years old. Think about the things you've gone through together. Where is that on the screen?" That's when Anders decided, "I'm gonna write a girl movie."[22]

Through her daughters the filmmaker began to learn more about the young neighborhood women. "Even before I met the Gang Girls, the real Gang Girls," she said, "I had seen these two fourteen-year-old girls with babies on their hips, yelling at each other. So finally I said, 'Devon, what's up with these girls?'" Devon's "translation" twists in the ethnographic thread that becomes the first of *Mi vida loca*'s three interlocking dramas: "Well, Christine and Marty were best friends since elementary school. Then Christine had a baby by Ernesto. But then Marty had a baby by Ernesto. And now they don't get along."[23]

"Getting along," as anyone knows who shares Rodney King's hope for peaceful coexistence in heterogeneous L.A., is both a utopic dream and a bare-bones strategy for survival. Anders's two fictive teens, Mona and Maribel (known respectively as "Sad Girl" and "Mousie"), not only figure out how to get along with one another, but how to resume being best friends—*co-madres* in the literal sense of the word—in order to fight for themselves and their kids in a world with increasingly scarce resources. Anders, for her part, besides figuring out how to get along in her neighborhood through her daughters, built her own relationships. After introducing herself to Nelida Lopez, one of the youngest girls in the Echo Park gang, Anders began to envision "getting along" in both real and cinematic terms. In Nelida (dubbed "Whisper"), Anders found her first "native informant," her connection to other gang kids in the community. In Anders, Whisper found her own "native informant": the film director who would cast the teen in a major role and introduce her to another world. While the power imbalances in these relationships have to be acknowledged—by the participant ethnographers on both sides of the paradigm and by those of us looking on—Anders's work demonstrates that "getting along" in culturally syncretic, resource-squeezed L.A. first and foremost requires engagement.

So she and her family became a part of the neighborhood, the filmmaker and the gang kids negotiating power relations that would span the entire range of the filmmaking effort. After establishing the terms of their engagement, says Anders, "my relationship with the girls in Echo Park, and the boys . . . continued to develop. They were involved in teaching me the slang, the clothes, the cars, the tunes. They posed for photographs and I videotaped them. I would deliver scripts to their homes and they would come to my house with scripts under their arms and pencils behind their ears. . . ."[24] In all, there were "about twenty kids, boys and girls, [who] helped me on every draft of the script."[25] They made form and content suggestions, some of which Anders would accept, some not. What mattered was the process her decisions filtered through. Her artistic sensibilities and choices as a director were consciously rooted in a community of which she was also a part.

These production details reveal something of the power relations at work in the film's creation. An "orchestration of multivocal exchanges occurring in politically charged situations,"[26] *Mi vida loca* operates simultaneously as a cultural project and an aesthetic creation. As a project, it responds to the filmmaker's responsibilities to community members who shared their expertise. Recognizing her debt to the neighborhood, Anders arranged benefit screenings to fund scholarships for local youth (she continues to provide five grants per year[27]), and connected cast and crew to IFP West's Project Involve (funded principally through her efforts), which offers a mentorship program for young women interested in filmmaking. As an aesthetic creation, the ethnographic elements of the melodrama permit us to see how "the subjectivities produced in these often unequal exchanges—whether of 'natives' or of visiting participant observers—are constructed domains of truth, serious fictions."[28] By linking Anders's role in her community with filmic evidence of interaction, we can better appreciate how the film—and the filmmaker—conceive of "getting along" in multicultural Los Angeles.

TAGGING THE TURF

Mi vida loca's opening credits display the signs by which we might choose to read this theatrically structured film. Pen and ink drawings of the Virgin, details of praying hands, enchained crosses, and figures representing *la muerte* share brilliantly colored space with images of lowrider cars, pairs of fuzzy dice, and bleeding hearts pierced by swords or crowned with thorns. These static icons belong to a highly expressive visual vernacular whose lexicon derives from Catholic and indigenous religious imagery as well as from the sacralized quotidian. Their hieroglyphic quality derives from and alludes to archaeological and historical signs such as those carved on pyramids, painted on *retablos,* or silk-screened onto posters. Anders's use of this symbolic system connects *Mi vida loca* to a particular interpretive community, suggesting that the film is "about" or "for" Chicanos/as, while her juxtaposition of cast, writing, direction, and production credits with this iconography suggests in addition that the film issues "from" a particular community, whose members' names themselves function as signs. Names of professional and nonprofessional actors are linked with stylized ribbons and chains of steel, thorns, and roses to claim the sort of community territory staked out by similar lists graffitied on walls. By not intercutting or breaking up names with moving images, and by not superimposing names over shots that privilege moving picture over static word (a strategy that would have resulted in the cinematic equivalent of "crossing out" and "de-meaning" gang members' tags), Anders fully credits those who made the film possible.

Musical cues further locate *Mi vida loca* in its specific community setting. Honking horns on the soundtrack, together with a Chicano band, The Crusados, invite viewers to enter the barrio: "Let's take a trip down Echo Park Avenue!" The horns, at once jubilant and cautious, ask viewers to consider the inclusiveness of the invitation as well as the significance of cruising what may be somebody else's streets. For community members whose Avenue spectators are about to traverse, there's a different invitation and significance in the crossover band's music. The Crusados's lyrics remind locals of the interconnected culture and history of all L.A.'s Latino neighborhoods. Their invitation is a recontextualization of the words of Thee Midniters's hit that invited '60s listeners to "Take a trip down Whittier Boulevard!" This reference to the two widely known groups (and the two distinct neighborhoods) simultaneously speaks to the unity with the larger Latino community these groups have engendered, as well as to the impossibility of some kind of essentialized, autonomous turf within any single barrio. While The Crusados have ushered us into a specific gang territory, bounded by specific street names with which gangs tend to mark their turf, all of us—gang members, filmmakers, spectators of all kinds—have links to other people and places. This linkage, Anders says through her credit sequence, is part of the eclectic nature of community itself. Yet however syncretic, however democratically cruised by anyone, the streets Anders focuses on constitute a decidedly local space within a global context. As her subsequent sequences suggest, and as one of Echo Park's homeboys will remind viewers, "You can come into our neighborhood as long as you respect us." The filmmaker's highlighting of community codes has set the stage for this respectful meeting of outsiders and insiders.

Anders gives us our first set of bearings with a series of postcard shots from the heart of the Echo. A static camera shows us the daytime L.A. skyline over the tops of trees crisscrossed by street lights and telephone wires. Fountains jet from Echo Park Lake in the next take, and California palms tower glamorously in a subsequent low-angle. A couple embraces near two young children in a long shot across the lake, and a close-up of a circling pair of pristinely white swans underscores the nostalgic voice-over narration: "This is the L.A. neighborhood where I grew up, Echo Park. We're east of Hollywood and near Downtown. We have a lake that's been here since the '20s, when movie stars had love nests in the hills."

Hollywood, movie stars, love nests in the hills; we're deep in Anders territory here. The filmmaker who gave us *Gas Food Lodging*'s love-struck '40s stars, comparing their movie angst with that of her "real" characters (again, by a series of static shots likening Laramie to a romantic film set), draws spectators into the realm of movie-inspired romance. As follow-up to these idyllic, signature sequences, Anders proceeds to subvert the very notion of authorship, undermining her own territorial authority as filmmaker. A young Chicana's voice-over addresses viewers directly, narrating yet another tale about storytelling: "Our homeboys take pride in telling the history of our barrio 'cause white people leave out a lot of stuff when they tell it." Will homeboys tell the story, we now wonder? Will white people (like Anders, like me) tell it and leave stuff out? Will our female narrator take us down Echo Park Avenue? Can she or anyone really tell the (whole) story? Just whose *vida loca* is this anyway?

The answer begins to unfold immediately, as the romance of the lake becomes mitigated by the realism of the streets. The shots are still tight, synecdochic. We stand under an overdetermined street sign marking Echo Park Boulevard, the low angle shot obliterating anything but the significance of the tag. A classic car, heavy with history and L.A. stories yet to be told, slowly cruises past the signpost. A man vending popsicles from a cart, Mexican style, walks past a motionless camera that also captures background advertisements. Writing as cultural signifier becomes more pronounced: shots are composed around signs for *La Guadalupana* market, Dr. F. Barreto's *clínica dental*, a presumably "pioneering" maternity shop next to a *taquería*, a street-corner newsstand, and a liquor store felicitously named "The House of Spirits." The final neighborhood snapshot takes in the writing on a cinderblock wall where the Echo Park Locos have tagged their names and claimed their turf. With these quite literal signature shots, the melodramatic ethnographer again credits the authorship of community members who take part in relating their *vidas locas*. Anders's metaphoric "credits" thus allow us to read the possessive of the film's title as a marker of community property. "My" crazy life becomes part and parcel of "our" *loca* existence, as the graffitied wall attests, *con safos.*[29]

The narrator continues to elaborate this fusion of the collective and the individual, establishing, in addition, an initial outsider/insider paradigm that eventually gives way to a configuration of a collective civic body: "On Saturdays and Sundays," she says, "*everybody* shops at Sunset and Echo Park Avenue. There's no reason to leave. You can get anything you need in *my* neighborhood." The words "everybody," "you," and "my" interact in a newly oriented map here. The first statement is at once inclusive and exclusive: "*everybody* shops." Before considering her next words, I count myself in, having some fifteen years of *La Guadalupana* groceries under my belt. Then inclusivity yields to a narrower definition of "everybody" as the narrator's subsequent sentence reframes the significance of the first: "There's no reason to leave—*our town.*" In this context "everybody" not only implies a "we," it also constitutes a "you"; insiders and outsiders here exist separately. (However many *Guadalupana* foodstuffs may have found their way home to my Highland Park refrigerator, I have always been an outsider on a shopping excursion.) But possibilities of interrelation between and among Los Angelinos surface in the third sentence, where the vernacular "you" democratically refers to insiders and outsiders alike. "You" can get, "one" can get, indeed, "we" can get anything in "my neighborhood."

Cultural citizenship is a product of transculturation. In the era of global migrations and immigrations, "We" are constituted and reconstituted by a confluence of narratives of tradition and travel.[30] If the place of the modern ethnographer, as James Clifford asserts, is to approach culture as a participant observer, and if participant observation is the business of "researchers" and "informants" alike, then we are all "in a state of being in culture while looking at culture," which is "a form of personal and collective self-fashioning."[31] This self-fashioning happens in the space "*between* cultures," and is precisely where we find ourselves in *Mi vida loca.* Again, though the film focuses on a single group of kids within the Echo Park gang, it considers the dialogic nature of what we might call a politics of *identities.* Not only do individuals merge with—and emerge from—collective subjectivities constructed within the neighborhood; self-fashioning depends on forces of transculturation from without. That "pervasive condition of off-centeredness in a world of distinct meaning systems" is expressed by our narrator, who migrated north from Mexico to become a part of the neighborhood: "When I first moved here from Mexico all the signs in the stores were in English and I couldn't read them." Lessons from her brand-new best girlfriend changed that, we later learn. But even as the barrio worked to fashion her, it too was shaped from the outside: "Now there's as much Spanish as there is English."

You can still get anything you want in our neighborhoods. On my most recent trek to *La Guadalupana,* I wanted to explore the workings of cultural hybridity, to reflect further on what it means, following Rosa Linda Fregoso, to "wrap a white girl's story in brown girls' drapes." Having shared the economic conditions of the barrio, I also wanted to keep in mind how class-based identities intersect with ethnic ones. If identity is a thing of conjunctions and not of essences, how did the wonderfully odd juxtapositions of our *rasquache,* make-do neighborhood—so closely allied with the cultural improvisations of other Latino neighborhoods—contribute to who we are and the stories we tell? Anders's literal detailing of the signs of barrio life encouraged me to look at other signifiers of cultural mixing that inform conjunctural identities in Latino communities. I proceeded to study the signs of syncretic exchange that marked the route from one barrio to another.

Heading out in my friend Esperanza's truck, I left the turf of my former students, members of Los Aves 43 gang, and my old house near the school. Cheech and Chong's big brown *Up in Smoke* palace disappeared in the rear view mirror, chased by a reflection of the housing project and its mural: Villa, Zapata, César Chávez, and the likenesses of the neighbors, all dominated by a reproduction of Swiss anthropologist Gertrude Blom's photograph of a Tzotzil holy man from Chiapas.[32] The Charles Lummis adobe, home of an early Los Angeles inventor and investor, sat around the corner protected behind iron gates, a point of interest on the tourist trail. On the other side of the freeway, Heritage Square Victorians—transplanted from their original sites downtown on Bunker Hill—begged the question of whose heritage we were to celebrate, all the while posing for Saturday morning visitors' cameras. South through Lincoln Heights, past sweatshops and Central American restaurants and Bank of America's nuclear-family-in-the-barrio mural, past the railroad tracks and industrial zones of the north inner city, past Olvera Street and Union Station, wound ancient crossroads of tourists and travelers. In the shadow of the Bonaventure Hotel, skirting the single most traversed freeway intersection in the world, Sunset Boulevard snaked a mile to Echo Park, a neighborhood in which the "pervasive condition of off-centeredness in a world of distinct meaning systems" constitutes meaning through its very diversity.

In my borrowed transport I reflected on dwelling and travel in these connected neighborhoods, where, to borrow Clifford's words, "the two experiences [and, we could say, the two barrios] are less and less distinct."[33] I thought about being a white girl telling one story about another white girl's stories regarding our brown neighbors, even as my homegirls' stories found their own way into this script, while a cacophony of other critical stories from journalists and academics resonated off-stage. I thought about folks real and fictional, about Anders's fictionalized dramas and her dramatic realities. How, for example, do we talk about Anders's friendships turned familial, as in the case of her own adoption of her deceased homegirl's three-year-old son? How do we understand alternative, interethnic families, like the one the filmmaker composed with her daughter's African American friend who needed to live with the Anders clan for a number of years? If our interventions in interconnecting worlds are constitutionally "inauthentic," as Clifford proposes, if we are "caught between cultures and implicated in others," not unlike those cultural artifacts that form our environments, then what matters is how our representations engage in a politics of location.

Anders has been extraordinarily careful to provide such a context. Her confusions between life and melodrama extend to self-aware stylistics within her films and also characterize extrafilmic (advertising, critical) apparatuses. Her standpoint vis-à-vis the community she portrays is evidenced in every interview she gives, in each press package her office sends to reviewers,[34] in her public appearances, and in other unusual direct communications (including published responses to critics and handouts given to audiences at screenings) that address spectators' questions about what a working-class white girl is doing making a film about working-class Latinas. Whatever reviewers—or audiences reached by the extrafilmic material, including the knowledge of other spectators—may think about the results of her work, Anders's self-disclosures invite us to think about the politics of representation.[35]

Yet as the filmmaker herself makes clear, all the disclosure in the world will not rectify power imbalances created since colonialism. When white people recount other peoples' histories, as *Mi vida loca*'s Mona reminds viewers, we categorically leave stuff out. The understatement speaks volumes: those with the power to narrate not only shape history but also public policies (based on those incomplete or misleading pictures) that further determine both the present and futures of those whose access to narration is compromised. Not until social and political policies—informed by communities speaking for and from any number of their multiple identities—enfranchise those whom they have systematically marginalized will power be democratically exercised. Working toward that goal, we can benefit from the strategies of progressive filmmakers like Anders whose lives and art struggle to denaturalize the process of representation.

Mona further prompts us to think about Clifford's "dwelling in travel" and "traveling in dwelling" when she offers, "When I show you all the crazy shit this truck can do, maybe you'll understand." Five shots of a gyrating camper top, embellished with the image of a gun-toting figure of a woman, preface what we're meant to comprehend in this film. It's the big stuff: crazy lives, insane deaths, binding love, all stirred up. Before the intertitle of the first act appears on screen, we glimpse—with a tracking shot focused *through* Echo Park vehicles—mourners embracing around a freshly dug grave. "We take life as it comes in my neighborhood," the narrator philosophizes, "The good and the bad. Like everyone else we have our ups and downs. We take it as it comes. You keep cool, knowing in your heart what goes around comes around. That's life in the Echo, eh?" Through the grim and transcendent realities that the details of this melodrama will unveil, we understand something about life in the Echo and in other *fin de siglo* urban locales, where the constructed domain of truth is indeed serious fiction.

ACT I: "SAD GIRLS, ¿Y QUÉ?"; OR, WOMEN IN LOVE

There is, in the first act of *Mi vida loca*, a bit of not-so-serious fiction that helps us think our way around the problems of representation and reality. Ever the ironic ethnographer, Anders has lifted a marvelous fake from her earlier melodrama to lend purposeful incredulity to *Mi vida loca*'s trysts with realism. It works like this: in love with love, *Gas Food Lodging*'s young protagonist spends her time, where else, but at the movie matinees, where 1940s-style Spanish language melodramas inspire her own love schemes. The film-maker, rather than inserting a sequence from any number of "real" melodramas, something from Mexico's Golden Age, for example, constructs her own movie-within-a-movie to further illustrate melodrama's metaphoric hold on reality. Screening her own "Elvia Rivero" picture at that Sunn Cinema of the exaggerated spelling, Anders plays tongue-in-cheekily with viewers who must employ melodrama's own aesthetic codes in order to discover the truth of fiction. Her use of the "mode of excess" particularly pressures spectators to consider relative truths.[36] The countenance of "Elvia Rivero," photographed in dramatically angled close-ups on posters that grace both the theater and Shade's bedroom, is actually an unknown face in an overwhelmingly identifiable Latina star system (Fig. 4.4). The actress's soft Spanish sibilants are an amalgamation of regional accents. "Elvia Rivero" plays a young woman who seeks love (but finds trouble) by looking at photographs of possible suitors, a strategy that Shade (and unwary spectators) may find tempting.

Lest *Mi vida loca*'s spectators succumb to such an illusion, Anders reconstructs this hyperreconstructed filmic reality and *reruns the "same" movie on TV in Echo Park*. As Mona prepares to leave her house to face off Maribel in a gun battle over their mutual lover, we hear "Elvia Rivero" greet the day ahead:

FIGURE 4.4. Sharing Shade's wall of honor with Bowie, "Elvia Rivero" stars in Anders's ersatz film *Sacred Dudes*. *Gas Food Lodging* frame enlargement.

"¡Qué día tan glorioso!, ¿verdad?" she emotes to the neighbor ladies. "¡Que tengan bonito día!"

As Mona continues to talk to her sleepy dad, dreaming of his deceased wife in front of the television, we further appreciate the seriousness behind Anders's humorously blurred boundaries between art and ethnography. With the flickering glow of the TV resembling the screening apparatus of film, Anders not only shows how melodrama courts "reality," but how "reality" mimes melodrama. The dialogue between Mona and her father (Carlos Rivas, a veteran film actor of latter-day Mexican melodramas as well as Hollywood vehicles) is linguistically sutured to the diegetic film. Their conversation brings to light melodramatic truths, where love, according to Mona's father, is expressed in the strangest ways: "I was dreaming that your mother was yelling at me," he laughed. "She always yelled at me, I don't know what about. It was her way."

Yelling and love are not at odds in this film, where Mona and Maribel's passionate friendship is declared at piercing decibels. Repeatedly, Anders contraposes their fighting words against romantic backdrops in order to heighten the intensity of their relationship and her serious fictions. Transforming the apartment window exchange of "Elvia Rivero's" sweet neighbor ladies, Sad Girl and Mousie scream at one another between street and balcony, while Mona's voice-over confides her true feelings: "We grew up together, her and me. There was nothing she didn't know about me, and nothing I didn't know about her. We were so tight people called us like we were one name: Mona'n'Maribel."

Post altercation, Mona is sifting through a box of photographs, treasuring memories. She tells the viewers, "When she got pregnant, I had a baby shower for her and all the homegirls got her presents for her kid, but I got her a real pretty ring for herself. It was the right thing to do, even if my homegirls thought it was stupid." Thus symbolically united, the two friends continued to make a pair until Maribel's baby was born. Then Mona, feeling somewhat jilted—"It seemed like she was gone forever. . . . I guess she was shining on Ernesto [Jacob Vargas] too"—looked to Ernesto to replace Mousie. "It wasn't like we planned it," she explained in voice-over. "I think we just turned to each other 'cause we missed my friend."

For her part, Maribel couldn't have been more connected to her homegirl. She has candlelight sex with Ernesto, but the force of intimacy lies with Mona. What's important to Mousie is communicated in voice-over, tracked in juxtaposition with her face, gazing away from Ernesto's intent body: "When I lost my virginity to him, she was the only person I told, and I told her the truth too, how it hurt and I was all embarrassed and shit." Then, as romantic melodrama demands, it's Mona who betrays her best friend. Now Maribel's voice-over grows angry—"It was right around that time that Sad

Girl fucked me over and got pregnant by Ernesto"—but visuals here underscore love, not anger. The sequence ends with close-ups of the photographs from Mona's store of memories. Two girls gaze passionately at each other and the camera in a series of automatic shots from a photo booth (Fig. 4.5).

The next time Maribel finds herself in bed with Ernesto, her postcoital bliss (reflected in remembrances of a neighborhood trip to Disneyland, a visit to the Planetarium, and Ernesto's tender accompanying kisses) is interrupted by anger that her boyfriend's betrayal has eternally separated her from Mona: "You lied, vato, you lied. Now I have to kill my best friend. She was my friend before I knew you, Ernesto. Now we're not friends no more. Now she's a bitch." These true confessions are hardly the indications of a gang's "iron grip" on its members' behavior, as one reviewer had it.[17] Nor are these articulated agonies indicative of any real choices the two friends will make. As Whisper, a homegirl and business partner of Ernesto, will chuckle, "Can you imagine Sad Girl killing anyone?!" Whisper's gentle mocking and Anders's self-conscious romanticism suggest that the only dramatic actions the inseparable friends are capable of will be metaphorical enactments of hyperbolic rhetoric.

FIGURE 4.5. Angel Aviles and Seidy Lopez as "Mona'n'Maribel": passionate friendship in a photo booth. *Mi vida loca* frame enlargement.

Mona'n'Maribel are indeed pressured, but it is the iron grip of the melodramatic imagination that holds them in sway.

With Peter Brooks, given this "spectacular excitement, the hyperbolic situation, and the grandiose phraseology," we might wonder what ends melodramatic "dramaturgy, situation, and language" serve.[38] Unlike ethno-exploitation films (movies like *Colors*, for example), ethnographic melodramas (such as Brooks's "'classical' examples of the genre") are not just about "thrills," but about "virtue made visible and acknowledged, the drama of a recognition."[39] The revelation of the good and the true arises from those pressured signs whose "very simplicity and exaggeration permits [their] use . . . as pure signifiers . . . [that] can be deployed in interplay and clash in such a manner that the struggle of moral entities is visible to the spectator."[40] In Anders's moral universe, signs are short symbolic sequences through whose interplay meaning surfaces. Shots of a peaceful Maribel in bed with her baby Junior ("I had something which was all mine"), a scene with her in harmonious residence with Ernesto's grandmother ("Abuelita told me stories of Ernesto when he was a little boy"), and a short sequence documenting the attempted sexual abuse by a family man with whom she lived after Abuelita died ("Spooky was kind of a dick") combine to tell a story of innocence threatened. In a society where teen mothers of color are routinely vilified in blame-the-victim maneuvers designed to "end welfare as we know it," Anders counters melodrama with melodrama. *Mi vida loca* directly and emphatically refutes the kind of hysterical claims that, for example, "'teenage mothers are more likely to be single, dysfunctional, and addicted,'" and worse, that "'they don't have the ability to give and receive love.'"[41] The film's eloquent signs crusade against vituperative conservatives' insistence that love and innocence and truth and beauty are the exclusive property of some kind of moral majority.

In Anders's world it is the moral minorities whose virtue is obscured and must be brought to light. Ernesto (aka Bullet Man), as we know from the outset, is no angel. He *is* a glib charmer, but he has to compete with his *rucas'* love for one another. He sells drugs, but he deals to keep his family going: "My job at the market paid all right . . . until I became a dad, and I needed more money. So I started a business to help out with my son and my daughter and my mom and my brother." He keeps his one pleasure, his minitruck "Suavecito," a secret from Mona and Maribel, but he brings home money that supplements their welfare. Anders doesn't apologize for her characters or condescend to them; she doesn't moralize about their behavior out of context. Instead, she provides a range of significant details that comprise a story. With one key monologue, shot in near reflexive-ethnographic style (cross cut with truth-defining flashbacks), she has Ernesto tell a story that explains—not excuses—what threatens virtue. Standing above his gang's tree-lined meeting place, amid brick and mortar ruins reminiscent of ancient indigenous palaces, Bullet Man teaches Whisper about what doing business with rich folks entails:

> You gotta have nuts for this kind of business. The white kids—the *güeras*—you can't trust 'em. The junkies are the worst kind, eh. They're too weak for the life. They got the nice pad to live in, always had it nice, got a bedroom just for them and their shit. Not sharing with no one. Then they get greedy. Nothin's ever enough for 'em. Just like that they're doing six, seven balloons a day. Like there's an unlimited supply. Come on, ain't no one's gonna give 'em enough *feria* to keep that up. So they come to you with the wet eyes, thinking you'll give a shit. That's how they do things in their neighborhood. That's how they get by: "Oh, Ernesto, please. I need it. I had a bad day; I had a bad week; I'm stressed." Sometimes, if I'm in a good mood, I'll let 'em bullshit me. Hey, if the chick's cute, I might go easy, 'cause the next time she'll give me head for it. But hey, I wouldn't fuck 'em. Not the white bitches, not the junkies, naw. But it gets me hard when they offer. It gets me hard just to say, *"al rato"* ["later"]; leave 'em standing there in my neighborhood all alone. Where they don't know nobody. Nothing they know means shit. Their wet eyes are everywhere and they don't buy you heaven. Not tonight, baby.

Significantly, the site of this monologue corresponds to what Peter Brooks identifies as one of melodrama's favored locales: "the enclosed garden, the space of innocence, surrounded by walls. . . ."[42] The "villains, the troublers of innocence" who "insinuate" themselves into this Edenic spot are not really the pathetic "white chicks" who plead with Bullet for drugs; here unacknowledged privilege is the real enemy. What restores Ernesto's trampled sense of self—*his* unacknowledged difficulties vis-à-vis rich white kids' desire for Ernesto to recognize *their* pain—is his ability to exercise turf rights. When the wealthy druggies suddenly can't have all their needs easily met by one more obliging servant, when they are left to stand alone in Bullet's garden, the privileged have to acknowledge their temporary lack, and thus their more characteristic plenitude.[43] Rich white people might flaunt their privilege in their own neighborhoods, Ernesto is saying, but not in his territory. With his serious mockery, Bullet renders real virtue visible; *Mi vida loca* strives to become a "drama of recognition" for any spectators with false notions about their superiority.

True to melodramatic form the privilege the white teens represent is not fully uncovered in Anders's first act. Since, as Brooks outlines it, "virtue has not yet established the full proof of its sign," the villain returns, "produc[ing] the topos of the interrupted fête, the violated banquet which, most often toward the end of Act I or in Act II, represents the triumph of villainy." In Anders's hands evil prevails at the end of Act I not when Mona and Maribel meet on a hilltop to engage in their deadly duel (which we later learn evolved into a recognition of love), but when a greedy blond, confident in her entitlement to get what she wants at any cost, wreaks revenge on a none-too-compliant Ernesto. In a symbolic reversal of media-hyped "reality," white girl kills brown boy.

The community of mourners in the initial cemetery scene takes on new significance in the light of Ernesto's death. We cannot assume, as gang films universally seem to do, that all violence in the barrio is the same, stemming from savage gang members killing each other. Taking life as it comes in post-Rodney King L.A. is a much more complex proposition; violence is everybody's domain. As is love, Anders counterbalances, through Mona's voice-over in the wilderness of gangxploitation. Having kept cool, having known in her heart what goes around comes around—a phrase we may have only associated with violence and its revenge—Mona's testimony over the grave in that initial sequence speaks of the resurrection and acknowledgment of love. Completing her narrative of *la vida loca*, she recounts what happened that fateful night when she went "one on one" to have it out with Maribel: "We stood face to face at the logs, and all I ever knew about Mousie and all she ever knew about me flashed before our eyes. We had a serious past, her and me, and I guess that's why we couldn't do it." When Mona implausibly claims to have heard "bullets echo through the hills," the imagined symbol is so powerful that it takes central stage in her drama of recognition. In that instant, everything becomes clear to her and Maribel: "It's like we both knew, we'd lost Ernesto for good."

Brooks, whom the filmmaker has studied with care,[44] has theorized melodrama's similarity to tragedy in a useful way, allowing us to understand what motivated Anders's characters toward the nightmarish abyss separating truth and anguish. It is only from the "full acting out . . . of basic emotions in their primal, integral, unrepressed condition . . . that a 'cure' can be effected."[45] Under cover of rain-slicked streets, silhouetted by ominous lighting reflected off stairwells, accompanied by relentless, driving music and a full moon, Mousie and Sad Girl indeed act out the twisted family romance where "basic loyalties and relationships become a source of torture." The realization of their love, born only in the moment before they are to die, is innocence unbound. When their uncanny sense of hearing informs them their lover is dead, "virtue can finally break through its helplessness, find its name, liberate itself from primal horror, fulfill its desires." Wonderfully conscious of twentieth-century transpositions of melodrama, Anders has her life-long friends reunited in the bright light of day, allowing Mona'n'Maribel (and the spectators) to "awake from the nightmare" on an Echo Park bench, kids in tow, their mothers' eyes upon them. For better or worse, Sad Girl and Mousie are united. Family romance doesn't get much better:

MARIBEL: [My son's] got the same eyes, like Ernesto.

MONA: A little bit the same.

MARIBEL: A lot the same; exactly. Hey Sad Girl. Mona. You want to come back to the pad and kick back with your daughter, it'd be all right.

MONA: Mousie. Maribel. I'm going to McDonald's right now.

MARIBEL: (misty-eyed) Burger King's better. It's not crowded.

MONA: They don't got what I like at Burger King.

MARIBEL: It's cheaper at Burger King.

MONA: Fine. You go to Burger King, and I'll go to McDonald's.

MARIBEL: (near tears of joy) We'll go to McDonald's!

Triumphal music. Fade to intertitle.

ACT II: "DON'T LET NO ONE GET YOU DOWN"; OR, (ALTERNATIVE) FAMILY VALUES

The second act of Anders's serious fiction, to redeploy the discursive arsenal of the right, constitutes a "focus on the family." Here "family" encompasses traditional relations as well as extended ties. Anders gives substance to the nearly mythic formula that gang life is family life without exacting the usual blood sacrifices demanded by family-values conservatives ("Kids form familial gangs to replace their own dysfunctional families."[46]). At the same time there is no mythification of *la sagrada familia*. Some of *Mi vida loca*'s families are troubled; some are not. We learned in Act I that Maribel's parents aren't much of a resource. Her too-young, impoverished dad (played in ironic cameo by Kid Frost) throws her out of the house when she becomes pregnant, but she eventually finds comfort with Ernesto's grandmother. Mona's father, a Mexican immigrant and Elvia Rivero fan, represents another kind of family, a compassionate widower in a loving relationship with his daughter.

Other functional family models emerge as the narrative continues. Act II introduces Rachel (Bertilla Damas), Whisper's thirty-something married sister. Her presence is key, and surpasses the largely symbolic roles of the other parental figures. A former gang member herself, Rachel has left the hardship of *la vida loca* to move with her police lieutenant husband (Ric Salinas) toward the middle class. Pregnant with her own incipient family, she mothers Whisper, doctors the young woman when she becomes wounded by gunshot, and cautions her sister's friends against the kind of violence that took the life of their brother, Creeper. During the four years their sister-in-law Giggles has been "locked up in prison for something stupid she didn't even do," as Whisper recounts in voice-over, Rachel has acted as full-time mother to her niece, who is Creeper and Giggles's child. A tattooed madonna, Rachel replaces traditional melodramas' proverbial *madrecita abnegada*. She is the image of the "older, compassionate, and understanding wom[a]n" who, despite Fregoso's claims regarding the absence of such women in the film, has "resisted and survived '*la vida dura*'" in order to sustain her extended family.[47]

Rachel's *comadre*, the angelic Giggles (Angélica of the rim-lit curls), is an even more beleaguered survivor of barrio wars. Her initial imprisonment was the result of "being in the wrong place at the wrong time." Then, having been released, an innocent walk to the corner market puts her back in police scrutiny for something else she didn't do. She and Whisper, also at the scene, get lucky this time when their brother-in-law the cop fishes them out of a line of kids waiting to be photographed by the police on the spot. Giggles's struggle to outwit the *locura* of poverty and assume her responsibilities as a working mother is the central issue in Act II, where gang life as work alternative is understood as a reasonable survival strategy in a discriminating and jobless society.[48]

Released from jail, Giggles shares her new-found wisdom with Whisper, with the reunited but still bickering Mona and Maribel, and with friend Baby Doll (Christina Solis), who drives the welcoming committee away from the prison in her River Valley boyfriend's 1940 sedan. While the girls expect to "learn a lot from Giggles—about love" or about extralegal entrepreneurial skills, they get lessons instead in female solidarity and the work ethic. Having arrived at a quintessentially American roadside café, the friends chat in a booth framed by the diffused reds, whites, and blues of translucent water glasses and sun-soaked gingham curtains. A glamour-lit Angélica/Giggles, her face softly shadowed perhaps to invoke our concern about the outcome of her dreams, emphasizes the importance of women's self-reliance with a confident wave of her all-American burger. "Girls," she says first to the crabbing Mona and Maribel, "you don't ever throw down with your homegirl over a guy. Guys come and go. They ain't worth it." She next refuses to let them romanticize her for "doing time for her guy," since Creeper's death robbed her both of moral satisfaction and worse, the company of her mate:

> I had a lot of time to think in prison, you know what I'm saying? We girls need new skills. 'Cause by the time our boys are twenty-one they're either in prison, disabled, or dead. That's fucked up, but that's the way it is. We're left alone to raise our kids; we gotta think about the future. Me, I really worked on my skills while I was away. I know what I need to do. Computers are the key to the future. Homegirls, I'm gonna get a *job*.

The cynically arched eyebrows on the homegirls' faces almost seem to anticipate some of the critical response that this oft-cited speech has garnered.

But the girls' mockery is different from the critics' derision. Anders's fictional characters appear to have an edge on the "reality" that many critics can only glean from the (sometimes equally fictive) discourses of social science.[49] Unlike Giggles, the girls in the café have not spent four years absorbing prison rehab discourse, and nothing in their experience convinces them that Yankee individualism will replace joblessness. Unlike the girls, critics schooled in the myth of the American success story expect that a positive attitude and a little training is all it takes for poor kids to pull themselves up by their bootstraps. What is remarkable about both these responses is that they operate out of a shared aesthetic, if not a shared ethic. Melodrama's moral absolutes can serve a number of masters, both radical and reactionary.

Let's consider critic Leslie Felperin's take on what she calls Giggles's "painfully preachy" stance. She urges her readers not to judge such attitudes too harshly since "it's easy to be scathing about the banal sentimentality and confused moral sense of [Giggles's] and other speeches, especially the [film's] concluding lines [that] 'Women don't use pistols to prove a point, women use weapons for love,' but even easier to forget that sometimes people talk like this, especially women reared on cheap romance and the religion of the gun."[50] Painful, indeed, is the notion that the boys Giggles refers to amount to so much "banal sentimentality," but this is not the grief that Felperin suffers. What gets her down is the apparently painful aesthetics of the girls' melodrama: confused morals are permissible but bad taste isn't. So while imprisoned, disabled, or dead boys' realities are left unexamined, girls with guns they don't shoot must be studied in ethnographic detail. Here conservative ethics combine with melodramatic aesthetics, and compel Felperin to construct her own cheap romance. "Women reared in the religion of the gun" is painful preaching at its zenith, a characterization designed to substantiate her barely concealed truth claim that the real essence of barrio family values is sacralized violence.

As if to circumvent such readings, Anders extends the concept of family and morality to represent the compassion and understanding of older males toward younger "brothers" still struggling with the toughest aspects of *la vida dura*. When Big Sleepy (Julian Reyes), an established father of three, comforts his friend Little Sleepy (Gabriel Gonzales) over the loss of Ernesto, the tenderness is palpable. The pair stand in homeowner Sleepy's backyard, a space dedicated to the sparkling cars and trucks (like Suavecito) that await his talented airbrush. Poised in front of a curling yellow electric wire that recalls the halo around the Virgin of Guadalupe's mantle, his naked torso suspended from his overhead grip on the garage door that suggests the stance of a redemptive Christ, Big Sleepy encourages his namesake's efforts in school, relates his own sadness about the death of one his homeboys, allows the young man his tears, and cautions him against retaliatory violence based solely on suspicion (Fig. 4.6). His voice-over reiterates the importance of family values to any spectators who may have missed his message: "When a boy's your namesake, you owe him. Least that's how I see it. Don't get me wrong, I have youngsters myself. You try to tell 'em not to write on walls, not to go looking for trouble. But you know how it is. All you can hope for is that they learn their lessons a little quicker and they don't fuck up too bad."

Big Sleepy's support of his extended family is repeated by others' actions throughout Act II. Rachel and Giggles discuss generational differences between homegirls with the auto artist's same affectionate ethos. Whisper honors Ernesto's brother's right to "the business," trying brilliantly but unsuccessfully to teach the sweetly dimwitted Shadow (Arthur Esquer) how to run things. Giggles steps in to organize her younger homegirls with their project to reclaim Suavecito for Ernesto's kids and family. Family life—in a number of its variants—is thus a real presence in *Mi vida loca*.

We have to wonder what's at stake for commentators to deny this so vehemently. Willie Martínez, an Echo Park social worker cited in a *Los Angeles Times* article by Leila Cobo-Hanlon, is one of a consequential few to miss *Mi vida loca*'s familial relationships. His opinions surface in Cobo-Hanlon's review mixed with this lead: "For many Echo Park youths, the depiction of

FIGURE 4.6. Julian Reyes as Big Sleepy tenderly comforts his namesake, played by Gabriel Gonzales. *Mi vida loca* frame enlargement.

their lives in *Mi vida loca* may be true but it misses the untold stories of compassion and understanding."[51] Martínez explains further: "'You don't see the extension of the other family members. But these family members are with them constantly. They're the ones who bail them out of jail, who take them to school and try to get them back in.'" Rosa Linda Fregoso echoes Martínez's position, emphasizing the importance of female family members in young Chicanas' lives:

> Anders misses the reality that the sisterhood captured so eloquently in the film is not created in a vacuum. If you are going to tell a story about Chicanas, you've got to understand that their survival in the barrio depends heavily on the kinship of older, compassionate, and understanding women who have also resisted and survived "*la vida dura.*" For some reason, Anders chose to portray Chicana teenagers as self-sufficient, having little interaction with adults. Untold is the story of the elaborate support network of mothers, grandmothers, and aunts who visit them in jail, bail them out, and take care of babies.[52]

Carmen, my young friend Elena's homegirl, has a very different take:

> Yeah, huh, we cut out the reviews and we read 'em all. And yeah, it was cool. We were in the papers. But they didn't interview me or Elena. We woulda said way different stuff about families. That guy they talked to [Willie Martínez] is singin' *la canción de siempre:* "Not enough family." Shee-it! Don't know what movie he was watchin'. What about that Rachel? She's just like Elena's Tía Espi. She's family! Or don't that count?

While she gazes at her charge asleep in the rebuilt stroller—the child is her neighbor's toddler, waiting for mom to finish cooking for everyone—it occurs to me that Carmen and her neighbor, Giggles and Rachel, my homegirl Esperanza and her niece Elena are part of that extended family Martínez talks of but doesn't seem to see in Anders's narratives. "What do you expect?" Carmen asks, when I wonder aloud about this, "He's a social worker. He wanted that *Mi familia* movie."

The lure of the Chicano family romance is indeed compelling. To name the concept is not only to mark the intrinsic value of the family, but to counter historical justifications of ethnocide.[53] Now, as "family values" conservatives increasingly claim the moral high ground—and concomitant economic benefits—for the family-minded "deserving poor," strategic redeployment of the notion of *familia* can still function as a survival technique. Willie Martínez, a grassroots bureaucrat struggling with the impact of government cutbacks, fights one kind of battle when he insists on the familial unity and morality of the poor. He challenges welfare reform logic that sociologist Frances Fox Piven calls a "slightly updated version of the nineteenth-century view that poverty is the result of moral breakdown, and moral breakdown is encouraged by helping the poor."[54] Under these terms, Martínez's morally upstanding poor may be judged "worthy," but the cost is high. Those who don't fit into the nuclear paradigm—that is, single women and children in alternative families—will pay the price by not being deemed "fit" to receive entitlements.

Not even Fregoso's emphasis on the female component of Martínez's model sidesteps the dangers of "*Mi familia*-ism." Reifying blood ties, male or female, still participates in the discourse of poverty "research" as established by those trying to dismantle the entitlement system. The risk in accepting the territory as defined by government policy-makers concerned primordially with economic bottom lines is dramatic. In the 1990s welfare accounted for a mere 1 percent of the federal budget, but cuts from this program ("Saving billions of dollars over the next decade!") have affected those individuals and families least able to bail out of the jobless inner cities that imprison the "worthy" and "undeserving" poor alike.[55]

Interpretations, offered by film critics, "native informants," or our-friends-the-spectators, are part of Clifford's paradigm of "orchestrated ethnographic texts" that not only "*occur* in politically charged situations" but *inform* them. Filmmaker Anders chose to live in Echo Park. When that community inspired her to make *Mi vida loca*, she joined her passion for Latino melodrama with the inevitable social realism that inner-city existence demands. Her own artistic sensibility combined with that of her characters, real and fictional, and she created an ethnographic melodrama, putting commentators who advocate the exclusive use of one or the other genre into something of a crisis. Whatever generic truths may guide competing politicized aesthetics, we can "get along," Anders suggests, if we talk with one another.

In the balance of the second act Anders shows how communication between people can be excited by charged objects. Here she gets even more metaphorical mileage from her fictitious truck, "Suavecito." Like a pressured symbol from a nineteenth-century drama of recognition, the vehicle sporting the image of a woman and the name of a Mexican movie melodrama[56] is rendered as a "token of a superdrama involving life and death, perdition and redemption, heaven and hell, the force of desire caught in a death struggle with the life force (Fig. 4.7)."[57] We have moved away from the realm of social realism to the place where "things cease to be merely themselves," becoming, instead, "metaphors whose tenor suggests another kind of reality."[58] The nature of this reality is, again, not immediately manifest; melodrama's task is to illuminate the darkest reaches of the moral universe. This is the other business of Act II, where Suavecito begins to emerge from both its figurative and literal concealments.

Initially, *Mi vida loca*'s viewers are not privy to a full, direct gaze upon this sign of the cosmos. Shuttered in an enclosed garage, the truck is spectacle pri-

FIGURE 4.7. Jacob Vargas as Ernesto, posing with "Suavecito," a "token of a super-drama involving life and death." *Mi vida loca* frame enlargement.

marily to Mona and Maribel, who must pry off a board even to peek at the promise of heaven. We watch them gazing at Suavecito, two girls framed tightly, the profile of one etched upon the other (Fig. 4.8). They discuss what they could do with such a truck, banal things that would make earth-shattering differences in poor mothers' lives. We expect a full countershot that would somehow confirm how righteously Suavecito would carry groceries, haul laundry, or ferry children to play. But the camera reveals only the figure of the gun-slinging *loca* adorning the camper top. Her presence exerts a power: Might women not use *the image of* pistols to prove a point? Might they not use *the metaphor of* weapons for love? Having just moments before supposed that their man had likely been "dogging" them both by sleeping around with other women, Maribel suggests slyly that they could use the truck to cruise Hollywood Boulevard and find a little love of their own. Mona is shocked: "Not in *Ernesto*'s truck!" But Maribel, poetic justice hers, is packing: "*Our* truck," she replies archly. In the wink of a conspiratorial eye, the pair vow to reclaim what is rightfully theirs: Ernesto's unintended legacy of self-determination and *amor propio*.

The truck as a metaphor for unbridled independence is thus more significant than the sum of its material assets. When Ernesto's homeboys appropriate Suavecito in order to enter the truck in a car show, hoping to gain prestige

FIGURE 4.8. "Mona'n'Maribel" gazing at "Suavecito." *Mi vida loca* frame enlargement.

and prize money, the girls, led by crusader Angélica, take particular offense. Money isn't the evil in their eyes, but if the truck is to be used for financial gain, it should be sold for *meaningful* profit. The girls thus enact their own democratic estate planning, not without a catch in the throat. "Some of the money should go to Ernesto's kids, some to Whisper's family to pay for hospital bills, and some to Ernesto's mother for her broken heart." Maribel's eye-rolling retort to such drama—her multisyllabic "Pl-e-ase!"—is enough to make the rhetoric all the more deliciously self-conscious.

Contrary to expectations about how "ladies' auxiliaries" might function, the girls get tough, self-reliant, and business-like. Giggles—whose path to the future is blocked not by her lack of job skills, but her prison record—has finally found an outlet for her work ethic. She facilitates the girls' first official meeting as efficiently as any of her male counterparts, but unlike the boys, she allows space for her friends' heart-felt responses to the truck's symbolic value. Once more, melodramatic affect is not so constricted as to lose sight of itself. In a humorous sequence that strains even the realism of ethnography, we get to see what no documentary would ever show. Giggles's All-American schoolmarmism is spoofed by girls refusing to raise their hands when the question about a meeting with the homeboys is called. Amid snorts of disbelief but approval of the motion, Baby Doll does her version of the minutes:

"Didn't I tell you girls that our homegirl Giggles would get our sorry shit organized?" On the soundtrack, "Girls, It Ain't Easy" revs up as snapshots of the now gang-draped Giggles flash on screen. She's united with Whisper in front of their graffiti-tagged turf. Giggles has returned to *la vida loca*, and as Whisper has wryly remarked about her own career as a dealer, the frustrated job-seeker has accepted a viable "opportunity to better herself in life."

ACT III: "SUAVECITO"; OR,
TRUE ROMANCE MEETS PULP NONFICTION

Within her demilitarized city limits, Allison Anders transposes what Monsiváis calls Mexican melodrama's "mythical environments" and its "ceremonial habits" to U.S. Latino locales and traditions.[59] In Act III the "Mexican *fiesta* filled with *mariachis* and *trios* and fierce women and fighting roosters" reincarnates in a party hosted by Los Lobos (the quintessential Chicano band), complete with jealous women and cocksure men. The Mexican dance hall is evoked here, scored by "libidinal sounds" stimulating the slow gyrations of dancers outfitted in the classic drapes of the 1940s. Reframing Monsiváis's idea of the "rural cantina" as a site of male self-fashioning, Anders documents the "fatal resolutions" of the boys meeting in their hillside club. There, among the decorated ruins of Aztlán's ravaged lands, Shadow will vow to avenge his brother Ernesto (believing him dead at the hands of a rival gang), invoking the historical legitimacy manifested in "primary school speeches" emblematic of melodrama's renditions of "ancestral history." His homeboys will pledge their fraternal support in similar style.

As we have seen in the previous sequences, the spaces of Mexican melodrama's streets and *vecindades* reappear here in force, concretized in rainwashed alleys and the living room where the *locas* plan their operations. From her "bedrooms of abandon," reconstructed throughout the film as places of romance *and* reflection, to her dance halls graced with representations of the anguished Popocatépetl cradling his tragically dead lover, Ixtacihuatl (whose pathos is mitigated by juxtaposed shots of lively *cholas* embracing boyfriends' cars), Anders's ethnographic melodrama reconfigures traditional sites, negotiating between cultures and subjectivities with respect.

Questioning the fantasy of reality and the reality of fantasy as she did in *Gas Food Lodging*, the filmmaker continues to use voice-over narration and point-of-view shots that privilege her protagonists' multiple perspectives. Mona returns in Act III to narrate the epistolary romance of her sister Alicia (La Blue Eyes), besotted with a prison inmate she's never met. Ernesto's brother Shadow claims his own agency and agony through speech; his voice-over erases the near-caricature presented in Act II, rendering his public suffering authentically human. Finally, the object of Alicia's affection, Juan Temido, addresses viewers in order to mark his barrio's turf and claim his rightful place therein. These highly subjective tales mediate "Suavecito's" two intertwined narratives: true romance meets pulp nonfiction.

The love story leads. After turning away from the corner mailbox where she has deposited the contents of her soul, Alicia is tracked in slow motion through the barrio. Mona narrates like a writer for *True Romance;* Anders provides the visuals of what readers of such a publication might look like. The two sisters, surrounded by baby blues and delicate pinks—Alicia clutching a pillow to her breast as she reads—are framed in the privacy of their bedroom perusing what we might take for a romance magazine. The voice-over adjusts our picture: "There was this magazine that shows how we were really like," Mona tells us, and we are pulled into the constructed world of nonfiction. *Teen Angels,* a close-up reveals, is something of a cross between a neighborhood yearbook and an annual collection of creative writing. Mona "can't believe it" when Alicia's beautiful blue eyes moisten as she reads "a poem some *torcido* [inmate] had sent in from prison." The distance between image and voice creates cognitive dissonance here; melodrama and life are again confused as one. But the camera stays with Alicia and her reading material, followed by shots of her letters and sequences of her reading and dreaming on the moonlit fire escape. Fiction informs life, Anders suggests with Mona's insight: "I think it was the book that did it. After he sent her that book, that's when she fell in love."

While Mona's skeptical voice lends viewers some distance from the lure, we're cautiously drawn into the romantic world by aestheticized silhouettes of Alicia and her postman. From the high contrast blacks and whites of a hallway reminiscent of a 1940s *vecindad,* the camera cuts to Alicia's hands as she unwraps the volume of poetry that was about to change her life. In untranslated Spanish, Juan Temido whispers a poem as we peer over his beloved's shoulder at a page blurred with pressed flowers:

> It is I, my love
> who knocks at your door.
> It is not the phantom, it is not
> the one who once paused
> before your window.
> I throw down the door:
> I enter all of the reaches of your life:
> I have come to reside in your soul:
> You cannot resist me.[60]

These words should serve as a warning of the fearsomeness of the fearless don Juan Temido, who would conquer innocence only to mock devotion. But

Alicia seems as oblivious to peril as are spectators without her translation skills. The Spanish words flow over the image of the text, saying all and saying nothing, wearing the exoticized guise of the irresistible lover. The villain in this drama of recognition is still not to be known as such, and even Spanish speakers who recognize Pablo Neruda's *Los versos del capitán* may not suspect Juan Temido's intentions. Has he chosen this volatile volume for its passions of love or fury? Does he employ the Nobel laureate's "real" missives to future wife Matilde Urrutia in order to mask the "falseness" of his own ardor? Of all the feverish verses, why does he choose "La pregunta"? The voice of that poem belongs to a suspected philanderer, returned home to break down the barriers a woman has erected to protect herself. Can Alicia trust, as the poetic voice maintains, that it will be her doubt—and not his *donjuanismo*—that will destroy her? ("Love, a question / has destroyed you.") Can she believe that the one who knocked down her door with the sheer weight of his letters is not a specter of her own desire?

Anders poses this last question and offers possibilities of answers that engage viewers' desires to collapse under the pleasurable weight of melodrama while simultaneously recognizing the filmic phantoms of such desire. Even as Juan Temido seduces with Pablo Neruda's words, we're left to wonder: Is it his selection or Alicia's choice that the voice-over recites? Does "La pregunta"—a poem neither from "El amor" or "El deseo" but rather "Las furias"—tell us more about Juan's self-knowledge or Alicia's knowledge about Juan's faithlessness that she can't yet bring herself to face?

Moving between romance and realism in the next sequences, the filmmaker uses Shadow's voice-over to narrate a flashback with Ernesto and his truck Suavecito in close communion. While we watch his older brother debate the merits of gold versus chrome-plated engine parts, Shadow, almost anticipating the comments of some Echo Park spectators, wonders why Ernesto "was so fucking crazy over the truck."[61] As his reflections change to present-tense anxieties, we see an aspect of the younger boy previously hidden by other characters' points of view. What reveals Shadow's humanity is not only the suffering he so publicly shares in this subjective moment, but his painful uncertainty with regard to other males' seamless self-confidence. When the cream-colored hood of a '40s sedan pushes into the frame, obliterating the shot of Suavecito's miniparts, Shadow's voice-over introduces us to its driver with a mixture of anger and trepidation. El Durán, Ernesto's brother explains, claims the truck as his own, notwithstanding his dislike of the mini. "He only drives classic cars, for that gangster, playboy vibe," the teen tells us, disturbing any untroubled pleasure we might derive from slow-motion shots of El Durán at the wheel of his "bomb." The man with a coterie of women dangling about him is danger, as Shadow says. El Durán is "on a mission to get this truck," and as Shadow appeals for support the camera at last obliges. Hunched on the hood of Suavecito, alone save for his young pal Chuco bouncing in pretended acceleration at the wheel, Shadow suffers: "Now it's all down to me: the truck, my brother's business, El Durán. Somebody give me a break."

But getting a break is not possible in these hard times. In the next key voice-over of Act III, El Durán mythologizes the chivalric code that organizes the barrio's feudal wars. He first historicizes his claim to legitimacy before aligning himself with the ancients: "Our *clica*, River Valley, is as old as Echo Park. But from the beginning we didn't get along. That was sixty years ago." Squatting next to the concrete-channeled stream that is the Los Angeles River, he frames his monologue in the magically real style of the poets and novelists he employs to woo women. "The rains would come and fill the river bed that ran through my barrio. An old *veterano* talks about it still—when L.A. *had* a river and the floods came. All the people would sit on the bank and watch all the things wash down from the city: mattresses, flower pots, hoods from *ranflas* [jalopies], even a piano. The old man claims that one day he saw a whole house." This fluvial speech is stemmed by snapshots of urban warriors whom we suspect participated in the pact to reward El Durán for single-handedly saving "a *torcido* from Echo Park . . . from a gang of *norteños*." The knight-errant's voice loses its charm as he gets to the point of his attempted beguilement of spectators, undermining, as did Shadow's words about him, the attraction of his slow-motion cruise through the Echo: "This minitruck, Suavecito, it's a dreadful machine. No class. But this is a matter of honor; the truck is rightfully mine."

Suavecito, as Anders demonstrates afresh in these sequences, is that loaded metaphor deriving significance from more than its painted or chromed parts. It is the flotsam and jetsam of Los Angeles that, river or no, runs through the barrios while astonished neighbors marvel at the way it divides turf, sweeping everyone along in its path. It is, quite literally, melodrama's vehicle, driving characters' emotions and actions in the manner of any number of such tropes that motivate plots and protagonists' responses. Like the eponymous mid-century Mexican melodrama, "Suavecito" sorts out the business of gangsters, womanizers, cars, and true innocents.[62] In Act III's denouement we'll see how this drama of recognition employs the truck to uncloak both the villains who threaten innocence and their tactics for instilling fear.

Voice-over narration and flashbacks stop at this point and we are again in the film's present time, witnessing the homegirls in Mona's living room relax after their meeting about Suavecito. A letter addressed to Juan Temido and marked "Return to Sender" sparks curiosity: What's La Blue Eyes doing still writing to this guy? Released from Soledad Prison, he's stopped corresponding and has come home, as Baby Doll realizes, to take up his philandering habits as none other than El Durán. The *locas* plan an operation in River Valley to disabuse Alicia of her romantic notions about the man "who steals your heart and disappears like a bandit."

From this moment forward the staging of "truth" and "fantasy" becomes increasingly overt. Lighting and music continue to differentiate the spaces of ethnographic and melodramatic constructions until the plot weaves both aesthetics into a single thread of serious fiction. In a series of a dozen cross-cut sequences, the homegirls take Alicia to a dance to expose Juan Temido as the villainous El Durán. The boys, learning of Shadow's discovery of a missing Suavecito and believing El Durán responsible for the theft, make their own way to the River Valley party. The scene is set for the revelation of truths.

That Anders chooses the dance hall as the site of revelation further links *Mi vida loca* to the filmmaking and viewing practices of Mexican melodrama. Lights outside the club are reminiscent of those director Emilio Fernández strings near the entrance of Salón México, whose zoot-suited dancers influence the stylish deliberation effected by the River Valley crowd. In drawing such parallels, Anders speaks also to Chicano syncretism; the dance hall is decorated with a combination of symbols from both Mexican and Chicano visual vernacular. Through a parking area filled with classic cars, beyond expressive paintings of crosses and signs (one memorial, entitled "Cry Later," prophesies the events of the evening), the Echo Park *locas* make their rendezvous with destiny. Spectators familiar with Mexican melodrama's recreational spaces and those who populate them can only suspect the worst: another woman's heart is about to be rent asunder, and someone will be made to pay for innocence lost.

Initially, Act III seems to be rehearsing nineteenth-century theatrical strategies, when third acts were generally devoted to "a full panoply of violent action which offered a highly physical 'acting out' of virtue's liberation from the oppressive efforts of evil."[63] In the remainder of Anders's third act, virtue is indeed emancipated, but violent action itself is ultimately seen as the incarnation of evil, not as virtue's liberator. Where post-revolutionary French theater could violently, cathartically purge evil from the universe, Anders's post-rebellion L.A. film is dedicated to showing the tragedy of such action. "Once you show violence," Anders asserts, "you've got an action sequence; you've got people waiting for the revolution. If you show violence, you can't talk about it."[64]

But exposing the folly of violence does not prevent the filmmaker from indulging in a little catharsis of her own. Under melodrama's chivalric codes, El Durán's demise is poetically justified. He is the embodiment of evil, the villain who "betrays and undoes the moral order"[65] by his suave seduction of countless women. When, on the dance floor, he romances Alicia—who still hasn't a clue about his real identity—he strikes a pose spectators love to hate. His devilishly lit face alerts us to unfettered danger; his sweet murmurings resemble satanic utterances designed to lure innocence from its domain. Like his nineteenth-century counterparts described by Brooks, El Durán is "strongly characterized, a forceful representation of villainy."

It is when he ceases to be a metaphor of evil that we have second thoughts about Juan Temido. The romantic music abruptly switches to rap, signaling the move from melodramatic fantasy to ethnographic fiction. The camera cuts to Shadow's bedroom, where we see the young man pack a serious-looking gun under his belt. His misapprehension of Suavecito's fate propels him into an action we are clearly meant to fear: a phone call to organize the homeboys' revenge. In the subsequent shot, a red light from an undetermined but menacing source casts doubt on his intent as he climbs into his truck to pick up the gang to head for what can only be trouble.

Tension continues to mount in a series of cross-cut sequences culminating with the arrival of the Echo Park *locos* at the dance. The boys are about to do their business; the girls have already done theirs. Baby Doll has revealed El Durán's true identity to La Blue Eyes, and the heartbroken schoolgirl has fled the scene to the comfort of her homegirls. The shots that next echo through the night have a double valence: evil is "recognized, combated, driven out" in the persona of El Durán, then made manifest in the actions of the boys who gun down the person, Juan Temido. Unlike traditional melodrama, where "the expulsion of evil entails no sacrifice," and where "there is no communal partaking of the sacred body,"[66] in this film uncovering and expunging violence exacts a price.

If we are initially relieved to see El Durán sink silently to his knees, his hand over his heart, mortally wounded, the true significance of Juan Temido's death has not yet been revealed. While Anders gently mocks the communal partaking of the not-so-sacred body of El Durán at a funeral attended by succeedingly more risible mourners (one leaves purple lingerie in the open casket while another's trembling grief threatens to revitalize the corpse), the filmmaker has yet to unmask the real villain of this film. It is not, in fact, El Durán, a *donjuan* who confounds innocence. It is not the young Chuco, who took Suavecito out for a joyride, letting his homeboys assume untruths. It is not even the rival River Valley *locas*, who will wreak their own terrible revenge on Echo Park in a "final" drive-by shooting. The real evil laid bare by *Mi vida loca*'s serious fiction is the violence that masquerades as the emancipator of virtue.

In the final sequences Alicia, La Blue Eyes, her flowered print frock replaced by a decisive red dress, floats love letters out to the sea of water lilies blooming in Echo Park Lake. In voice-over, Mona synthesizes the liberation of Alicia's innocence. It is love, not violence, that puts her on the shore, inhabiting a new moral universe: "Once her pain was gone, it didn't matter to her who he really was. Her heart was stronger for the love she gave." What truth is at work here? Is "Suavecito" a tale of true romance or cheap nonfiction? Mona herself doubts the answer. Ethnographic melodrama is a slippery genre: "Some people say when he died they found her love letter in his coat pocket over his heart. I guess we'll never know if it was the truth."

Melodrama's verbal truth claims, Anders seems to be saying, are sometimes as unreliable as the narrators who espouse them. Melodrama without some staged ethnographic context is a kind of violence. If *Mi vida loca* ended with Mona's voice-over (as critics like Felperin appear to believe), we'd be left with merely a woman's version of violence's supposed virtues: "Women don't use weapons to prove a point, women use weapons for love." But a gun is a gun in anyone's hands, Anders shows in her next sequences.[67] Its lethal potential can be used to destroy the very things it purports to protect. In agonizing slow motion, the camera makes us see the consequences of Mona's words gone awry. What Anders calls "melodrama's truthful moment" is to be found in the "truth of feeling, the reality of the emotion" we're meant to experience as a classic Thunderbird filled with River Valley *locas* cruises vengefully to the sidewalk where Little Sleepy has just greeted Big Sleepy's tricycling daughter.[68] A villain in disguise smiles disarmingly at the pair in front of the market.

A pistol is drawn, a target missed, a little girl lies dead. We watch the sequence in near silence, recognizing fully the villain veiled in Mona's speech moments before. The truth of her words—the truth of any words that justify violence—is brought into question: "By the time my daughter grows up, Echo Park will belong to her, and she can be whatever she wants to be." Concluding at the cemetery where it began, this (melo)drama of recognition offers up the image of its final moral message: a child's coffin, a life of infinite possibilities suddenly rendered nil. The communal sacrifice in this real-life melodrama is almost palpable.

CODA

Gang films are inevitably about turf wars, about zones militarized and demilitarized by cops and kids who are terrorists all. *Mi vida loca* wages different battles. Unlike a gangxploitation flick or a governmental report on the "culture of poverty," Anders is not interested in delivering action-packed (statistics on) violence in the fashion of filmic or political rhetoric. In an era when violent movies and violent public policies are becoming increasingly hard to differentiate, *Mi vida loca* stakes out its own generic boundaries. Within ethnographic melodrama, the materiality of violence gives way to a consideration of the unpredictable destruction it wreaks.

While the depiction of physical violence is the favored domain of the corporate media ("If it bleeds, it leads"), *Mi vida loca* is concerned with the epistemological violence that incites material violence in the first place. As kids from all parts of embattled L.A. can attest, and as legislators profess to believe, fightin' words are sometimes more powerful than semiautomatics.

How else can we explain the violent impact of radically conservative film-makers, lawmakers, critics, journalists, and "moral majoritarians" on life in jobless inner cities? Consider the dramatic times we live in: highest indices ever of people living in poverty, coupled with the highest amount of entitle-ment cutbacks; greatest division between the "underclass" and the "ruling-over-class"; most pronounced demonization of supposed "welfare queens," together with the most emphatic beatification of the allegedly "responsible individuals" living in nuclear familial bliss. These scenarios of competing truths are the stuff of the melodramas of our times, where politics and aes-thetics meet. To understand their force, we might take a last look at a key crit-ical response to *Mi vida loca*, where a conservative political agenda has been cloaked as an offering of liberal film criticism.

In "The Road to *Mi vida loca* Paved with Good Intentions" *Los Angeles Times* staff writer Kevin Thomas bases his analysis on this plot outline:

> . . . Sad Girl and Mousie, who've been best friends since childhood, grow up in Echo Park and join a gang, a kind of ladies' auxiliary for the local male gang. But now Sad Girl and Mousie have become deadly enemies, all set for a potentially fatal showdown to resolve their rivalry for the same young man, Ernesto, who has fathered a child out of wedlock with each of them. . . . What's going on here? Two lifelong friends, both with infants, prepared to snuff out each other's lives all because of their love for a glib charmer whom we have every reason to assume would take up with yet another woman in a flash. Can their gang's code of behav-ior have them in such an iron grip that they cannot conceive an alternative to such a drastic course of action?[69]

In this violent allegation of violence, Thomas gives us "deadly enemies" and "fatal showdowns," selecting the ultimate in pornographic murder *m.o.*'s, the "snuff out," to describe a gang's "iron grip" on the "drastic" behavioral choices of a pair whom members of the film's targeted audience see as "two women in love." For Thomas, whose reading of *Mi vida loca* is filtered through the media of which he's so much a part, no love exists in this. Even without evidence, he sees what he's seen before: a gangxploitation flick. Yet *Mi vida loca* is premised on the fact that women in gangs don't always form "ladies' auxiliaries," and that organizations of female solidarity exist in their own right, as Anders's experiences (and other reports from the barrio, includ-ing scholars' work) thoroughly document. And regardless of their relative autonomy, neither boys' nor girls' groups demonstrate many signs of top-down leadership, to say nothing of draconian domestic politics. Young men like Ernesto are free to invest their time in individual entrepreneurship, bear-ing out findings by epic studies like those of Martín Sánchez Jankowski and Joan Moore, whose decades in the barrio as participant ethnographers have convinced them of the importance of separating individual from group behaviors.[70] Finally, as hierarchical leadership practices and rigid rules characterize few Los Angeles Chicano/a gangs, they do not mark those of Anders's serious fictions.[71] Thomas's "Good Intentions" are really fighting words that criminalize all gang activity and, by extension, anyone who might be a member.

Overt moralizing is not all the writer accomplishes; he also advances a subtext. The mortal enemies ready to do each other to death "all because of their love for a glib charmer" are emphatically women "with infants" born "out of wedlock" who belong to that threatening class of unwed barrio mothers. Why else underscore their motherhood if not to categorize, as he subsequently does, their deplorable behavior and values? Perhaps Thomas wants to prepare readers for his assessment that Anders acts to "confirm rather than dispel our impression that these two women and all their friends are none too bright." But after reading numerous reviews of this film and talking to friends and other viewers, I can't imagine what consensus he refers to here. His words not only attempt to speak for (and naturalize the presumed existence of) a unified spectatorship, they also try to essentialize (and naturalize the presumed existence of) unified objects of scrutiny. Yet it's Anders, he repeats, who "has ended up *confirming* a decidedly negative stereotype of young Latinos as aimless, dangerous, and incapable of thinking for themselves, not to mention welfare-dependent." How could *Mi vida loca* be so "downright offensive," he wonders.

Invoking the rhetoric of one of the most melodramatic social policy debates of our time, it is Thomas's characterization, not Anders's, that demonizes. Welfare "dependency," in his lights, and in the view of the conservative welfare reformers whose politics he soapboxes, is in itself an evil. Being on the "dole" (not to be confused with, say, receiving social security entitlements or government grants for research) is not a creative survival mechanism that the poor use to manage scarce resources in jobless economies, but a near ontological state owing to character flaws. Yet what is becoming clearer is that, among other reasons, welfare needs arise because economic and social policies favor unemployment and low minimum wages.[72] Ignoring these realities, "dependency" models only see the "addictions" of the allegedly "undeserving" poor.[73]

I have dwelt at length on Thomas not because his opinions are representative of *Mi vida loca*'s critical response—the film has garnered largely positive reviews[74]—but because of his wide readership in the Los Angeles area. Even the savvy who read between the lines of Thomas's good intentions may still have been put off by his review, choosing to stay away from what promised to be another depressing portrayal of the barrio. Others may have interpreted the piece as just another bit of media-inspired "proof" that impoverished youth are without "dreams or aspirations," and that those without jobs have no desire to work.

Unwilling to let such bad press about kids' attitudes prevail unchallenged, Anders responded to Thomas in a *Times* "Counterpunch" article. The move was refreshingly unusual; no false decorum about a filmmaker's "place" silenced a woman who is committed to community conversations that could promote understanding among Los Angelinos. Her words, like her film, put a human face on suffering, defusing the moral panic that Thomas tried to provoke:

> Thomas was offended by the fact that my characters, Latina gang girls—some of whom are teen-age mothers—are welfare dependent. . . . Speaking from experience as a teen-age welfare mother, I can assure everyone that the demoralization that comes with your AFDC [Aid to Families with Dependent Children] check . . . is far more offensive than what he would consider an unfair onscreen representation. I would have given the moon to see a mother with food stamps on the screen when I was a teen-age kid with a baby to feed—instead, all I got to see were options available to him [Thomas], not to me.[75]

The logic of Thomas's parting shot that "*Mi vida loca* makes the case for how important it is that ethnic and minority filmmakers get the opportunity to tell stories of their own people" is the logic of an essentialism that further divides how we understand community. Without elaborating how membership in an ethnic group might indeed provide a filmmaker insight about the cultural identities she represents, without advocating the importance of "minorities'" full-fledged participation in all aspects of the disproportionately white world of filmmaking, without discussing how intra-ethnic community coalitions might work, without locating himself as a white male critic who speaks for poor Latinas, without understanding Anders's relationship to Echo Park kids vis-à-vis her own acknowledged identities, Thomas leaps to theorize that ethnicity is constitutionally linked to class. Only "minority filmmakers," his logic proceeds, can respond to "all the questions [Latina gang girls'] identit[ies] and situation[s] inescapably raise."

The ramifications of this argument effectively ghettoize filmmakers of color, who by definition could not make films of anyone besides "their own people." Even if they focused on members of their ethnic group, if we read such efforts through Thomas's strictures how would we then interpret their representations of a class or gender or any other identity they don't themselves claim? Could we, in Thomas's paradigm, accept a middle-class Latino's portrayal of Latina welfare mothers? Other consequences of this ludicrous reasoning are brought to light by Anders's response, mocking the critic's moral outrage with humorous clarity: "If I am to be confined to only make films about my own race, gender, and class, then I demand to be reviewed by white working-class girls from Kentucky who were raised by single mothers and who were themselves single mothers on welfare."

Although I don't quite fit that bill, when I phoned her for an interview Anders was only too happy to discuss community politics. Though her then-current release, *Grace of My Heart* (1996), could have been expected to be her primary interest, she was still intensely invested in discussing how people from a variety of communities might work together to effect change. "I yearn for old-fashioned liberalism," she said, referring to the kind of racially integrated activism we saw in '60s civil rights campaigns that incorporated a range of progressive people from different class backgrounds, "including compassionate white males who would use their power and privilege for the social good." In a nation where 20 percent of the population controls 80 percent of the wealth, Anders worries about how cutbacks will affect those least likely to survive: "I know what it's like to have food stamps; I also know what it will be like for the poor not to have them."

As (melo)dramatist, ethnographer, and humanist, Allison Anders, in her films and public comments, reveals her personal stake in community conversations. If her democratic ideal of cultural citizenship is to replace the impossible dream (or nightmare) of cultural authenticity as a token of legitimation in our hybrid society, we all—spectators, critics, and filmmakers alike—have everything to gain by thoughtfully listening and talking to each other, directly and in translation, in the demilitarized, increasingly transculturated zone we call civil society.

CHAPTER FIVE

◥

The Last Judgment:
Marcela Fernández Violante's
Requiem (for) Melodrama

THE ART OF POLITICS AND THE POLITICS OF ART

Melodrama endures. Following the close of a very secular century our yearning for meaning seems as acute as our suspicion that postmodern contingency is all there is. While the aesthetics of minimalism are again in vogue—recent independent films stage particular moments of transcendent quiescence[1]—the excesses of global melodrama still hold power for spectators desiring some kind of narrative explanation of an increasingly nonsensical world.

Indeed it is the realm of the senses, in all the permutations of that word, to which the melodramatic sensibility seeks to gain access. Given our emotional stakes in sociopolitical economies, we still feel a sense of rightness or outrage or resignation or optimism in the face of great global shifts in our daily paradigms. Cinematic melodramas exploit this, and their self-aware strategies clue us in to their punchlines even as we knowingly yield to their empathetic impetus. If we accede to the cynicism of our times, the movies can make us weep over the loss of significance. If we indulge in eternal hope-against-hope, cinema asks us to ponder the pragmatism of faith. In the regime of this new melodrama we are sentient beings in a sense-able world.

Civic melodrama can function much the same way, shaped by anyone who assigns meaning to an extrafilmic situation through the imposition of a narrative. The discursive strategies of politicians and the media famously rely upon the aesthetics of excess, aggrandizing and demonizing almost by force.

Smart melodramatizing (that is, however our own personal savior of a politico puts things) is cogent and complex, appealing both to our sentiments and our good sense.

Throughout this book I have assumed a contiguity not only between the form of cinematic and civic melodrama, but, more emphatically, between the concerns that the genre and the sensibility address. It's the big stuff—revealed in the *pars pro toto* formula—that ignites melodrama. So it is that my own frankly excessive narrative on excess has been brought to life by what interests me most profoundly: a place in time and space that exists on (what feels like? what appears to be?) the edge of a melodramatic denouement. At the end of one century and the beginning of the next I write in what *fin de siglo* monumentalism describes as an in-between time, hoping, against evidence to the contrary, that our chronological in-betweenness does not also herald an ontological pause between one revolution and the next. Nearing the end of my project, with its undercurrent of social, secular prayer, I can't help worrying about the outcomes of some of the dramatic scenarios that have driven my own search for meaning in this Mexamérica that I and millions of others call home.

While my apprehensions are sometimes evident in the plots of the new border movies—say, the melodramatizations of (im)migration and citizenship in films like John Sayles's *Lone Star* or María Novaro's *El jardín del Edén*—my concerns often resonate with the practices of daily life. The great melodramas of our times are political, including decisions that legislate everything from peoples' entitlements to their basic human rights. Having traced some of the political antecedents of post-revolutionary and post-rebellion (trans)nationalist melodrama, I've been especially troubled by the overarching question of "home" in what is becoming an undemocratically post-national age. The legal transnationalism of corporations, for example, is as fluid as that of a Mexican factory worker is not, and being at home—or making oneself at home—in today's global economies is commensurately harder for those whose claim to world citizenship is tenuous.

For first-world, passported, and visa-ed world travelers of all sorts, understanding the far-reaching implications of waiting one's turn in an immigration line (or having to manage without such legal niceties) may well rely on narrative. But whether that narrative is an ethnographic melodrama, or a lucid, moving documentary about the injustices faced by *maquiladora* workers on the border,[2] or a heart-rending, critical analysis of Arizona ranchers acting as death squad vigilantes bent on "hunting" humans who cross political borders,[3] we are spectators of, and actors in, more than narrative representations. Ultimately the materiality of melodrama's excess—public and private policy as lived experience—is not to be contained by the spectacles produced in radio, television, newsprint, or in movie theaters.

At my least hopeful I find this confluence of art and politics a prediction of impending tragedy. Are the wounds occasioned by third worlds grating up against first worlds, as one critic indelibly wrote,[4] festering sores symptomatic of an as-yet-undiagnosed antebellum nationalism? Are the tensions of local, daily life that we see represented on film or discussed in the media poised to explode into bloody civil conflict on a transnational scale?

While progressive, self-aware melodrama's morality tales may warn of apocalypse, in the end its sensibility sides with optimism, not doom-saying. If such melodrama describes the conditions of evil, it also offers the promise of common good. And while its concerns are of epic scale, it sees life in its details, investing the simplest object with transcendent significance: metaphor as metamorphosis.

As I entertain these thoughts I am also in transition, and my movement from here to there is marked by many of the border crossings I have been writing about in this book. Decades have passed since I began my journey to mid-century Mexico by way of matinees at the local Spanish-language theaters in Los Angeles. Later another life took me to Mexico to live and study and happily "waste my youth at the movies," as my biology professor insisted, by watching old movies out of time if not place. Still another life returned me to my L.A. barrio to share new melodrama with old friends. And years after attending the Tijuana film fête that inspired this book I am a traveler once more, driving through my old neighborhood to the airport, bound for Mexico City and the completion of one story about melodrama and the inauguration of a new one. On this May afternoon of the millennial year, I find myself again on the perfectly monstrous Arroyo Seco Freeway, whose pulse toward the heart of Los Angeles beats so listlessly in the midday traffic that the world around me reveals itself as if in a slow-motion movie. Here, near the most-traversed artery on the globe, I begin to ponder life in its grand proportions, so fixed on instances of evil and promises of common good that I nearly miss life in its transcendent detail: winking brake lights that signify the inception of one last L.A. narrative.

When Worlds Collide

It's summer, the meanest of that cruel quartet of seasons—fire, flood, earthquake, riot—imagined by city cynics. The man in a rusting Pontiac next to me is visibly beginning to sweat; he reaches back to lower a window while trying to prevent a cool black El Dorado from nosing into his sluggishly moving lane. Gentle curves in the road, designed when the parkway was meant to charm Pasadena motorists past riverside sycamores to afternoons, perhaps, at downtown cinema palaces, prevent us from seeing what's ahead. But when forward motion all but ceases, we anticipate the worst: the effects of road rage in several different languages.

It doesn't quite happen. Yet an intent Acura applies pressure on the Caddie from the rear, nudged on by the mounting traffic behind us, none of which, I presume, is bent on a relaxing lunch and movie. Whatever lies ahead, I worry about my little local threesome. One eye on their drama, and another on the car in front, I glance about, looking for a space I can slip into to diminish the tension around me.

No such graceful concession is possible. We edge 'round the bend and the accident appears as if from a film set. It's minor—a souped-up Chevy and a bakery van; nobody hurt, nobody rubbing her neck, just mashed marzipan and people walking on the roadway—but until the tow trucks arrive, all three narrow lanes are blocked. We are forced to patience, witnesses not of a tragedy but another drama of the quotidian.

Under such circumstances Los Angelinos become surprisingly calm. No horns, no yelling, no rude gestures. The mishap has transpired; our lot is to survive with a bit of class. This freeway etiquette is so pervasive that even out-of-towners seem to adapt. Those who don't are oddities who make the nightly news.

There's nothing for it but to make the best of this situation. I've budgeted five hours to drive fifteen miles and make a plane bound for Mexico City. I can afford to relax into this freeway parking lot. So can a few others; an elderly Hornet has inched up to allow the Pontiac to cede ground to the El Dorado. Resigned détente is achieved. Better yet, we're stopped where else but within view of Charles Freeman's *Return to the Light*. The mural is as vibrant in summer 2000 as it was in 1994 when the human figures it represents went to war with the Mexican government under the banner of the Zapatistas.

I am moved, as always, by the sight of those migrant souls, dominating the frame of the Carlota Park Apartment wall as imposingly as figures on a grand Mexican mural or the screen of an L.A. drive-in movie theater. They stand impossibly together in such solidarity. The Tzotzil healer seems particularly present today, holding in his embrace peoples from the still-besieged Chiapas to the streets of this increasingly impoverished barrio. Linked to the most decisive call for participatory democracy since Emiliano Zapata organized indigenous resistance against the Porfiriato nine decades earlier, the leader's eloquent gesture also assumes a challenging stance with respect to the Mexican government's current—and contradictory—appeals for peace in the region. His face on one fighter's tee-shirt (caught by Univisión television cameras) speaks for the Zapatista's plan for democratic national unity: restored human rights, fair electoral processes at both local and national levels, socioeconomic programs including long-deferred land reform, release of political prisoners, return of municipalities taken by the military and paramilitary groups, self-determination, and legal enfranchisement into the nation.

Objects of his gaze, two countries pause on the eve of national elections, the Mexican contest just over a month away.

The moment feels monumental. Not for me a placid drive to the airport or pious silence in light of the fender-bender. Freeway etiquette aside, I fantasize leaping out of my car and launching a community debate from the hood of my rented Festiva. I want to use this unexpected halt in the blind race to the metropolis to talk about what exists on the road between here and there. What's happened to the welfare-reformed families, the economic and political immigrants, those left behind in Free Trade América? The transculturated figures on the mural, connected with Mexican, Chicano, and antiwar resistance movements, force us not only to rethink democratization in a national context, but to consider the need for inclusive transnational citizenship in an increasingly undemocratic new world order.

Given this globalization of national subjects, how might we understand the current implications of the celluloid (trans)nationalisms of Emilio Fernández's, Matilde Landeta's, and Allison Anders's melodramas? Fernández's indigenous peoples, however apotheosized, still speak out against the injustices of *caciquismo*, a sociopolitical system promoting chiefdoms that Zapatistas resist even today. The filmmaker's representations of a people whose water (not to mention land) rights have been stolen cannot but remind us of similar struggles of native peoples throughout the Americas. Screened more than forty years after its Mexico City debut in a Border Film Festival in the very region where Mexicans have had to fight the United States for their fair share of a pollutant- and saline-free river, *Río Escondido* takes on expanded significance to serve as a symbol of the truly "Hidden River"—the Colorado—whose riches rightfully belong to both nations.

Lola Casanova's proposal for national unity, however interested in indigenous assimilation, still imagines the possibility of traditional peoples' sovereignty in a multiethnic nation. As the filmmaker herself remarked in retrospect, "the Seris in my first feature anticipated today's Zapatistas . . . guerrilla fighters defending indigenous rights."[5] Landeta's polyvalent recreation of an Edenic past, in contrast to more monochromatic views produced by mid-century image makers, prompts us to look even further for representations of a less nostalgic *México profundo* produced by native artists. Explorations might begin with studies of indigenous broadcast journalism (one of the first media that communities have used to chronicle and disseminate information about their own lifeways), and move on to native groups' use of the Internet.[6]

Landeta's and Anders's narratives of solidarity also assume a special meaning given our current political context of transnational "wars on poverty" rendered as wars on the poor. The devastation left in the wake of Free Trade (Mexican women have been particularly affected as small businesses go under and large assembly plants pay downsized wages[7]) and the hardship that the near welfare repeal is beginning to cause in the United States (women and children particularly are suffering[8]) almost preclude the possibility of engaged citizenship for marginalized women. Both *Trotacalles* and *Mi vida loca* function to dramatize the effects of governments' abandonment of the poor, the narratives urging empathy for those forsaken by draconian public policy. Landeta's documentation of the "legitimate" business failure of the once-productive Plaza de las Vizcaínas resonates in Anders's portrayal of Echo Park Boulevard's similar demise. What's clear in these visions of besieged streets is that the creation of a second-tier economy threatens everyone's public space: a war on the poor could spark a kind of civil war devastating the entire society.

The Pontiac in the next lane is starting to heat up, keeping pace with the driver's damning of his exhausted machine. I shut off my rented air conditioner and roll down my windows in unity with his blistering car. The guy's not impressed. My real car is an un-air-conditioned '78, I want to tell him; I share your pain. The look we exchange is complex, but in the end the ostensibly middle-class white woman gets a break as the presumably poor brown man shrugs an eloquent *ni modo*. Oh well, he finally gestures, and I know he's not holding anything against me. His anger has a point, though; there are forces worthy of condemnation, here on the freeway or in a film. I flash on an image of us all getting out of our cars and speaking to those issues.

But this is L.A.—not Mexico City—and drama in the pre-election streets is still a plane trip away. Anyway, how would one manage? A privileged Festiva driver and a man in a boiling Pontiac don't make a rally. Even if my old-guard girlfriends and diehard former neighbors, at work this afternoon in their mostly social service jobs, were home to help organize an impromptu street discussion, there's still a chain-link fence separating the unhurried, barrio access road from the speedway where I'm now fully stopped. And though faces in the late-model cars around me turn toward the neighborhood, the longing I read in them is about getting the hell out of here, not about staying and taking it in. Finally, we drivers are Los Angelinos, compatriots if only while on this freeway. We form a car culture that dictates our distance from one another while defining our disparate rates and modes of travel. In the midst of the mass, each of us is alone.

Yet our auto-imposed separateness seems to break down in cases of emergency. Even before the police and rescue crew arrive, first-at-the-scene motorists have already alighted from their cars, escorting folks to the roadside, running back down the freeway to place flares, to direct traffic. Since no one is hurt, what could have been a tragedy turns out to be a fine show of solidarity. Melodrama in action, complete with strains of rap music issuing from the gutsy speakers of the Pontiac. We've a kind of peoples' bread and circus here that bests any opportunistic grandstanding I might have imagined. Having stepped from his Lexus to help the bakery driver, for instance, a conservatively dressed man in a display of lightheartedness stoops to pluck out a croissant from the damaged van. A slow pitch and a whimsical grin console the Chevy driver. A few croissants tossed to the crowd make us all smile, as does the guy's ironic self-disclosure: "Always been good at giving away other peoples' bread." When the authorities do arrive, there's a respectful handing over of duties as drivers return to their cars and the cops take charge. An extraordinary gentleness in the way an officer leads the equally grateful Chevy and bakery van drivers off to the side of the freeway nearly moves me to tears. Guilty or not of reckless driving, the men who have just collided with one another stand comforted in the light embrace of the policeman until they get their bearings. This is not the Los Angeles seen on TV.

It's also not the L.A. of criminalizing news melodramas or of commercial movie spectacles, where either citizens or police are represented as fantastically good or horrifically bad. This is an L.A. in which nothing much—and yet everything—has happened, an afternoon when the whole world seemed sublimely mundane.

A lane opens; I let the freshly anxious El Dorado pass. I crank up the soundtrack of *Mi vida loca* and horns blast from my tape player as Los Lobos lead me down the freeway. An interested spectator of this melodrama of the transcendent everyday, I blow my first-ever kiss to a cop and make my way to Mexico.

"AMEMOS AL MONSTRUO":
DE CUERPO PRESENTE, MELODRAMA RESURRECTED

Years after its inception I am concluding this book in the places that inspired my study of melodramatic representations of nation and citizenship. Now, in the summer of 2000, I've come to Mexico to witness the final weeks of what has proven to be the most dramatic presidential campaign since the institutionalizing of the Revolution under the State party in 1929. My purpose is to see the audacious turn-of-the-new-century films that, like the melodramas before them, make art out of politics. How, after decades of civic and cinematic melodramas, do these parallel worlds still collide? How might a current director view the national melodramatic tradition? Moved to glimpse the next chapter in the national narrative, I'm in the capital to interview one of Mexico's most accomplished political filmmakers, artisan-scholar Marcela Fernández Violante. I spend my mornings with a stack of newspapers or at public conferences, my afternoons at film archives or in video stores, my evenings at movie debuts or political cabarets. I'm frequently in the company of Fernández Violante, the animated director whose six feature films, three documentaries, and numerous scripts have starred in a quarter century of cinema in Mexico.

How is it then that I don't see many copies of her films on display when we hit the neighborhood Blockbuster? En route to locally owned *Librería Gandhi* where she will help me sort through video collections of Golden Age melodramas, she explains the glut of Hollywood movies in not-so-freely-trading Mexico. Not only does Blockbuster's inventory consist of more than 95 percent foreign films, but the country's movie theaters screen mainly U.S. productions. Bringing me up to date on the "Leyes Cinematográficas" promulgated in 1992 under President Salinas de Gortari, Fernández Violante paints a bleak picture of a government still disinclined to safeguard its own patrimony. "Protection" spells only destruction for the domestic market, the President of both the Authors' and Adapters' Guild and its umbrella union, the STPC (Sindicato de Trabajadores de Producción Cinematográfica), tells me.[9] But since 1995 in her capacity as Union leader, Fernández Violante has been able to effect change. Working with two industry lawyers, she has drawn up new regulations that have passed into law. Though some of these protections have yet to be seen—in violation of anti-dubbing regulations, for example, *Mission to Mars's* (2000) Don Cheadle can be heard conquering the universe in Spanish[10]—under the direction of Fernández Violante the STPC continues to defend the national cinematic heritage.

When sobering tales of life on the wrong side of NAFTA get to be too much, we lunch. *Comida* with Marcela is an intimate drama. She shares expansive ideas, extensive meals. We savor talk and food as unhurriedly as if she were not scheduled to discuss the state of the film industry with the presidential candidates. We reopen debates we enjoyed almost a decade ago when our conversations circled around Matilde Landeta's dining table: melodrama, politics, the intellect, the emotions.

Mati's absence still seems palpable to her friend and colleague of more than twenty years (Fig. 5.1). Eight years since my last face-to-face interview with a director debuting her final film *(Nocturno a Rosario)*, Marcela and I share memories of Matilde and her movies, speculating on the new government's willingness to support studies about the first century—and production in the second—of Mexican filmmaking. Whichever party prevails, the politics of neoliberalism and transnational trade, established since Salinas's reign of economic and other terrors, threatens art worlds. Political and affective melodramas have become a lived genre, a sensibility for all seasons.

In the midst of writing an article for the alma mater where she had recently been celebrated for twenty-five years of teaching, Marcela was eager to talk about tragedy and melodrama during one particularly stimulating luncheon.[11] We discussed the qualities of each genre, the unequivocal denouements of tragedies, the ultimate optimism of melodrama. We considered elements of her own films, the (neo)melodramatic tensions of love and crime in the tragic *Nocturno amor que te vas* (Nocturnal Love Departing; 1987), and the

FIGURE 5.1. Three generations of filmmakers: Matilde Landeta is flanked by Marcela Fernández Violante on her right and María Novaro on her left. Courtesy Landeta.

tragic consequences of the Salinas government reflected in *Golpe de suerte* (Stroke of Luck; 1991). In commenting on the genres employed in her work we found ourselves reviewing seventy years of filmmaking and politics since the inception of sound and the consolidation of the post-revolutionary state. As we returned to her movies, I began to wonder if "commenting," in its most resolute form, is not exactly the aim of the best of the new films, including a wickedly perceptive Fernández Violante documentary about the politics and procedures of melodrama.

If stellar mid-century melodramas, as the filmmaker sees things, were dedicated to imparting to their viewers both civic and "sentimental" educations (that is, of the senses), insightful new movies are devoted to revealing the pedagogy of that education. Fernández Violante's latest film is an exemplary case in point. Reverberating with the same kind of self-aware stylistics as Landeta's melodramas and echoing the biting expositions of Luis Buñuel's tongue-in-cheek Mexican tear-jerkers, *De cuerpo presente: Las espirales perpetuas del placer y el poder* (Present in Body: The Perpetual Spirals of Pleasure and Power; 1997)[12] is a witty tribute to—and unflinching critique of—seven decades of melodramatic *educación sentimental*. Long on analysis, the black and white short is the crown jewel of a two-hour anthology of other Latin American short documentaries about the last century of filmmaking in the hemisphere, *Enredando sombras* (Intertwining Shadows; 1999). Choosing sequences from nearly eighty melodramas dating from the early 1930s to the end of the century, the documentarian works in black and white 35mm to reshoot her "found footage" (intensely memorable moments from both black and white and color films), editing images and layering sound to bring forth a sort of monstrous new melodrama. This hybrid film "illustrates," as she writes in her script synopsis, "the curious paradox between the political profile and the social landscape proposed by the national cinematic culture."

De cuerpo presente transforms that curious sociopolitical space into a metaphoric body politic: here the moral universe is exposed through a painstaking script that aligns cinematic specters with their corporeal spectators. In nine visceral movements the film documents melodramatized bodies from conception to death. Their point of physical and psychological contact with other bodies is fierce; they move from the abyss of violence to the apex of tenderness and back again. In the film's lush melodramatic excesses we are made to feel their pain, their pleasure. We are mesmerized to complicity when we regard the characters in their original contexts; we're amused beyond hilarity when we watch them through our current perspectives. Bold juxtapositions of images and renarrativizations of plots engage us in a whole new cinematic experience.

It is in the reframing of these films' manichean morals that Fernández Violante's documentary metamorphoses into its own ethnographic neomelodrama. Where previously we may have understood the movies' symbolic systems in the narrow terms that commercial cinema defined for itself (*machismo* is all-pervasive, the mother is sacrosanct), *De cuerpo presente*'s iconoclasm reveals complexity. This is not to say that Fernández Violante's study of Foucauldian "spirals of power," as suggested by the short's subtitle, exposes some consummate truth about what last century's melodramas really represented. But like Buñuel, the filmmaker purposefully perverts the grammar and syntax of filmic violence to show us how intricate social orders apprised—and were informed by—representational practices.[13]

Cuerpo's perverse form is consistent with its thematic drive. Using melodrama's own aesthetic of excess to demonstrate how previous films melodramatized their moral fables, the short concatenates a selection of mainstream movies' "succession of plurals," to borrow from Benedict Anderson's taxonomy of the representational strategies of nationalism, in order to emphasize how cinema "imagined" nation and citizen through its own system of "sacred signs." Where pre- or extranational entities, as Anderson explains, began to consolidate their identities through immutably significant icons featured in "this relief, that window, this sermon, that tale, this morality play, that relic,"[14] post-revolutionary filmic production, Fernández Violante shows, solidified the idea of "Mexico" and "Mexicans" through its own lexicon of stable stereotypes. In a traditionally ordered state, where the expression of gender was regarded to be as binding as national affiliation—and as inextricably tied—the citizenry was often portrayed *enacting* a succession of plurals, all in the service of the nation or in the embellishment of the gendered national character. In an endless succession of movies that consolidated national identity through immutably significant icons, this man dominates that woman, that woman subjugates this man. Mexican melodrama's insistent repetition of similar characters engaged in similar battles motivates *De cuerpo presente*'s own multiplication of some of these same images, which serve to articulate the documentary's world view and claim its spectators as enfranchised members of its (trans)national community.

If significance is indeed derived from detail, and if it is the accumulation of details that mount to the expression of a world viewed, I now propose a microscopic analysis of *Cuerpo*'s macrobodies: some 275 shots stitched seamlessly together to make up thirteen of the most saturated cinematic minutes in the history of Latin American film. However hydra-headed this celluloid beast, its intellectual acuity is as sharp as its heart is empathetic. It witnesses how the movies managed morality, how they sought to express the relevance of violence and suffering, how they proselytized the masses. And the documentation does more than testify. It interrogates. Rectitude and turpitude are no fixed points on *Cuerpo*'s moral compass; violence is multivalent and suffering may have no meaning at all. What is notable in the ethic and aesthetic of Fernández Violante's reimagined cinematic body is her incorporation of spectators' psyches and social bodies in the flesh of her text. While suffering or savoring the farragoes of life may not carry transcendent significance, in this film the viewers' pain and pleasure matter and can be indulged or mitigated with a little ironic distance.

It is distancing irony that draws us into the oxymoronic world of this documentary. Through repetition that nearly moves us to the brink of delirium we get to think closely about what the melodramas of the last seventy years have encouraged us to feel profoundly. It's important to note that the depth of all this thinking and feeling relies on the proximity of the spectator to the heart of the matter. "We the viewers" of the *cuerpo presente* are imagined as friends and family of the corpse, which lies in state under the aegis of the Pan-American film anthology. One of ten shorts by recognized Latin American directors (including another thoughtful piece on Mexican cinema by María Novaro), *De cuerpo presente* is by far the most inventive and the most sought-after offering of the collection. Beyond its exhilarating audacity, it owes its popularity to a continent of spectators who have imagined their Latin Americanness through the prism of Mexican celluloid nationalism. And though *Cuerpo*'s "friends and family" may be ideally of national or Pan-Latino origin, with the help of English subtitles others may also enjoy a kind of naturalized kinship with the filmic body. While our relative distance from the film's entic-ingly distancing mechanisms may temper our intimacy with the documentary, we are all nonetheless quite democratically invited to the requiem celebration of a life born of the movies. I like to think that the secular psalm of this short movie offers global spectators an opportunity to practice a little regionalism, exercising our citizenship in a community imagined without borders.

"Cuerpo moral, cuerpo social"

The documentary's originating moment (and we must remember that we are dealing with seconds of footage here, flickers from a collective dream) situates the film in an aberrant biblical beginning. In that beginning there was light-ning; blackened heavens rend themselves to flood the earth and drench an icon of mortal divinity resting upon it. Instantly recognizable as Mexican melodrama's foundational figure and goddess-citizen *por excelencia,* the alabaster likeness of a kneeling, nude María Félix suggests from the outset that the human creatures spawned in this film will be something other than blessed. But there's compassion here for protagonist and audience alike. Con-demnation has its redeeming qualities, the short implies, and the film moves on to reveal the pleasures in sin and sanctity. *Cuerpo's* primordial *Moral Body, Social Body*[15] is consecrated in the startling image of the adulterous protagonist of *La diosa arrodillada* (The Kneeling Goddess; 1947), serving as an ironic *¡Viva!* to the carnal progeny of this celluloid *Chingada* (Fig. 5.2). "Long live smart, suffering spectators who relish their weekly penance at the altars of sentimental education," Fernández Violante seems to say. Her documentation of the public display of private power salutes viewers' fidelity to their heart-*and*-head responses to the religion of cinema.

Appeals to spectatorial participation are yet more legible in the next sequence, selected from *Apasionada* (1952), when a negligéed Leticia Palma invites us, by extension, to identify with Jorge Mistral and "get comfortable" in our own theater seats as the character settles into his home movie house. The actress, playing an actress, turns on a 16mm projector. As we watch the pair watching an impassioned Palma dance alluringly across the diegetic screen in a Mexican homage to Hollywood's 1943 *Stormy Weather* (complete with sleazy orchestration), we become aware of the sequence's multiple time-and-place frames. Our awareness of the cinematic apparatus—and I'm talking about all the elements that make film function—extends from our apprecia-tion of the dual national contexts to the multiple historical subjects that inhabit that strangely familiar space. We "make ourselves comfortable" in the delightfully uncomfortable world of Palma's sexually charged silhouette (graphically matched with the previous female nude), gyrating in cane and top hat under a streetwalker's lamppost across from the distorted image of a

FIGURE 5.2. The adulterous protagonist of *La diosa arrodillada*, María Félix. Courtesy Cineteca Nacional.

church (Fig. 5.3). As her body fills the frame to black, we cut to the terrified eyes of a tough Ninón Sevilla (*Sensualidad;* 1950) superimposed over storm clouds in celestial address of the audience. Her stare, incarnating our return look, is contrasted with the next shot of a hand uncovering the defeated face of *Salón México*'s (Dance Hall "México"; 1948) much-martyred Marga López. The moment passes quickly as we try to recall Emilio Fernández's film about abuse and abnegation: is this the hand that metes out violence or the one that soothes a sorrowful taxi dancer? Or are we spectators of this new ethnography of violence witnessing some kind of see-no-evil hand that warns us of the dangers of looking? What demons will we liberate when, comfortable or not in the final seconds of this prologue, we lower our eyes together with *El diabólico*'s Jorge Humberto Robles (1976) to peer into a keyhole through which we cannot resist gazing?

Circles of hell and heaven open to us as the body of the film, however truncated, extends seamlessly from the prologue through nine distinct but fully integrated "Estaciones." These Stations, Fernández Violante notes in a screenplay so fully turned out that it can stand on its own, are linked with

FIGURE 5.3. An impassioned Leticia Palma dances across the diegetic screen in *Apasionada*. *De cuerpo presente* frame enlargement.

Christian soteriology that describes Christ's redeeming progress to Golgotha and his eventual crucifixion and death on the Mount. Although we are clearly meant to make the connection between the suffering body of Christ and the tormented cinematic and spectatorial bodies of the documentary's universe, Fernández Violante's *Via Dolorosa* is intentionally dissimilar from the journey to the biblical Calvary. Where the Church's first Station of the Cross represents the juncture when the adult Jesus is condemned to death, the film's first Station, *The Regime of the Body*, portrays souls condemned from the instant of their progenitors' thrillingly unoriginal sins.

Stained by conceptions wrought in violence, mainstream cinema's damned have little bulwark against Satan. Only the grace of the resacralized State, granted through the intercession of the movies' divas, can save the wretched. Cognizant spectators of these films' excessive moments, though, brought to awareness by highly conscious editing and reasoned manipulations of sound, can savor sin without consigning our souls to commercial movies' theology of damnation and redemption. *De cuerpo presente*'s rearticulations of moral universes deliver us from the evils of binary thinking. The best of these new universes: ironic tales moralizing against hypocrisy. As Ana Martín of *Los indolentes* (1977) unself-consciously bares her breasts while undressing in the privacy of her room, nuns in voice-over from the 1976 *Las noches de Paloma* (hard at prayer since the *Sensualidad* sequence) recite in perfervid monotone: "Forbidden fruit; it is indecent to show our shameful parts needlessly. [Hold fast to] ablutions of the body as symbols against the filthy stains of sin." But transgression in "The Body in Abstinence" is the cross the nuns must bear. Through cleansing Cristina Baker's body, suggests *Las noches* director Alberto Isaac in a sequence that Fernández Violante employs for its wit, the nuns commit offenses against the very strictures they seek to impose. A tight camera frames Baker's bath-soaked legs with a view of her suggestively covered pudendum, so apparently stained that the hand introduced into this composition, which we subsequently learn belongs to a nun, seems compelled to scrub with purpose (Figs. 5.4 and 5.5).

The apple thus consumed, generations of Eves start paying for their sins. The body in the next segment, "The Body Beaten," is that of the punished woman. Here, as ethnography, *De cuerpo presente* displays the panorama of the cinema of violence. As neomelodrama the film speaks to the dangers of movies that "meditate" on violence only to exalt it. An image of the vainly supplicating, bound wrists of a woman about to be raped recalls *Violación's* (Rape; 1987) violent "fable of violence" without eroticizing—unlike that box-office hit—the bodies of brutalized women.[16] Instead of punctuating the shot

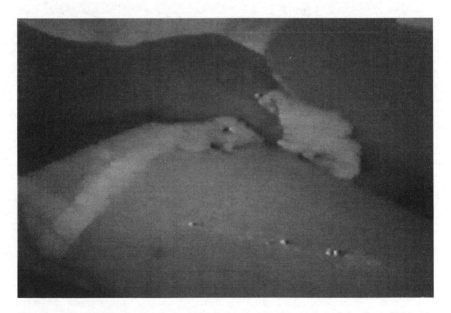

FIGURE 5.4. Scrubbing with purpose: nuns removing the stain of sin from Paloma's (Cristina Baker) body. *De cuerpo presente* frame enlargement.

CONACINE y DASA FILMS presentan a
BRUNO REY y PANCHO CORDOVA en **"LAS NOCHES DE PALOMA"**
con Cristina Baker como Paloma y Gregorio Casal • A COLORES • Distribuída por Clasa-Mohme, Inc. • C1817
PRINTED IN U.S.A.

FIGURE 5.5. Paloma's compromising positions multiply. Courtesy Agrasánchez Film Archive.

of the helpless wrists with images of women who are "never more attractive than while being raped," Fernández Violante's choice of painful portraits of violated women are superimposed over dramatic night skies where storms rage in protest against the abuse of power.

However legible, Fernández Violante's *neo*melodrama doesn't oversimplify, and the film is no humorless tirade. Even as we hurtle toward the next Stations, we have to deal with anomaly. What are we to make of the insertion of an image from Chano Ureta's pseudohistorical terror-comedy, *El signo de la muerte* (The Sign of Death; 1939), where spectators who recognize the film and know of its mad conception[17] are not quite certain if Elena D'Orgaz's mouth is muzzled to prevent her from screaming or from chortling at the thought of her impending sacrifice to "Aztec" gods? What are we to do with the close-ups from Ismael Rodríguez's sly *La Cucaracha* (1958), where character actress Emma Roldán is made to produce a fabulously hideous grimace that opens to screech a sweaty "¡Aguántate!" ("Bear up!") to the violated women Fernández Violante has edited into earshot?

The savvy spectators with whom I first saw this documentary, trained in the satirical melodramas of Buñuel, Rodríguez, and Isaac, knew just what to make of such moments: everyone roared. In Fernández Violante's sensationally monstrous film Roldán's "¡Aguántate!" constitutes searing black humor. Other instances from *La Cucaracha* sensationalize differently. Within the scope of two contrasted shots Rodríguez encourages us to empathize with the experience of pain and intellectually appreciate its role in creation. When La Cucaracha (María Félix) screamingly gives birth to a child, we wince. When we recall that the father of that child is none other than longtime Félix director Emilio Fernández, playing a revolutionary general, we smile. When Félix's opened-mouth "¡Aaayy!" transforms by sound-over and graphic match into a shouting soldier's "Aaahhí . . . viene Pancho Villa," we delight in the cut that encapsulates the pedagogy of movie *maestras* instructing us in the political-sentimental tenets of the mid-century nation and its state-supported cinema.

In case none of this is quite clear, the final sequence sutured into this Station's marvelously mutilated body further elucidates a violated mother's ambiguous feelings toward her alleged *hijos de puta*. But before showing us that complexity, Fernández Violante reminds us of commercial melodrama's passion for absolutes. In one of the most overwrought scenes in the whole of Mexican cinema, "victim of sin" Margarita Ceballos, counterpoised against a Monument to the Revolution in towering condemnation of its weakest citizens, tearfully agrees to throw away the fruit of her union with her pimp into a refuse barrel (*Víctimas del pecado;* 1950). Choosing "between 'that' and me—garbage belongs in the trash!" she obliges her *padrote,* so degraded that only her masochism remains intact. "Hit me," she sobs to Rodolfo Acosta, "I deserve it all, but don't abandon me!" Viewers familiar with the film can relax, remembering that the infant (that is, Mexico, *de cuerpo presente*) will be rescued by Saint Ninón Sevilla just seconds before the trashmen arrive.

In order to illustrate the vicissitudes of power and pleasure, Fernández Violante subsequently employs a detail from a Felipe Cazals ethnographic fiction (*Los motivos de Luz;* 1985), where a calm Patricia Reyes Spíndola ruptures the piety of sin-and-salvation discourses. The image of a loving mother murmuring into her male infant's ear is at once reassuring and unsettling. We wonder what kind of mother would coo, "One day you'll grow up and become just like other men. Instead of giving you *chichi* to suckle, I should cut off your prick, my weakling."

Facetious word play, serious sadism, or sweet nothings? If we read only the iconographic significance lent by Reyes Spíndola as an actor, recalling her intelligence and humor (qualities that Fernández Violante herself sought for the protagonist of her *Nocturno amor*), we may well find the sequence satirical.

If we consider Cazals's ultimately indeterminate narrative, based on a real case about a woman accused of killing her four children, we may view the scene as a precursor to a mother's power—or that of her prosecutors—gone awry. However the moment strikes us, what's important to note is that Fernández Violante has seeded enough possibilities to make ambiguity itself articulate.

This is the pleasure of the rest of the text. Pastiche here has both purpose and possibility. The film's reconstructed body is by turns tragic (its flaws fatal to the grave), horrific (inspiring condemnation and compassion), cryptic (straightforward and ironic), and finally, melodramatic (its moral banner aloft regardless of the circumstances). Eight Stations form the documentary's main corpus, linked together in uneasy pair bonds like so many mismatched limbs. The body displayed incarnates all fashion of mothers and fathers *(Home Fires; Power and its Representations)*, registers multiple permutations of human desire *(The Permitted and Prohibited; The Body Alive with Desire)*, and presents a continuum of female and male violence *(Fury and Wantonness; Punishment and Control)*. Thematically and aesthetically similar, the last two Stations *(The Flagellated Body; Sacrifice and Expiation)* also relate more directly than any others to Catholicism's final Stations of the Cross.

Having served as a sort of catechism for interpreting the balance of the film, the first Station gives way to an increasing concentration of mainstream cinema's odd blend of sacred and profane icons and mythologies. The saintly subject of *El fuego del hogar*, the figure of the mother, is juxtaposed with provocative maternal images that offer comparisons beyond generic dichotomies of matriarchs as honorary virgins or mothers as honorable whores. The genius of the documentary is that while Fernández Violante milks classic cinema for its gender archetypes, she also takes the trouble to suggest that not all melodramas achieve the same effects. Her use of a radio announcer's paean to Mexican motherhood from Juan Orol's hugely popular *Madre Querida* (premiering Mother's Day, 1935), for example, does more than serve as straightman for her comedic sketches of mothers who regard their offspring with less affection—or wickedly, with rather more—than they ought. Blasphemy be damned, says the monstrous *Cuerpo;* neither motherhood nor a movie extolling its unblemished virtues is sacred. Whatever the director's intentions, *Madre Querida*, prototype of a host of maternal tragedies, is risible. And on their own terms the films from which she borrows to demonstrate Orol's "humor involuntario"[18] are considerably less droll than they appear here. Yet how better than through these recontextualizations are we to understand the mercurial ways of power and pleasure as exercised between and among filmmakers, protagonists, and viewers?

With the final rearticulations of the second Station's bodies, when our *madre querida* transforms into that Medea presaged by Patricia Reyes Spíndola, spectators become accessories to crime. Though Gabriel Figueroa's subjective camera lends us the perspective of a murderous mother (*La casa del pelí-cano;* 1977), our complicity lies less with her actions than with the documentarian's point of view. Our "crime" here consists of perversion, a persistence of vision that, thanks to Fernández Violante's resurrection of the moribund cinematic body, sees the conventions and contradictions of decades of cinema and society incarnated in a single moment. For spectators who followed national news reports about the late Enrique Álvarez Félix's allegedly difficult relationship with real-life mother María Félix, it may be hard to ignore the irony of Álvarez Félix's character suffering castrating stabs by his angry mother's hand (a risibly young Jacqueline Andere [Fig. 5.6]). And against all "appropriate affect," it may be tough to resist laughing at the satirical role the reshot footage plays—to the beat of *Abandonadas*'s Víctor Junco in a voice-over elegy to divine motherhood—in revealing the sanctimony of many Mexican mommie dearests. Here the power of analytical editing allows us our pleasure in gossip-column prurience, but at the same time underscores both the perversity of melodramatic yellow journalism and our attraction to it.

Black humor lightens melodrama's burdens and gives spectators something to think about in addition to our cathartic good time at the movies. Without Buñuel's double-edged Mexican melodramas, I wonder, would we ever have appreciated the full vigor of Golden Age cinema? Fernández

FIGURE 5.6. Motherly love in *La casa del pelícano. De cuerpo presente* frame enlargement.

Violante doesn't seem to think so. Not only does she use bits of Buñuel's films to flesh out *Cuerpo,* but she pays homage to an overall Buñuelian sensibility when she treats such themes as subjugation and submission. Nodding to the surrealist in a sequence from his *Una mujer sin amor* (A Woman without Love; 1951), the third Station ventures into the infrequently explored territory of paternal power and male masochism. As in Buñuel's film, the sons represented in "El padre: cacique" suffer repression at the hands of omnipotent, Freudian father figures who, weighted with their own unresolved feelings toward their wives and mothers, rouse their children's sentiments of desire for, and dread of, the maternal. Because Mexican social and cinematic ideology limits boys' and men's access to the traditionally feminine realm of emotion, males' longing for what is coded as women's warmth becomes perverted into cravings for carnal possession, desires that will be worked out literally or symbolically with the mother or her surrogate. Whatever choice he makes, the child of this paradigm will be punished. And whatever form that punishment takes, this male will be represented as at least resigned to—and possibly even pleased with—his fate. Since Fernández Violante makes subtle points emphatically—this is a melodramatic ethnography—her third Station ends not only with the death of an incestuously libidinous son at the hands of his father (the object of desire here is a very unmaternal Isela Vega), but with the young man's erotic affections transferred to the patriarch (*La India;* 1974). In spite or perhaps because of the ultimate in sadism, the son suffers in ecstasy as he confesses in voice-over during the slow-motion knifing, "And along with the pain of death, as my father penetrated my flesh and my blood, I was flooded with great joy . . . because . . . for the first time he cared about me." Composing subjective shots of the father in monumental low angle, our ethnographer intercuts the agonizingly slow death sequence with reminders of paternal passion run amok. In quick succession Pedro Infante is belted by an off-screen Fernando Soler (*La oveja negra,* Black Sheep; 1949 [Fig. 5.7]), Rodolfo Acosta beats up his ashcan-surviving issue *(Víctimas del pecado),* Pedro Armendáriz gets it from Miguel Ángel Férriz (*Flor silvestre,* Wild Flower; 1943), and *Una mujer sin amor*'s Julio Villareal is back at it with his abused son. That melodrama deserves the unexamined sobriquet "*women's weepies*" is challenged here in full force.

After such fulsome pathos the tone of the documentary shifts to a minor, more subdued key. The transition is marked much like the third Station's initial image of a searching eye, but in *Lo permitido y lo prohibido* the orb peering through a knot in a wooden wall is female. Where in the previous segment we might have recognized the voyeuristic gaze of a child pining for a glimpse of his undressed mother, with the tableau Fernández Violante proposes as countershot to this eye we begin to wonder if we're not witnessing an instance when a young girl, about to be violated by a repulsive old man (*La mujer per-*

PRODUCCIONES RODRIGUEZ HNOS. PRESENTA A
PEDRO INFANTE y **FERNANDO SOLER** en **"LA OVEJA NEGRA"**
con AMANDA del LLANO, ANDRES SOLER, DALIA IÑIGUEZ y VIRGINIA SERRET · Distribuída por CLASA-MOHME, Inc.
PRINTED IN U. S. A.

FIGURE 5.7. Paternal passion run amok: here the production still tells all. Courtesy Agrasánchez Film Archive.

fecta; 1977), might be looking *out* from the place of her imprisonment. If we observe this sequence empathetically, in accordance with melodrama's solicitation of spectator identification with the female subject, we feel her entrapment. Notwithstanding the next scene's ejaculating champagne (splashing merrily between pinup Pedro Armendáriz's legs and onto the ladies at his side), Fernández Violante purposefully spoils *Abandonadas*'s original, festive moment. We know—the movies have taught us—what comes of an excess of drink or a saturation of other exuberant fluids (Fig. 5.8). When the Station concludes with images of a lone bride contemplating her circumstances in the face of a crazily spinning mirror that also elicits audience reflection (*Días de otoño,* Days of Autumn; 1962), the sensation of imprisonment is complete.

Not one for letting her viewers sink into a miasma of despair, the filmmaker gives us a breath of refreshing tranquillity in her fifth Station, *El cuerpo vivo del deseo.* Without its "Intensity of Pleasures," embodied by the seductive waters of ocean, rain, river, and rose-petaled tub, we might be hard-pressed to

FIGURE 5.8. Pedro Armendáriz uncorks with abandon. *De cuerpo presente* frame enlargement.

move on. But this quiescent bridge between the fourth and sixth Stations gives us as much relief as *Potemkin* spectators find in the misty calm of Eisenstein's transitional, middle act.

Waters, though, torment as well as soothe, and the parts that form *Cuerpo*'s desire have been ripped from stormy melodramas whose very titles testify to turmoil: *Amok* (1944), *Amor salvaje* (Savage Love; 1949), *El callejón de los milagros* (Dead-End Street of Miracles; 1994). When *Días de otoño*'s mirror spins 'round again, this time without the reflection of the single bride, we know we're in for the *Fury and Wantonness* of the sixth Station. In smart homage to the Russian filmmaker who influenced—and was influenced by— Mexican filmic iconography, Fernández Violante introduces an Eisensteinian "collision" of shots of women's unleashed passions of the mordant kind. Teeth flashing, Katy Jurado, María Rojo, and Marga López sink their carnivorous *dentata* into flesh that bleeds its ecstasy. This sensual carnage from Buñuel's *El Bruto* (1952) and *Nazarín* (1958), together with Luis Alcoriza's *Lo que importa es vivir* (What Matters Is Living; 1986), is interrupted between bites by another example of classic Eisensteinian punctuation: a word. Like the transitional moment in *Potemkin*'s Odessa Steps when "Suddenly!" signals the shift between civilization and savagery, *Cuerpo* women's blood lust transforms to men's castration fear when, in a voice-over from the appropriately named *El hombre sin rostro* (The Man without a Face; 1950), Arturo de Córdova breathes an ominous "Suddenly." Suddenly it is men who are filled with fearsome blood lust, and their desire doesn't stop with a few nibbles. Playing *Crepúsculo*'s and *La diosa arrodillada*'s besotted adulterers, Arturo de Córdova joins a succession of other men bent on choking the life out of their projected personifications of temptation. At the point of consummating their evil deeds, the men stop short and the balance of power briefly returns to the distaff.

If this power shift is initiated by a moment in male masochism—*Profundo carmesí* (Deep Crimson; 1997) protagonist Daniel Giménez Cacho on his knees to Regina Orozco, begging that she "walk on him like a worm"—a second swing back to cinema's opprobrious men draws protest from *Cuerpo*'s defiled women. Abused Alma Muriel defends herself forthrightly to her resigned mother in a sequence from *Retrato de una mujer casada* (Portrait of a Married Woman; 1979). "¡Es que ese cabrón pudo matarme!" ("That bastard could have killed me!"), she says to a mother counseling that her daughter return to her husband's ultimately "benevolent" embrace. Spliced into the end of the succession of plurals—women battering men, men buffeting women—that constitutes *Furias y desenfrenos*, Station Six, and *Castigo y control*, Station Seven, the sequence is crucial. It not only disturbs the commonly held notion that Mexican melodramas have offered no resistance to dominant gender paradigms, but it underscores Fernández Violante's reminder of cinematic violence as wreaked, relished, and cursed by villains and victims alike.

That women and men share acquaintance with civility and savagery may be a fine object lesson, but however initially satisfying such a moral may be, the filmmaker knows that strategies such as rape-revenge schemes have their limits. What seem infinitely more compelling are questions of spectator pleasure that derive from genres that exceed mere gender-reversal tactics. How violence can spark so much gratification has less to do with some kind of spectator sadomasochism than it does with our enjoyment of satire, itself sometimes an avenging angel. What better critique of power than to laugh in its face? Having learned from Buñuel that, as she says in a new interview about his work, "black humor is a potent, caustic instrument," Fernández Violante shows in her own film how "grotesque excesses and blasphemy lead to disbelief and from there to eruptions of laughter."[19] As the seemingly innumerable women in Station Eight's "The Fall" tumble trampled to the ground, the "grotesque excesses" of their brutalization defy melodrama's overwrought reality: we're moved to mock even the truth of violence in order to mitigate its force. With the blasphemous linking of that Station's *Flagellated* secular *Body* to the Catholic Stations of the flagellated sacred body—Jesus literally falls three times under the cross and the whips on his journey to Golgotha—we're also asked to reread Christ's agony in the face of cinema's "fallen women," a dazzling pun that dispenses with sanctimonious sermonizing from any orthodoxy.

Blasphemy begets blasphemy in "Blame and Repentance," Station Eight's final hosanna. In the space of some literally incredible excesses, *Nazarín*'s Noé Murayama, whom we earlier saw bloodily deflowered in the mouth by an hallucinatory Marga López's incisors, has now been transformed into satiric *Tlayucan*'s (1961) blind beggar. In Fernández Violante's cinematic reconfiguration, the gory lips of Luis Buñuel's chosen figure transmogrifies into the saint-venerating lips of Luis Alcoriza's protagonist, suggesting a graphic link between the sexual and the sacred. This juxtaposition does not go unnoticed within the diegesis of the sequence; in a film interested in making fun of filth and fastidiousness, an "old maid" (Anita Blanch) approaches Santa Lucía's statue and disinfects its feet with a little alcohol before applying her lips in a kiss where the beggar has just pressed his now bloodless mouth. Spectators who know the film will remember that both holy woman and blind man will themselves soon be steeped in alcohol, so drunk that their carnal pleasure will overwhelm any of the pious "cleanliness" they earlier exhibited. Uniting the two Murayama roles in the same way Alcoriza demonstrated his philosophical ties to Buñuel—he cast wife Janet Alcoriza and Buñuel spouse Jeanne Rucar as gringa tourists who motivate *Tlayucan*'s plot—Fernández Violante sketches a kind of family tree that incorporates ironic filmmakers, a stable of familiar stars, and an audience that, by virtue of faithful commonlaw spectatorship, seems incestuously related to everyone.

Having invoked iconoclasts Buñuel and Alcoriza in preparation for the ninth Station's final dismemberment of dogma, the ethnographer plots her penultimate representation of the cinematic body's arduous *Via Dolorosa*. Far from any accusations of murderous motherhood, *Nocturno amor*'s Patricia Reyes Spíndola now screams in the righteous agony Fernández Violante imagines that the real-life wife of a "crucified" taxi driver must have felt when, like Antigone attempting vainly to entomb her brother, her mate's corpse could not be properly buried. We move from the optimism of melodrama to the doom of tragedy as Cosmic Law is flouted and Christ-like women and men suffer on their own crosses. The storms of the first Station rage again as Eisenstein's image of a cross-bearing man casts his eyes heavenward in a silent ¡Qué viva México! to this condemned *familia de tantas* that is the national cinema. When the nude torso of self-flagellating *Las lupitas*'s (1985) Lyn May appears in one of the short's most shocking shots, the "grotesque excesses and blasphemy" of the Stations of *Cuerpo*'s Calvary conduct us "to disbelief and from there, eruptions of laughter."

"Forgive them, Lord" (the protagonists? mirthful spectators?), says *El Mártir del Calvario*'s (1952) Jesús in Station Nine's first wicked cut, "for they know not what they do" (Fig. 5.9). With this, the sacrificial filmic body expires in endless consecutions of death rattles. The progression moves from serious to sensational. If we are disturbed by initial images of dead and dying women—including a quick reminder of *Trotacalles*'s tubercular Ruth, complete with Mariachis that now play *Las golondrinas* to the bitter end—the *Miserere* of the requiem chant ceases its dolorous sound when supplanted by the *Te Deum* of a celebratory chant: Luis Buñuel's wryly amusing *Ensayo de un crimen* (Rehearsal for a Crime; 1955). Here Ernesto Alonso plays close to type as a man who couldn't harm even the least of Buñuel's cherished insects, not to mention the flesh-and-blood women he impotently tries to do in (Fig. 5.10). For one particularly irreverent moment, Landeta fans can't help rereading Alonso's role in *Cuerpo*'s reprised *Trotacalles*. Can we believe the truth of Rudy's (Alonso) supposed violence? Surely Buñuel—and Fernández Violante's reiterated, recontextualized Buñuel—would require our most considered reflection on any aspect of the rejuvenated corpus of melodrama. If not, how do we reconcile our laughter in the face of a mannequin's consignment to the flames in the gently neurotic Alonso character's home kiln?

ENRIQUE RAMBAL JR. y CONSUELO FRANK en "EL MARTIR DEL CALVARIO"
con M. ANGEL FERRIZ, FELIPE DE ALBA, CARMEN MOLINA y MANOLO FABREGAS · Distribución: AZTECA FILMS, Inc.

FIGURE 5.9. *El Mártir del Calvario* before *De cuerpo presente* has its way with Him. Courtesy Agrasánchez Film Archive.

FIGURE 5.10. Poster for Luis Buñuel's wry *Ensayo de un crimen*, doubly satirical in *De cuerpo presente*'s mutilations. Courtesy Agrasánchez Film Archive.

I think this is precisely Fernández Violante's point: whatever the intent of classic sentimental education, filmmakers and spectators have a hand in their own schooling for scandal. If Jesus has been said to weep, in this documentary he also has a fine sense of humor. Given the ubiquitous state of suffering that the movies mirrored and invented, a little saving grace is not an evil thing. Borrowing an image from Buñuel's *Nazarín*, our filmmaker crowns *De cuerpo presente* with the icon of a cackling Christ whose snickering—and not his suffering—becomes the ultimate in redemption.

Satire as survival strategy: a filmmaker's potent response to a Saturnine State that appears intent on devouring its cinematic child. Whether the death sentence imposed on the film industry has issued from legislation that protects foreign film over national production, or whether Mexican cinema's seemingly planned demise is the product of a vengefully paternalistic government refusing to support its unruly offspring, the sardonic power of a little monster of a movie that refuses to die at the end of the last act gives rise to melodrama's sweetest conceit: optimism.

At first glance, though, *Cuerpo*'s last visage is more tragic than hopeful. A young man (*La otra virginidad;* 1974), his back to a stage and his eye to a Super 8 camera, films a diegetic audience, capturing by extension *Cuerpo*'s spectators in his direct pan to the camera. We cut to a close-up of wax melting on the incinerated face of *Ensayo de un crimen*'s simulacrum of a corpse, and our filmmaker involves us in this mannequin's murder by eliciting our split subjectivity. We can accede to the Super 8 filmmaker's point of view— he seems to be shooting the burning body—or observe the scene from our own vantage point. However we choose to look, we have seen. There's no going back, no return to innocence. Guilty by association, we have witnessed the death of a cinematic body; only its fetishistic nature saves us from more than a metaphoric crime. In the next frames the serious young filmmaker raises his small camera to his temple and shoots; blood gushes from the suicidal wound. Do we behold the death of the filmmaker? Has post-Golden Age Mexican cinema been so orphaned as to come to this?

By fetishizing the filmmaker as Buñuel fetishized the cinematic corpse, Fernández Violante gives us ironic distance from the not-so-metaphoric death threats of a government little invested in promoting national cinema. When an image from her own successful *Nocturno amor* seems to ratify the "death" of the young filmmaker—blood gushes ominously from under a closed door—what might have been read as autobiographical tragedy can also be read as an instance of autobiographical blasphemy. And what blasphemy! What "prayer in reverse," as Buñuel compatriot and poet Antonio Machado once said of believers' curses. The blood that washes from under the door acts as a sacramental testimony to the body and blood of the living cinema. Herein the optimism: however beleaguered, Mexican filmmaking exists and our director's work is a part of the body that declines to give up the ghost. In spite of infanticide, patricide, matricide, and suicide—mimetic or metaphoric—marvelously monstrous movie-making survives. *De cuerpo presente* is not so much the moribund corpse as the resurrected spirit of melodrama. As a charwoman from *Mujeres sin mañana* (Women without a Tomorrow; 1951) casually sweeps bits of litter off a floor so recently awash in the blood of the last shot, that spirit ascends from a body represented by the most mundane of symbols. From trash to ash the corpse is consumed. "Fin" marks a gravesite. The transcendent spirit remains as a memory when, in *Cuerpo*'s epilogue, *Apasionadas*'s Leticia Palma turns off the 16mm projector whose purpose has been to restore her companion's recollection of life before amnesia.

Lest we forget the soul of Mexican cinema, I want to complete this analysis by invoking assistant scriptwriter Alfonso Morales Carillo's requiem remarks, pronounced over *De cuerpo presente* as a commentary included as a formal part of the script. Spectators for whom excess is never excessive will thrill to his panegyric for the movies, which adds yet another layer to the monster's mottled epidermis. The essay is the thick-skinned eulogy one might deliver in honor of a beloved relative whom everyone cherished and feared in uneasy measure. His encomium to the movies' "cripples, the incapacitated, the blind, the trampled, the paralyzed, the handicapped, the scar-faced, disfigured beauties [and] scandalous machos" in "innocent" but incestuous carnal congress gives us quite a body to weep over.[20] At the end of his memorial, where paragraph-long sentences mount one upon the next in yet other acts of beastly creation, he breathes an eloquently simple benediction that speaks to a century of Mexican melodrama: "Amemos al monstruo" ("Let us love the monster"). Indeed, with Marcela Fernández Violante, with her eighty passive directorial collaborators and her active filmmaking team, and with one hundred years of solidarity as lovers of latin movies, let us love the monster who has brought us so much pleasure, even at the price of a little pain.

EPILOGUE

N

Deeds that Inspire Confidence

The Mexican elections are over. On the night of July 2, 2000, an effigy of the ruling political party was laid to rest in a gaily decorated (tricolor) casket held aloft by the jubilant hands of the conquering heroes. Outside the circles of the PRI and the third-party PRD a festive wake issued in a new national order. Born under the monument to Mexico City's "Angel of Independence" and celebrated throughout the nation, this "Alliance for Change" trumpeted the birth of a Moral Universe, the likes of which the demoralized country has yet to experience.

However relieved by the death of despotism, PAN-supporters themselves are still reservedly optimistic about the coming era. Those who now form the opposition express greater doubt. It is not only the leftist PRD who worry about how democracy will supplant "la impunidad" of a morally bankrupt system. People supporting the PRI out of fear that the rightist PAN would decimate even the few weakened public programs still functioning in Mexico (including the State-supported cinema, such as it has become) join those who are concerned about the PAN's track record of intolerance (including a not-so-clandestine movement for the reunion of Church and State, expressed by Vicente Fox himself). It is a time when questions of ethics and their restoration to the body politic hold paramount importance. The bloodless coup of fair-play elections having been ratified by the majority of citizens, Mexico now also lives another post-revolutionary epoch when the articulation of "truth" will become an increasingly coveted and contested activity. What more fecund conditions for melodrama?

Given the growing sophistication of spectacles' spectators, I wonder if conventional melodrama, or even straight-faced neomelodrama, will satisfy

195

our post-post-revolutionary, post-postmodern desires for a new, secularized sacred. Working in troubled Mexamérica as a transborder scholar, I have yearned for a cinema that would express a sense of the moral realm without doing itself in with too much solemnity. A few days before leaving the country, I find this possibility incarnated in the latest examples of cinematic satire. Blockbuster now carries the national hit *Todo el poder* (All Power; 1999), a humorous look at the grimly rising crimes of the police. *Amores perros* (Dog Loves; 2000), back home from Cannes with top prizes, opens to packed houses eager to follow its dark moral tales about love, violence, and hope in the time of hopelessness. And an hour before I leave for the airport, my street-market video dealer looks me square in the eyes and swears that the thirty-four-peso copy (U.S. $3.40) of another daring political satire I hold in my grasping hands has been obtained legitimately. I suspend disbelief to shell out the price of a movie date so as to possess the on-and-off censured *Ley de Herodes* (Murphy's Law; 1999), a film situated in the late 1940s but very much concerned with current scandals. Without giving me time to observe that the back of the video jacket advertises some other movie and that the tape itself bears no production information, let alone copyrights, the vendor stuffs my prize purchase into a recycled pharmacy bag complete with the reassuring moral, "Hechos que dan confianza" ("Deeds that Inspire Confidence"). Scheming how I will get through customs on both sides of the border, I tuck the booty into the deepest reaches of my bag and join the criminal class.

Were this the plot of a mid-century melodrama, I would be writing these words from the slammer. As it is, I have become an actor in the kind of twisted "democracy in action" that *Ley de Herodes* recounts. In this film a lazy but honest manager of a garbage dump is chosen by the PRI to act as puppet mayor of a backwater village. While my lowlife career has had its heyday (having studied the video for academic purposes I destroyed it forthwith), the PRI's pawn cannot escape participating in corruption that leads straight to his assumption of the highest ranking posts in the land. If we are not left with images that inspire the confidence of a mid-century melodrama, what remains in *fin de siglo* Mexamérica to restore our sense of meaning and moral value?

I suggest that however generically distinct, neither the new satirical movies nor the new civic endurance tactics differ much *in effect* from the moralizing of mid-century conventions. It is the self-conscious episodes of melodramas of all persuasions that reveal the regime of righteousness, moving us to comprehend excess, to understand viscerally and intellectually the high stakes of citizenship and democracy in post-sacral societies where (im)morality has become the business of the corporate State. Whether or not we (cinematic) citizens are saints or sinners is ultimately less crucial than our awareness of how celluloid truth and other fictions sustain or interrupt claims of national coherence in an increasingly transnational world.

NOTES

—— ▧ ——

Though I have designed this book as a (chrono)logical exploration of some of the concerns and strategies of Mexamerican melodrama, and though I share the genre's creed that meaning lies in the accumulation of detail, I also hope to serve readers for whom melodrama's single token—say, one chapter—manifests significance. To these disparate ends, the chapters, each with full-citation notes, serve either in concert or as discrete movements that may be approached as the spirit moves.

PROLOGUE

1. Freeman's SPARC- (Social and Public Art Resource Center; 1976–present) sponsored mural, a culmination of a project that honors founding muralist Judith F. Baca, painter Christina Schlesinger, and filmmaker Donna Deitch's vision that public art should "arise from within communities" rather than being "imposed upon them," could not have been better imagined nor better placed. Not only did the mural incorporate local residents' ideas in its conception and completion, but the work seems to engage a dialogue with other artistic projects in the neighborhood. A few paces from Lummis's Arroyo Seco home, it stands in eloquent debate with this greatest of L.A. mythmakers. Writer, archeologist, historian, Charles Lummis (1859–1928) trumpeted the city's magnificence to mask its misery. Los Angeles historian Mike Davis debunks the "impresario who promoted the [California mission] myth as the motif of an entire artificial landscape." He discusses how Lummis's contribution to mission literature, with its insistence on "race relations as a pastoral ritual of obedience and paternalism," influenced local literati. That the "Arroyo Set" could argue racial superiority of Euro-Americans while elevating the image of indigenous people is the kind of foundational paradox Freeman's work seeks to unveil. See Mike Davis, *City of Quartz: Excavating the Future in Los Angeles* (1990; London: Verso; New York: Vintage, 1992) 24–30. For an opposing outlook on Lummis as "advocate and promoter of the splendors of the Southwest," see "Charles F. Lummis," *Southwestern Wonderland,* University of Arizona Library's Special Collections Pamphlet and Travel Brochure: n. pag., online, Internet, 29 July 1998, which points out that Lummis "was quick to scold the American public

about their ignorance of their own backyard." For a view of the city's very different champions, including Charles Freeman, see Robin Dunitz, *Street Gallery* (Los Angeles: RJD Enterprises, 1993) and Robin Dunitz and James Prigoff's *Walls of Heritage, Walls of Pride: African American Murals* (Rohnert Park: Pomegranate Communications, 2000).

2. Novelist Arturo Islas defines "migration" in its widest sense. His saga of the Angel family's life in the Mexican/U.S. borderlands forces us to rethink how the binaries of "migrant" and "immigrant" affect the enfranchisement of "citizens" in "nations." Islas's narrator observes that "The Río Grande—shallow, muddy, ugly in those places where the bridges spanned it—was a constant disappointment and hardly a symbol of the promised land to families like Mama Chona's. They had not sailed across an ocean or ridden in wagons and trains across half a continent in search of a new life. They were migrant, not immigrant, souls. They simply and naturally went from one bloody side of the river to the other and into a land that just a few decades earlier had been Mexico. They became border Mexicans with American citizenship." *Migrant Souls* (New York: William Morrow, 1990) 41.

3. A celebration of 140 years of foreign photographers' images of Mexico, the catalogue features prints and autobiographical material from forty-nine artists. Gertrude Blom, whose image of the Tzotzil religious leader adorns both the book and the poster made of the traveling exhibition, has documented life in Mexico since she made her home there in 1940. Having chronicled women's work in factories as a government-sponsored investigator, she became a photojournalist in 1943, traveling on behalf of the State on her first of more than seventy expeditions into Lacandón villages in Mexico and Guatemala's border region. Over the years, her interventions have helped to preserve both indigenous culture and the rain forest where these native peoples live. See Blom's "The Jungle Is Burning" in *México: Through Foreign Eyes*, ed. Carole Naggar and Fred Ritchin (New York: W. W. Norton, 1993) 144–53; 292.

INTRODUCTION.
OF MELODRAMA AND OTHER INSPIRATIONS

1. Charles Freeman's most recent political art extends transcultural dialogue. Jefferson Middle School in South Central L.A. is host to a new mural that honors African American and Mexican American heritages as linked to each other in present time (embodied in the figures of two young people reading key sociohistorical texts from the works of W. E. B. Du Bois to Guillermo Bonfil Batalla), and as joined together by parallel continuities of the past (coded by symbols of the ancient worlds from pyramids to hieroglyphs). I am grateful to Freeman and his assistant muralist Noni Olabisi for an inspiring Sunday morning with them at work at the site. Informal interview, 14 Oct., 2001.

2. The Cananea Mine stood in the border state of Sonora close to Arizona. At issue in 1906: U.S. workers held some of the key positions Mexican workers wanted

to share, and miners from the States earned more than Mexican miners. As Latin American historian James D. Cockcroft recounts, the PLM (a party led by, among others, the radical Flores Magón brothers) backed the strike that was initially subdued by "some 275 armed U.S. volunteers under the command of six Arizona Rangers [who] temporarily occupied Cananea, before being replaced by 2,000 Mexican soldiers who crushed the strike. Nearly one hundred workers were killed." For one of the most compelling reexaminations of Mexico's last century see Cockcroft's *Mexico's Hope: An Encounter with Politics and History* (New York: Monthly Review, 1998) 91.

For a complex dramatization of this particular strike see Mexican filmmaker Marcela Fernández Violante's award-winning film, *Cananea* (1977).

3. Lázaro Cárdenas's progressive presidency (1934–1940) incorporated radical change while sustaining a capitalist economy. He fostered agrarian reform for peasants *and* offered protection for landholders; he promoted "socialist education" *and* interpreted this in much the same way that U.S. conservatives today hail "school to work" programs; he expropriated foreign-controlled oil *and* advanced the nation's reliance on foreign trade. He was beloved by *campesinos,* appreciated by the business elite, and damned by those few whose material or ideological interests he could not serve. With the election of General Manuel Ávila Camacho (1940–1946), the era of astute politics and radical rhetoric gave way to a full embrace of monopoly capitalism and conservative discourses on national unity. Though the ideological Revolution continued, in practice Cárdenas's advances became Ávila Camacho's retreats. See Cockcroft 111–38.

4. Cultural historian and Student Movement participant Carlos Monsiváis chronicles the significance of the events that led to the government atrocities of 1968. From his portrait of Ruiz Cortines, a man whose comprehension of the world "mixes the ideology of *Reader's Digest* with History as . . . anecdote," we see a leader who "never humanized the dissidents," whom he regarded as "incomprehensible." If students are more comprehensible in 1966, if still inhuman, it is because Díaz Ordaz has constructed their image in the demonizing language of the Cold War, as Monsiváis so singularly details. See Carlos Monsiváis, "El 68: Las ceremonias del agravio y la memoria," in Julio Scherer García and Carlos Monsiváis, *Parte de guerra: Tlatelolco 1968. Documentos del general Marcelino García Barragán. Los hechos y la historia* (Mexico City: Nuevo Siglo/Aguilar, 1999) 119–264. (The translation here is mine, as are all others in the chapter unless noted.)

For a testimonial of voices speaking about the tragedy that reveals the powerful response to oppression, see Elena Poniatowska's *La noche de Tlatelolco* (Mexico City: Era, 1971), also available in Helen R. Lane's translation with an introduction by Octavio Paz, *Massacre in Mexico* (New York: Viking, 1975).

5. Monsiváis, "El 68" 138.

6. Though the subordination of indigenous people is fundamental to record, the history of resistance to such violence is indispensable. As Carlos Monsiváis observed on the seventh anniversary of the Zapatista uprising, "Before January 1, 1994, Mexico had never problematized indigenous issues with the enthusiasm, the production of historical texts, the multiple debates, and the accumulation of knowledge and under-

standing that these [post-uprising] years [have occasioned]." With the proliferation of intelligent analyses and with the advent of the Internet where direct addresses from the Zapatistas urge an inclusive national project, the State's legitimation of its oppression of indigenous peoples has been nearly impossible to sustain. For continual updates on the seemingly ceaseless civil war against native peoples in Mexico, including many Zapatista communiqués since 1994, see the web site "¡Ya Basta!" (available http://www.ezln.org.) Monsiváis's and Hermann Bellinghausen's interviews with Sub-comandante Marcos are anthologized on this comprehensive, multilingual site (though the translation here is mine). See "Marcos: 'gran interlocutor,'" *La Jornada* 8 Jan. 2001: n. pag., online, Internet, 18 May 2001.

7. Cedric J. Robinson, "Race, Capitalism, and the Antidemocracy," *Reading Rodney King/Reading Urban Uprising*, ed. Robert Gooding-Williams (New York: Routledge, 1993) 73.

8. Robinson 77. For a visual precursor of Robinson's analysis see Noni Olabisi's powerful mural, "Freedom Won't Wait (1992)," at N. 54th Street and Western in Los Angeles. The mural is also anthologized in Dunitz and Prigoff, 186.

9. Peter Brooks elaborates melodrama's expansive nature in *The Melodramatic Imagination: Balzac, Henry James, Melodrama, and the Mode of Excess* (New Haven: Yale UP, 1976) 15.

10. Brooks 15.

11. That transnational banks count their own character flawless is an irony that seeks to be concealed by these institutions' use of melodrama to highlight detail—the individual—as paradigmatic of the big picture—the corporation. While the banks' pauperization of nations is quietly proceeding, the upstanding nature of their individual clientele redounds to the institutions' "good standing." The mockery of such a pose is nowhere better revealed than in the U.S.-controlled Citigroup's "rescue" of Mexico's once-national Banamex-Accival in August 2001, constituting a major incursion of a foreign firm in the Mexican market (purchase price: 12.5 billion dollars in cash and stock) and one of the largest, *tax-free* financial acquisitions in the history of Latin America. Yet imperialistic buyout isn't the only issue here. U.S./Mexico bank melodramas crawl with villainy on both sides of their laundered coins. For a complete narrative of institutions "caught with their hand in the narco-till," see Cockcroft 336–39. For a popular response to banks' "Character Counts" sloganeering, consult the work of your local taggers. Graffiti also knows melodrama.

12. Although these terms offer comfort zones in which to think about "postcolonial resistance," they can also obscure the workings of multinational colonialism, as Masao Miyoshi cogently points out in "A Borderless World?: From Colonialism to Transnationalism and the Decline of the Nation State," *Global/Local: Cultural Production and the Transnational Imaginary*, ed. Rob Wilson and Wimal Dissanayake (Durham: Duke UP, 1996) 78–106.

Claire F. Fox's compelling *The Fence and the River: Culture and Politics at the U.S.-Mexico Border* (Minneapolis: U of Minnesota P, 1999) describes how "celebratory metaphors of border-crossing and migration [that] are in common use among groups with widely divergent political, national, and class affiliations" can lead to a "globalization of the border" that denies "site-specific" reality. Where the border as "space" deterritorializes the border as "place," she argues, "space is almost always [seen] as universal." Such essentializing projects "neglect that the deleterious effects of economic restructuring [as produced by trade agreements like NAFTA] will be felt in some geographical areas more than others." See Fox 6, 119, 136.

13. Ana M. López traces the history of Mexican cinema's influence in the Americas in "A Cinema for the Continent," *The Mexican Cinema Project*, ed. Chon Noriega and Steven Ricci (Los Angeles: UCLA Film and Television Archive, 1994) 7–12.

14. In her study of *¡Que viva México!* (the film Eisenstein intended to make with Eduard Tissé and Grigori Alexandrov, which was eventually completed by the latter), Laura Podalsky asks us to invert our usual perspective, reflected in numerous critics' claims that Eisenstein indelibly marked Mexican productions, and regard Mexico's influence on the Soviet filmmaker. See "Patterns of the Primitive," *Mediating Two Worlds: Cinematic Encounters in the Americas*, ed. John King, Ana M. López, and Manuel Alvarado (London: BFI, 1993) 25–39.

15. Charles Ramírez Berg discusses the classic example of such mixing. Mexico's first sound film, *Santa* (1932), is the product of the Compañía Nacional Productora de Películas's foraging in Hollywood for cast, crew, and filmmaking equipment. The expedition netted "a Spanish actor turned director (Antonio Moreno), a Canadian director of photography (Alex Phillips), and two Mexican actors who were working in Hollywood, Lupita Tovar and Donald Reed." See *Cinema of Solitude: A Critical Study of Mexican Film, 1967–1983* (Austin: U of Texas P, 1992) 13.

16. Emilio García Riera's eighteen-volume *Historia documental del cine mexicano* (Guadalajara: U de Guadalajara, 1992–1997) must be credited as the most extensive and thorough compilation of contemporary critics' work where these ideas resonate.

17. Ana López points out that Cuban critics Enrique Colina and Daniel Díaz Torres regarded "old" Mexican and Argentine melodramas not only as obstructions to the "'development of people's political consciousness,'" but as arms of Yankee cultural imperialism. See both "A Cinema for the Continent" and "Tears and Desire: Women and Melodrama in the 'Old' Mexican Cinema," in King, et al. 147–63.

18. Charles Ramírez Berg graphically illustrates how Mexican cinema "adapted" classical Hollywood style and didactic purpose. Eschewing Hollywood's linear perspective in favor of a curvilinear one, Golden Age cinema "attack[ed] the unity of the viewing subject" and therefore "challenged Western artistic traditions and the dominant ideology they conveyed." See "Figueroa's Skies and Oblique Perspective: Notes on the Development of the Classical Mexican Style," *Spectator: Journal of Film and Television Criticism* 13.1 (fall 1992): 24–41.

19. Mexican economist Federico Heuer offers the most precise documentation of this partnership in his study of the Banco Cinematográfico (that in 1942 formalized State subsidy and protectionism begun with the production of sound film a decade ear-

lier). By 1970, as Charles Ramírez Berg points out, such governmental support had vanished. See Heuer, *La industria cinematográfica mexicana* (Mexico City: Policromia, 1964), as well as Berg, *Cinema of Solitude* 6.

20. López, "A Cinema" 10.

21. See Alex M. Saragoza (with Graciela Berkovich), "Intimate Connections: Cinematic Allegories of Gender, the State and National Identity," *The Mexican Cinema Project*, 25–32; Ariel Zúñiga, "De la madre en el melodrama mexicano: *Nosotros los pobres* (1948)," *Archivos de la Filmoteca* 16 [Valencia, Spain] (Feb. 1994): 20–29; Julianne Burton-Carvajal, "La ley del más padre: melodrama paternal, melodrama patriarcal, y la especifidad del ejemplo mexicano," *Archivos de la Filmoteca* 16: 50–63.

22. Claire Fox explores some of the distinct perspectives that contemporary "border geographers, historians, artists, writers, and activists" have with regard to nation formation. These "cultural workers" offer innovative contestations of the kind of monolithic nationalism promoted by such exhibitions as "Mexico: Thirty Centuries of Splendor," a 1991 Metropolitan Museum of Art (New York) show sponsored by the Salinas de Gortari government. See Fox 32–37.

23. James D. Cockcroft, citing a parallel analysis of Italian Marxist Antonio Gramsci, sees the struggle for power in post-revolutionary Mexico as an example of "'catastrophic equilibrium.'" In the 1920s various groups vied for "hegemony," a Gramscian term based on a theory that Cockcroft usefully synthesizes: "Such a hegemonic project normally takes form in times of crisis, often during a transition from one stage of economic development to another; also, during a period of political transition (itself related to economic change). In the course of a given crisis, a particular class or class fraction (often the ascendant one) attempts to carry through the transition and the class goals it seeks through ideological combat, alliance-building, and other forms of political struggle. The aim of the project is to gain dominance over the state and its ideological apparatuses, to transform the state in corresponding ways, to subordinate or defeat rival projects and the class interests behind them—in sum, to alter the balance of power in society as a whole." Though members of the "victorious . . . [but initially] . . . weak" bourgeoisie were indeed rising to power, as evidenced by the Vasconcelos story that I recount in the text below, Cockcroft points out that their "hegemonic project was not necessarily clear or well-articulated, since it was confused by different contestants' formations of new alliances of class and social forces—new 'power blocs.'" See Cockcroft 111, 125, and 395.

24. Benedict Anderson, *Imagined Communities: Reflections on the Origin and Spread of Nationalism* (New York: Verso, 1983) 18.

25. Anderson 19.

26. Virtually all historians consider the election of the little-known Pascual Ortiz Rubio fraudulent. The final "incredible" vote count, as Cockcroft records: 1,948,848 to 110,979. Engineering the contest, President Plutarco Elías Calles established the political party (the National Revolutionary Party, or PNR) that (as the PRI) would govern Mexico for more than seventy years. See Cockcroft 118–19.

27. Such "rehabilitación del pensamiento de la raza," as José Joaquín Blanco notes, citing Vasconcelos, was the express mission of the Ateneo. The group's Popular University "survived until 1920, when Vasconcelos incorporated the school into the National University, which he served as its Rector." See *Se llamaba Vasconcelos: Una evocación crítica* (Mexico City: FCE, 1977) 42; 56–57.

28. Octavio Paz details this period in "Pintura mural." See *México en la obra de Octavio Paz*, t. III. *Los privilegios de la vista: Arte de México* (Mexico City: FCE, 1987) 221–319.

29. Books, as national treasures, and Vasconcelos, as treasured national librarian, are still lauded in the new century's disquisitions on the importance of Mexican print culture. As keynote speaker introducing Vicente Fox's *Programa Nacional de Cultura 2001–2006*, novelist Carlos Fuentes recently advocated that *"la lección vasconcelista"* be adopted by the current government. Fuentes urged the expansion of State-sponsored "literacy [programs], the edition and distribution of [affordable] books, as well as the promotion of artists." Even "the possibility of such a new cultural policy," Fuentes said with eternal optimism, would venerate that "José Vasconcelos who told the majority of Mexicans: 'One day you shall be part of the center, not the margins [of this nation].'" See Arturo Jiménez, "Una biblioteca nombra al mundo," *La Jornada* 23 Aug. 2001: n. pag., online, Internet, 26 Aug. 2001.

30. Vasconcelos made this declaration at the inauguration of the new Education Building in July 1922. See Paz 249.

31. Gabriela Mistral, *Lecturas para mujeres* (1922; Mexico City: Porrúa, 1976) xv.

32. Vasconcelos, *Ulises Criollo* (1936; Mexico City: Botas; Mexico City: FCE, 1983).

33. Martha Robles, *Entre el poder y las letras: Vasconcelos en sus memorias* (Mexico City: FCE, 1989) 67.

34. Qtd. in Sylvia Molloy, "The Unquiet Self: Spanish American Autobiography and the Question of National Identity," *Comparative American Identities: Race, Sex, and Nationality in the Modern Text*, ed. Hortense J. Spillers (New York: Routledge, 1991) 27.

35. Blanco 18.

36. Vasconcelos 32.

37. Molloy 34.

38. Vasconcelos 123–28.

39. Molloy 36.

40. Licia Fiol-Matta, "The 'Schoolteacher of America': Gender, Sexuality, and Nation in Gabriela Mistral," *¿Entiendes? Queer Readings, Hispanic Writings*, ed. Emilie L. Bergmann and Paul Julian Smith (Durham: Duke, 1995) 201–39.

Jean Franco, *Plotting Women: Gender and Representation in Mexico* (New York: Columbia UP, 1989) 102–28.

41. Franco 112.

42. Franco 128.

43. Franco 127.

44. Qtd. in Franco 126.

45. Franco 116.

46. Blanco 57.

47. Blanco 63.

48. Anderson 21.

49. Qtd. in Anderson 21.

50. See José Vasconcelos, *La raza cósmica: Misión de la raza iberoamericana. Notas de viaje a la América del Sur* (Barcelona: Agencia Mundial de Librería, c. 1925) and *La raza cósmica; The Cosmic Race,* trans. Didier T. Jaén (Los Angeles: California State UP, 1979).

51. Blanco 98.

52. Anderson declares that "sacred silent languages were the media through which the great global communities of the past were imagined." The term is still viable in a modern Mexican context. See Anderson 21.

53. Blanco 100.

54. See Antonio Rodríguez's presentation of the *Guía de los murales de Diego Rivera en la Secretaría de Educación Pública* (Mexico City: SEP, 1984) 118. Emphasis mine.

55. Paz discusses Vasconcelos and Rivera's relationship in detail (*México en la obra,* t. III, 256), but it is Rivera's North American biographer who describes the events preceding the caricature. Bertram D. Wolfe's *The Fabulous Life of Diego Rivera* (New York: Stein and Day, 1963) documents that "when Diego finished the revolutionary ballads on the top floor of the Education Building, José Vasconcelos . . . denounced the work. He had never liked Diego's painting, but had hitherto claimed credit for it. As [Diego's work] was becoming more 'revolutionary,' Vasconcelos was becoming more conservative. To the [almost] completed work Vasconcelos dedicated the following oft-repeated phrases: '. . . In Mexico . . . [artists] have fallen into the abjection of covering the walls with portraits of criminals. . . .'" Wolfe finishes dryly, "Diego responded by painting Vasconcelos's portrait . . . among the disseminators of false knowledge." See Wolfe 211.

56. Blanco discusses how *vasconcelismo,* particularly its *"mística educativa y cultural,"* would find a place in Manuel Ávila Camacho's government: "With Ávila

Camacho and [Secretary of Education] Jaime Torres Bodet the Secretariat dismantled [former President Lázaro] Cárdenas's programs and Education became . . . an insipid and timid version of Vasconcelos-style nationalism." See Blanco 81 and 127.

57. Like Vasconcelos, Fernández also lived with his family for a while in Piedras Negras. In contrast with the Creole, *El Indio* had no Indian horror stories to plague him given his mother's indigenous roots, the Kickapoos' friendly relations with the Mexican government (from whom they successfully gained land as exiles from the United States), and their alliance with the military. "Integrating into Mexico's historical process as mercenaries," writes Adela Fernández in her biography of her father, "the Kickapoos . . . were a combative force designed to end the terror imposed by bellicose Indians [Comanches and Mescaleros] from North America." See Adela Fernández's *El Indio Fernández: Vida y mito* (Mexico City: Panorama, 1986) 34, as well as Julia Tuñón's 1988 interview with Fernández, *En su propio espejo* (Mexico City: U Autónoma Metropolitana-Iztapalapa) 19.

58. At the very least, Fernández's memory of Adolfo de la Huerta's advice, as Carlos Monsiváis explained to me in a December 1991 interview, is "undoubtedly embellished."

59. Emilio García Riera cites Margarita de Orellana's unpublished interview with Fernández here. García Riera calculates that the future filmmaker must have crossed the Río Bravo *"a nado"* in 1924. See *Emilio Fernández: 1904–1986* (Guadalajara: U de Guadalajara, and Mexico City: Cineteca Nacional, 1987) 13.

60. José Natividad Rosales's 1970 interview appears in the magazine *¡Siempre!* (2 Dec.) and José Luis Gallegos's 1985 interview is part of the daily *Excélsior*'s Sunday Supplement (1 Sept.), as García Riera's meticulous study reveals. See *Emilio Fernández* 15.

61. José Luis Gallegos's interview is cited in García Riera, *Emilio Fernández* 15.

62. Adela Fernández 56.

63. García Riera, *Emilio Fernández* 15.

64. Anderson 21.

65. Postmodern scholar/filmmaker Ariel Zúñiga made these comments in 1992 at the working conference on Mexican melodrama organized by Julianne Burton-Carvajal at the U of California-Santa Cruz. By week's end his resistance to alternative filmmakers seemed to diminish, thanks to the cogent discussions regarding the politics and aesthetics of oppositional cinema.

66. Qtd. in Berg, "Figueroa's Skies" 25. This idea is slightly more emphatic in an expanded version of the piece, where the film scholar uses critics cited in Emilio García Riera's work to support his embrace of *El Indio*. See "The Cinematic Invention of Mexico: The Poetics and Politics of the Fernández-Figueroa Style," *The Mexican Cinema Project* 13–24.

67. García Riera cites scriptwriter Mauricio Magdaleno's unhappiness with the project. Backed by Diego Rivera, Magdaleno was adamant that *María Candelaria*'s theme—that of an indigenous woman ostracized by her people because her mother was a prostitute—"seemed artificial . . . that Indian women would not hold such theories." Tellingly, though, Magdaleno would have given up authenticity for allegory, if only the film were representative of some "area very far from Mexico City, nameless; something like Chiapas, Chihuahua." It took the Soviet Ambassador Ousmansky's panegyric for locals to understand that, for the world, Mexico City's nearby indigenous population *did constitute* a sort of nameless, symbolic lot. With the exception of the opinions of a few, the film finally won recognition in the eyes of the urban Mexican elite. See *Emilio Fernández* 45–62.

68. In addition to the work on Landeta that I cite in the body of my text, Luis Trelles Plazaola records a thoughtful conversation with the filmmaker in *Cine y mujer en América Latina: Directoras de largometrajes de ficción* (Río Piedras, Puerto Rico: U de Puerto Rico, 1991).

Carmen Huaco-Nuzum unites psychology and "race" in her provocative analysis of *La Negra Angustias*. See *Mestiza Subjectivity: Representation and Spectatorship in Mexican and Hollywood Films*, diss., U of California-Santa Cruz, 1993, 79–110.

Eduardo de la Vega Alfaro and Patricia Torres San Martín completed a comprehensive study on Adela Sequeyro as journalist, silent screen actress, and pioneering female filmmaker of the 1920s and 1930s. Their work is centered at the CIEC (Centro de Investigación y Enseñanza Cinematográfica) in Guadalajara, where Sequeyro's '30s films are being restored. See *Adela Sequeyro* (Guadalajara: U de Guadalajara, 1997).

69. Landeta explained that the Cineteca featured the cinema of women filmmakers from Italy, France, Germany, Sweden, and the United States, "but at first they couldn't find a filmmaker from Mexico where the conference was hosted!" Personal interview, 17 July 1992.

70. Patricia Reyes Spíndola has featured in numerous films, including one by the second Mexican woman to be professionally trained as a director, Marcela Fernández Violante's *Nocturno amor que te vas* (1986). Among other roles, Ofelia Medina is internationally known for her portrayal of Frida Kahlo in *Frida: naturaleza viva*, Paul Leduc (1983).

71. In fact *Nocturno a Rosario* never saw its commercial debut. The theater where it was to premiere was sold to U.S. interests that immediately began programming Hollywood films. Commenting on this in 1995, Landeta expressed hopes that the nation "would soon have more screens to exhibit Mexican cinema" so that *Nocturno*, as well as other nationally made films, could be shown. Three years later the national cinema scene had not improved. A few months before her death in January 1999, the filmmaker spoke out against the Free Trade Agreement: "Europe won [sovereignty] over their own culture with the GATT [General Agreement on Tariffs and Trade]; we lost our culture with the TLC [NAFTA]. . . . Now we have to beg to have the treaty require [foreign-controlled theaters] to give us 30 percent screen time." In the

event, Mexican-made films now account for less than 5 percent of the total movies projected in the nation. See both Bety Garfias Ramírez, "Matilde Landeta, toda una vida entregada al cine," *El Universal* 22 Oct. 1995: n. pag. and "Con el TLC, México perdió su cultura," *La Jornada* 22 Sept. 1998: n. pag.

72. Julianne Burton-Carvajal's "Daughter of the Revolution: Matilde Soto Landeta," Part I of *Three Lives in Film: The Improbable Careers of Latin America's Foremost Women Filmmakers* (forthcoming in English and available in Spanish as *Matilde Landeta: Hija de la Revolución* [Mexico City: IMCINE and CONACULTA, 2002]).

73. Landeta's extended-familial ties are rich. Not only did she and Peralta sustain a long friendship, not only did she assist Peralta in the completion of the documentary *Islas Revillagigedo* initiated by Peralta's longtime companion, the writer Luis Spota, but she worked with Spota to write *Trotacalles*, as I discuss in Chapter Three. I'm indebted to Elda Peralta for her memories of Landeta that she shared with me during our lively and informal discussions in Mexico City in May and June 2000. With regard to the prolific Spota, see Elda Peralta, *La época de oro sin nostalgia: Luis Spota en el cine* (Mexico City: Grijalbo, 1988) and *Luis Spota: Las sustancias de la tierra. Una biografía íntima* (1989; Mexico City: Grijalbo, 1990). For a compelling fictional view of a film actress and her politico paramour through Peralta's eyes see *Nocturno mar sin espuma* (Mexico City: Morgana, 1997).

74. Burton-Carvajal, "Daughter of the Revolution" 21.

75. Burton-Carvajal, "Daughter" 43.

76. Here the filmmaker's self-comparison referred to the women soldiers of the Revolution. Matilde Landeta, personal interview, 22 July 1992.

77. My comparison of Education Minister Vasconcelos's and Filmmaker Fernández's ideologies is certainly not new, and certainly not as audacious as the characterization of the two offered by Diego Rivera. In an interview challenging José Vasconcelos's denigration of filmmakers (they were apparently as "uncultured" as the citizens-in-the-making whom they narrativized), Rivera describes both Fernández and Vasconcelos as those who "intellectualized Indians," working against realistic portraits of their lives. If in Rivera's lights the usually intelligent Fernández made occasional poor judgments (*María Candelaria* was a "*porquería de* film," but the director's *Flor silvestre* [1943] was a triumph), Vasconcelos was more singularly described: "My friend Pepe is very affected. We're talking about an authentic bourgeois cretin who doesn't even go to the movies. . . ." Qtd. in García Riera, *Emilio Fernández* 53–54.

78. Drafted as infantry in the crusade for nationalism, Mexican women could not vote for their leaders until they won the hard-fought right to do so. As *Río Escondido*'s protagonist mediates citizenship in a desert municipality in the 1947 film, so too do women begin to exercise their suffrage in municipal elections in that same year. Despite concerted efforts from the forging of the 1917 Constitution on, women were unable to vote for the President of the Republic until 1953. See Shirlene Ann Soto, *Emergence of the Modern Mexican Woman: Her Participation in Revolution and Struggle for Equality, 1910–1940* (Denver: Arden, 1990).

79. Impassioned scholarship did, of course, exist prior to this time. More than a decade ago, for example, Guillermo Bonfil Batalla's *México profundo: Una civilización negada* (1987; Mexico City: Grijalbo, 1990) called for a "new national project" that would address a "negated civilization's" struggle for sovereignty. Bonfil Batalla militates against an "imaginary [but hegemonic] . . . minority Mexico" whose nation-building is constituted at the expense of another nation-within-a-nation: that of "Deep Mexico," indigenous Mexico, the forgotten "majority nation."

80. See Subcomandante Marcos and EZLN (Ejército Zapatista de Liberación Nacional) communiqués, 29 Apr. 2001: n. pag., online, Internet, 17 July 2001. Available http://www.ezlnaldf.org.

81. In this Landeta's representations both illustrate and exceed Benedict Anderson's paradigm connecting "imagined political communities" with "religious imaginings." As I examine in Chapter Two, her portrayals of indigenous sovereignty both depend on and depart from an evocation of Mexico's Edenic past. For further insight on the relationship between national and religious iconography, see Anderson 18.

82. Brooks argues that the genre's characteristic *"tout dire,"* as expressed by Rousseau, "is a measure of the personalization and inwardness of post-sacred ethics." Landeta's conviction follows suit. See Brooks 16.

83. The discourse of National Unity is discussed by virtually every observer of the first half of twentieth-century Mexico, but its delineation is particularly interesting in the context of Chicano (Neo-)/(Post-)/(Anti-) Nationalism of recent years. See, for example, Juan Gómez-Quiñones, *Mexican National Formation: Political Discourse, Policy and Dissidence* (Encino: Floricanto, 1992) 308.

84. Joanne Hershfield marks one vital deviation from the norm in "The Construction of Woman in *Distinto amanecer,*" *Spectator* 13.1 (1992): 42–51.

85. In addition to the extensive Mexican Cinema Project at UCLA and the Paris exhibition of Golden Age Mexican film at the Centre Pompidou, interest in the decade's aesthetics also prompted an outpouring of "Frida Kahlomania" such as that displayed at the modest-sized Mexican Museum in San Francisco (summer 1992), where opening night festivities alone attracted more than 1,500 people. Again, catalogues and essays were prepared for these events, serving both as artifacts of the fêtes and as scholarship on 1940s art and culture. See *Pasión por Frida*, ed. Blanca Garduño and José Antonio Rodríguez (Mexico City: Bellas Artes, 1992).

86. See E. Ann Kaplan's "'Healing Imperialized Eyes'": Independent Women Filmmakers and the Look," in her *Looking for the Other: Feminism, Film, and the Imperial Gaze* (New York: Routledge, 1997) 218–55.

87. The word is Kaplan's. Her "distanced" response to the film seems to stem from her understanding of its "emotional flatness," a point to which I return in the text below.

88. See especially Kaplan's thoughtful preface to *Looking for the Other.*

89. Kaplan xx.

90. Moving from Jane Gaines's seminal 1988 article, "White Privilege and Looking Relations," Kaplan regards "looking" as "relation" in ways coincident with Judith Mayne (*The Woman at the Keyhole*, 1990, and other writings, 1993) and Toni Morrison (*Playing in the Dark*, 1992) to conclude with ideas in concert with those of Jessica Benjamin (*The Bonds of Love*, 1988). See Kaplan xvi.

91. Kaplan 16.

92. Kaplan 240.

93. Kaplan 241.

94. Kaplan 300. Emphasis hers.

95. Kaplan 242.

96. This charge is somewhat mitigated by Kaplan's observations about "tender" moments in the film regarding other women's "capacities for emotional sharing." See 242 and 244.

97. Although only appearing in a cameo role, Ric Salinas's presence in *Mi vida loca* is significant for viewers who are also fans of the popular actor. These spectators not only see "hope" in the lieutenant, but life-saving humor in the Salvadoran-born, San Francisco Mission District-reared man who plays that character. While Salinas's role in *Mi vida loca* is a serious one, the appeal of this member of the Chicano/Latino comedy troupe Culture Clash adds to the depth of audience response to his cameo. Readers unfamiliar with Salinas's art can find him with Clash members Richard Montoya and Herbert Sigüenza in two of their numerous satires, elaborated in concert with—and filmed by—Lourdes Portillo: *A Bowl of Beings* (premiering on stage at the Los Angeles Theater Center, June 1991; shot in 1992) and *Columbus on Trial* (directed by Portillo in 1993 and written in collaboration with the cast and creative team). For script material from these *actos* and two others, plus an interview by Philip Kan Gotanda, see the troupe's *Culture Clash: Life, Death, and Revolutionary Comedy* (New York: Theatre Communications Group, 1998).

98. Elissa J. Rashkin's *Women Filmmakers in Mexico: The Country of Which We Dream* (Austin: U of Texas P, 2001) provides the first comprehensive study of the current generation of directors while offering analysis of earlier filmmakers' antecedents to their work.

99. For a useful comparison see Patricia Rodríguez Savaria's *De piel de víbora* (Mexico City: Sansores y Aljure, 1998).

100. See Martha M. de Ketchum's interview in *Mexicanos creativos*, Volumen II (Mexico City: EDAMEX, 1996) 113.

101. Underscoring the affinities between the two filmmakers, in July 1999 New York's Guggenheim Museum screened Fernández Violante's *De cuerpo presente* as prelude to a Luis Buñuel retrospective in the cinematic exhibition "Muestra Mexperimental."

CHAPTER ONE.
RE-BIRTH OF A NATION:
ON MEXICAN MOVIES, MUSEUMS, AND MARÍA FÉLIX

1. Nevertheless, a notable few '40s films have examined relations between dominant and subordinate groups. In addition to Matilde Landeta, directors Julio Bracho and Alejandro Galindo made particular effort to imagine and project images that questioned the status quo.

2. Venezuelan novelist Rómulo Gallegos's 1929 *Doña Bárbara* became Mexican patrimony with Fernando de Fuentes's 1943 film adaptation.

3. Claudia Schaefer outlines this idea in the introduction to her "'Monobodies,' Antibodies, and the Body Politic: Sara Levi Calderón's *Dos mujeres*," Feministas Unidas Panel, MLA Convention, San Francisco, 29 Dec. 1991. Schaefer's *Textured Lives: Women, Art, and Representation in Modern Mexico* (Tucson: U of Arizona P, 1992) also acknowledges the exhibition as motivating the United States's current fascination with Mexico.

Rubén Martínez pursues the point of "Free Trade Art: The Frida Kahlo-ization of Los Angeles," in the lead story of *The L.A Weekly* 17 Nov. 1991: 16–26.

The "official" view of "Mexico: Splendors of Thirty Centuries" is promoted by Octavio Paz and others in the catalogue of the same name (New York: The Metropolitan Museum of Art, 1990).

4. Only after touring outside Mexico were national "Splendors" available for national consumption. Not until August 1992 did construction workers begin to feverishly prepare the National Preparatory School as the Mexican site of the "Splendors" show. The exhibition's opening was initially scheduled to coincide with the pinnacle of the quincentennial celebration on El Día de la Raza (Columbus Day), October 12. In the event this desire proved over-optimistic.

5. As I argue below, this rhetoric particularly informs Antoine Tzapoff's exhibition of Mexico's "disappearing" Indians. See the catalogue of the collection "Cuando la danza se vuelve rito," ed. Álvaro J. Covacevich, *Cuando la danza se vuelve rito: Los indios de México* (Mexico City, Madero, c. 1990).

6. See Paco Ignacio Taibo I's work on María Félix in his sequentially complete, if somewhat cursory, *María Félix: 47 pasos por el cine* (Mexico City: Joaquín Mortiz, 1985).

7. Spectators who memorize *la Doña's* speeches often contextualize them by quoting these lines from *Doña Bárbara's* initial sequences.

8. Beatriz Reyes Nevares, interview of Emilio Fernández, cited in *Trece directores del cine mexicano* (Mexico: Secretaría de Educación Pública, 1974) 22–23. English translation here by Carl J. Mora and Elizabeth Gard, *The Mexican Cinema: Interviews with Thirteen Directors* (Albuquerque: U of New Mexico P, 1976) 14. Again, following Monsiváis, the story of Adolfo de la Huerta's participation may well be an enabling fiction.

9. James D. Cockcroft usefully defines this concept: "In Spanish and Latin American thought at that time, socialistic education meant 'rational and secular,' as distinguished from 'religious and clerical.'" See Cockcroft, *Mexico's Hope: An Encounter with Politics and History* (New York: Monthly Review, 1998) 121.

10. For a contrasting view of celluloid consumer capitalism in Hollywood see Mary Ann Doane, *The Desire to Desire: The Woman's Film of the 1940s* (Bloomington: U of Indiana P, 1987) 22–33.

11. These initial sequences have been excised for export. Early video versions of *Río Escondido* made for sale in the States eviscerate Fernández's most didactic affirmations as found in the original film's opening and closing scenes. Worse still, newer videotapes issued in Mexico evidence the same bankruptcy. Is "México, S.A.," as pundits are calling the "Incorporated" State, not only consuming imported rice and beans but imported national culture as well?

12. Jean Franco, *Plotting Women: Gender and Representation in Mexico* (New York: Columbia UP, 1989) 148. The entirety of Chapter Seven, "Oedipus Modernized," dealing with Emilio Fernández's *Enamorada,* makes for particularly useful comparison here.

13. Carl J. Mora's mistaken identification causes him to "prove" an overlap of the State's ideology with Fernández's discourse. The overlap certainly exists, as Mora's fundamental history suggests, but it is even more complex: in the midst of controversy about the film, Alemán gave his seal of approval. See Mora, *Mexican Cinema: Reflections of a Society, 1886–1988* (Berkeley: U of California P, 1989) 78, and Ignacio Taibo I 115.

14. Fernández's insistences are recorded by many biographers. Three effective texts include Julia Tuñón's interview, cited in the notes to the Introduction, *En su propio espejo* (Mexico City: U Autónoma Metropolitana-Iztapalapa, 1988) 27; Paco Ignacio Taibo I's *El Indio Fernández: El cine por mis pistolas* (Mexico City: Joaquín Mortiz, 1986); Emilio García Riera's *Emilio Fernández: 1904–1986* (Guadalajara: U de Guadalajara, 1987). (The translation is mine, as are all others in the chapter unless noted.)

15. These comments represent the few negative responses the film received. See García Riera, *Emilio Fernández* 125.

16. Qtd. in Tuñón 78.

17. Benedict Anderson, *Imagined Communities: Reflections on the Origin and Spread of Nationalism* (New York: Verso, 1983) 21.

18. Rodolfo Stavenhagen, *Derecho indígena y derechos humanos en América Latina* (Mexico City: Colegio de México, 1988) 303.

19. Stavenhagen 313. As mentioned in the Introduction, little has changed with respect to the government's stance regarding indigenous incorporation into the national body politic. With the promulgation and protests of the "Ley Indígena" in

August 2001 (originally designed as a Constitutional reform to extend human and property rights to native peoples, but, with its redrafting and subsequent Senate approval in April 2001, rendered ineffective and even harmful public policy), liaisons between native peoples and the State are breaking up. In a stunning action echoing protests from civil society to clerics, Mixtec lawyer Francisco López Bárcenas resigned in August 2001 as juridical head of the government-sponsored *Instituto Nacional Indigenista* (INI), stating emphatically that Fox's promised public policy is no different than that of previous governments. "Civil society," he wrote in his twelve-point objection, "no longer believes in the government, and the government does not take civil society into account." See "Por qué renuncio al INI," *La Jornada* 22 Aug. 2001: n. pag., online, Internet, 22 Aug. 2001.

20. Néstor García Canclini, *Culturas híbridas: Estrategias para entrar y salir de la modernidad* (Mexico City: Grijalbo, 1990) 158. Translation here is mine, though the work is available in English. See *Hybrid Cultures: Strategies for Entering and Leaving Modernity*, trans. Christopher L. Chiappari and Silvia L. López (Minneapolis: U of Minnesota P, 1995).

21. For a "strong, self-wrought description" of Tijuana, see García Canclini's study of what he calls the second most postmodern city in the world (after New York), 297–305. In the course of that investigation he finds an interesting "vehemence with which everyone rejected 'the missionary intent' of cultural activities advanced by the federal government. In the face of national programs designed to 'affirm Mexican identity' in the northern border area, Baja Californians asserted that they are as Mexican as anyone else, just different." García Canclini 304.

22. See Fernando Gamboa, "Antoine Tzapoff," *Cuando la danza se vuelve rito*, 15.

23. Carlos Monsiváis, *Escenas de pudor y liviandad* (Mexico City: Grijalbo, 1988) 162.

24. Elizondo (qtd. in Tzapoff Catalogue) 21. For a lucid critique of this position, see Trinh T. Minh-ha, "The Language of Nativism: Anthropology as a Scientific Conversation of Man with Man" in her *Woman, Native, Other: Writing Postcoloniality and Feminism* (Bloomington: Indiana UP, 1989) 47–79.

25. *La Jornada* 1 Sept. 1990.

26. This 1965 Monsiváis article (cited in García Riera, *Emilio Fernández* 125) interests particularly because of its clarity and decisiveness. Twenty-six years after its publication, however, Monsiváis "repented having written it," as he stated to me in an interview in Mexico City, Dec. 1991.

27. Paz asserts, *la Chingada* "*is* Nothingness. And yet she is the cruel incarnation of the feminine condition." Tracing the history of Mexican women's essential lack, Paz writes, "If the *Chingada* is representative of the violated Mother, it is appropriate to associate her with the Conquest, which was also a violation, not only in the historical sense but also in the very flesh of the Indian woman. The symbol of this violation is doña Malinche, the mistress of Cortés. It is true that she gave herself voluntarily to the

conquistador, but he forgot her as soon as her usefulness was over. Doña Marina [Malinche's Spanish name] becomes a figure representing the Indian women who were fascinated, violated or seduced by the Spaniards. And as a small boy will not forgive his mother if she abandons him to search for his father, the Mexican people have not forgiven La Malinche for her betrayal." See *El laberinto de la soledad* (Mexico City: FCE, 1950) or Lysander Kemp's translation: *The Labyrinth of Solitude* (New York: Grove, 1961) 86.

28. Norma Alarcón, among other feminists, reclaims Marina/Malinche/Malintzin in "Chicana's Feminist Literature: A Re-Vision through Malintzin; or, Malintzin: Putting the Flesh Back on the Object" in *This Bridge Called My Back: Writings by Radical Women of Color*, ed. Cherríe Moraga and Gloria Anzaldúa (Watertown: Persephone, 1981) 182–90. She also addresses the role of the mediating Malintzin in "Traddutora, Traditora: A Paradigmatic Figure of Chicana Feminism" in *The Constitution of Gender and Modes of Social Division*, ed. Donna Przybylowicz, Nancy Hartsock, and Pamela McCallum. Special issue of *Cultural Critique* 13 (fall 1989) 57–87.

29. Jean Franco poses this question of women's control of their own narrative in *Plotting Women*.

30. I have purloined significant parts of Carlos Monsiváis's fascinating accounts of María Félix's cultural activities: "Crónica de sociales: María Félix en dos tiempos." The two juxtaposed essays, written respectively in 1977 and 1984, also provide the italicized passages that I appropriate below. (To differentiate between written and oral discourse, I have transcribed subsequent passages from the Tijuana conference and placed them in quotation marks and italics.) The first chronicle, "La Doña está molesta," focuses on the occasion of a street-naming ceremony in Ciudad Netzahuacóyotl that honored María Félix. The second article captures the actress—and her admirers—in completely different settings in the elegant neighborhoods of Mexico City. Félix is recorded in her capacity as Patron of the Arts as she introduces the French-Russian painter Antoine Tzapoff to Mexican society. Monsiváis, *Escenas* 161–68.

31. Edmund White, "Diva Mexicana," *Vanity Fair* Nov. 1990: 210.

32. White 212. Either Félix does not remember the scene or she chooses to rewrite it. Her character did not approach the president for a favor; he specifically called upon her to perform a service to the nation.

33. Elena Poniatowska, *Todo México* (Mexico City: Diana, 1990). The interview with María Félix, which took place in 1973, is partially a parody of Carlos Fuentes's *Zona sagrada* (Mexico City: Siglo Veintiuno, 1967). *Todo México's* relationship with Fuentes's *Myself with Others* can also be read as parody.

34. Poniatowska 161. The critic's disbelief is underscored by her freshly employed cliché about the indigenous dances that take place in Chalma, Morelos. ("Ay, ¿a poco?" she says, "¡Eso que dice usted no se lo creo ni yendo a bailar a Chalma!") One goes to dance in Chalma to petition Nuestro Señor de Chalma (the Spanish replacement of Osototocteotl) for rain and other favors, which occasionally those "great leaders" see

fit to deliver. Her retort is a mock reference to miracles. The event is memorialized by Fernando Leal in one of the murals encouraged by José Vasconcelos in the Escuela Preparatoria, Mexico City.

CHAPTER TWO.
LAS DE ABAJO: MATILDE LANDETA'S MEXICAN REVOLUTION

1. Mexican anthropologist Roger Bartra has developed a compelling analysis of the history of the Mexican "national character" as seen by a century of essayists. Endemic to their mythification and the concomitant political legitimation of the State lie myriad tales of Mexico's subverted Edenic past. See *The Cage of Melancholy: Identity and Metamorphosis in the Mexican Character*, trans. Christopher J. Hall (1987; New Brunswick: Rutgers UP, 1992) 17.

2. Bartra 17.

3. Matilde Landeta's screenplay of *Lola Casanova* follows Francisco Rojas González's novel with a good deal of precision, although she occasionally embellishes and independently exercises her own interpretation of his anthropological findings, as we shall see below. See Rojas González's *Lola Casanova* (1947; Mexico City: FCE, 1992). (Translations in this chapter are mine unless noted.)

4. Combining these two archetypes of Mexican womanhood that are most often dichotomized in the virgin/whore paradigm, the figure of Lola parallels Malintzin's positive aspects as she acts as a cultural translator for native peoples much as the sixteenth-century native woman served as translator for the *conquistador* Cortés. But where myth maligned Malintzin as the "Malinche," *"la Chingada,"* and the betrayer of her people and her Spanish consort, with Rojas González and Landeta, reworked myth attempts to rehabilitate Malintzin in the person of a redemptive Creole. This is dicey business at best; La Malinche is most usefully "refleshed" in her own skin (see Alarcón, Chapter One, n. 28). As film scholar Elissa Rashkin clearly sees, Rojas's and Landeta's "substitut[ing]" a white *conquistadora* with benign intentions for the alternately vilified and victimized Malinche" does constitute a "fundamentally patronizing and racist" stance. See Rashkin, *Women Filmmakers in Mexico: The Country of Which We Dream* (Austin: U of Texas P, 2001) 46–52.

Yet however eurocentric, the "Raza Cósmica" imagined in *Lola Casanova* is achieved through an unusual proposition. To the degree that *mestizaje*, or "racial" mixing, is desired (and Landeta, as we'll see, also appreciates Seri sovereignty), transculturation should be exercised democratically. Part of this plan is linguistic and indicates a point of view not usually represented in mainstream movies: Creoles have to recognize themselves as "Yori" for the narrative to function.

5. Rojas González, *Lola Casanova* 8.

6. Joseph Sommers's *Francisco Rojas González: Exponente literario del nacionalismo mexicano* provides us with further details. Dr. Fortunato Hernández's historical

work, *Las razas indígenas de Sonora y la guerra del Yaqui* (Mexico City: J. de Eliazalde, 1902), not only fueled "the legend of Lola Casanova" for Rojas González's novel, but inspired Armando Chávez Camacho's 1948 *Cajeme*. See Sommers, trans. Carlo Antonio Castro (Xalapa: U Veracruzana, 1966) 96.

7. Manuel Gamio, *Forjando patria* (Mexico City: Porrúa, 1916) 6.

8. See Brooks's *The Melodramatic Imagination: Balzac, Henry James, Melodrama, and the Mode of Excess* (New Haven: Yale UP, 1976) 12–20.

9. Brooks 9.

10. Brooks 15.

11. Bartra shows how these ideologues created the "myth of the modern man" (perhaps the greatest melodrama of all). They found it "necessary to reconstruct the primordial original, to generate a tragic sense of the opposition between the barbarian and the civilized man, and to create for modern man a mythical past, so that this very modernity can, apparently, shed such myths and confront rationally the construction of the future." See Bartra 53.

12. "Barefoot ["cracked-hoofed"] Indians" and "Frenchified Spaniards" are derogatory terms that, through their persistence and commonality in the language, attempt to naturalize racism.

13. My authorship of these observations and of many other conclusions I have drawn in this chapter must be clarified. If my analyses and rhetoric, including select vocabulary and idiosyncratic phrases, sound virtually identical to numerous statements made by Patricia Torres San Martín in "Adela Sequeyro and Matilde Landeta: Two Pioneer Women Directors" (anthologized in Joanne Hershfield and David Maciel's *Mexico's Cinema: A Century of Film and Filmmakers* [Wilmington: Scholarly Resources, 1999]), it is, as she told me at a conference where I first asked about similar borrowings in her presentation, because she had access to a draft of what now constitutes my Chapter Two. I had given this draft to Matilde Landeta (who confirmed that she'd passed along my essay) and had provided copies for others who helped me circulate my work so I could establish a dialogue with scholars in our field. A colleague and I had translated this early version of my chapter from English to Spanish in 1992, and it subsequently became part of a special issue on Mexican Melodrama in the Spanish film journal *Archivos de la Filmoteca* 16, [Valencia, Spain] (Feb. 1994): 36–49. In addition to a number of unreferenced citations, the Torres San Martín piece also contains another of my long-pondered topic sentences lifted from a second source: an unpublished, but copyrighted, essay that I had shared with Landeta and others in Mexico and at conferences in the United States. My previous essay now forms the base of my Chapter Three. All material that I authored and that was used without attribution made its first appearance in my previously copyrighted dissertation and its early drafts, dated and held by colleagues in the United States and Mexico (*Celluloid Nationalism and Other Melodramas: From Post-Revolutionary Mexico to Post-Rebellion Los Angeles*, diss., Stanford U, 1997. Ann Arbor: UMI, 1998). That my work was copyrighted and published first is small comfort. And while I'd like to believe that the use of my argu-

ments and phrases represents nothing more than imprecise scholarship, their whole-sale deployment as the thesis of "Two Pioneer Women Directors" and their (mis)use in the essay's concluding pages precludes even that optimism. This is a violation that strikes at the heart of the intellectual enterprise. I only hope that the double oblitera-tion of agency that this act has occasioned—the erasure of my subjectivity and that of the other writer—might metamorphose into useful consideration of the nature of authorship and intellectual property. Moreover, I'd like to think that the very discus-sions our writing seeks to promote are not foreclosed before they've begun.

14. Octavio Paz's highly influential *El laberinto de la soledad* (Mexico City: FCE, 1950) has a perspicacious reader in Roger Bartra, who systematically reveals the work-ings of Paz's paralyzing paradigms. See especially the discussion of *la Chingada* in Bar-tra 147–62. For an English rendering of Paz, see Lysander Kemp's translation: *The Labyrinth of Solitude* (New York: Grove, 1961).

15. Brooks 15.

16. Founded in 1942, The National Film Bank was nationalized under President Miguel Alemán after the war. See Heuer, *La industria cinematográfica mexicana* (Mex-ico City: Policromia, 1964).

17. The significance of these facts cannot be underestimated; a first film especially requires a showcase. Landeta recounted these aspects of *Lola Casanova*'s debut in almost all her print and filmed interviews, including our conversations during the sum-mer of 1992. As she had in her public interviews, Landeta emphasized the importance of one of the only other women working in a creative capacity in the film industry at the time: editor Gloria Schoemann, who re-edited *Lola Casanova* when an entire reel of disparate, key sequences was "lost" in the lab.

18. Patricia Torres San Martín captures these comments in an "Interview with Matilde Landeta." See *Pantalla* 16 (1992): 29.

19. Torres San Martín, "Interview" 29.

20. As discussed in the introduction, Matilde Landeta, dressed as a man, pre-sented herself before the union and attempted to show that in filmmaking the differ-ences between male and female directors should be as superficial as clothing. It was not until 1945, after some eleven years as "script girl" and general factotum, that she rose to the position of assistant director. And then it took another fourteen films working with renowned directors before the guild would permit her to direct on her own.

21. After the National Film Archive's "rediscovery" of Landeta during the special programming in conjunction with the International Women's Year (1975), critics and writers from Jorge Ayala Blanco to Cristina Pacheco began to reevaluate Landeta's impor-tance in the history of Mexican film production. Eventually Landeta was honored and recognized in film festivals from Japan to Italy. In 1991, enthusiasm intact, she returned to directing with *Nocturno a Rosario,* tracing the life of patriotic poet Manuel Acuña.

22. We owe this ideological construction, as I outlined in the Introduction, to Secretary of Education Vasconcelos. *La raza cósmica* argued that national unity—as

well as a kind of global oneness—would result in the harmonious blending of the races (achieved, necessarily, through groups' "assimilation" or even through the "erasure" of some of their "least desirable characteristics"). José Vasconcelos, *La raza cósmica: Misión de la raza iberoamericana. Notas de viaje a la América del Sur* (Barcelona: Agencia Mundial de Librerías, c. 1925) and *La raza cósmica; The Cosmic Race,* trans. Didier T. Jaén (Los Angeles: California State UP, 1979).

23. Adoration of *la Doña* continues without pause. Carlos Monsiváis, unique among the actress's many admirers, grants Félix a bit of tongue-in-cheek homage in his "María Félix: Pabellón de la imagen," where he invites us to reflect on the mythic woman and upon our engagement with her as spectators. See *Intermedios* 6 (1993): 12–17.

24. With *El monje blanco* (1945), as *Doña* historian Paco Ignacio Taibo I relates, there arises a "curious movement to deify María." See *María Félix: 47 pasos por el cine* (Mexico City: Joaquín Mortiz, 1987) 74. The other María, demon-woman, appears in the title roles in *La devoradora* (1946), *La diosa arrodillada* (1947), and *Doña Diabla* (1949).

25. Jean Franco best outlines the gender paradigm that conventional filmmakers subscribed to. See especially "Oedipus Modernized" in *Plotting Women: Gender and Representation in Mexico* (New York: Columbia UP, 1989).

26. Brooks 15.

27. Carlos Monsiváis locates *La Negra Angustias,* for example, among the few films "with a clear demythifying sense," noting Landeta's "betrayal" of Rojas González's original plot. See "Las mitologías del cine mexicano" in *Intermedios* 2 (1992): 12–23.

28. Discussing her alteration of the script, Landeta remarked that she "didn't want to repeat the history of a Mexican Cinema that produced great films yet always featured humiliated women, women ready to put up with any degradations that the Mexican male might inflict upon them, women who based their value on being resigned mothers, tearful washers of diapers." Landeta herself, while giving her friend the novelist his due, was quite unready to resign herself or her script to a subordinate status. She made these comments during the round table homage to Francisco Rojas González on the fortieth anniversary of his death. See "Francisco Rojas González y su cine," *Homenaje a F. R. G.: 1903–1951* (Guadalajara: Secretaría de Educación y Cultura, 1992) 18–20.

29. Joseph Sommers sees the novel as pertaining to the "romantic tradition" while the novelist is imbued with certain "anthropological interests." With its marked "romantic indianism" on one hand and its "socially conscientious indigenism" on the other, such an outlook "generates an incongruity that spoils the novel." See *Francisco Rojas González* 96. Arriving at different conclusions, Carlos Monsiváis appreciates the "complexity" of the novel's dual nature: *Lola Casanova* is "a novel of betrayals, of acculturated passions, of loyalties that are visions of the world." *Homenaje a F. R. G.* 15.

30. This is the (possibly unpublished) opinion of E. Noguera, from the archives of Matilde Landeta.

31. This kind of analysis has not lost its appeal even to the present. As we have seen with Tzapoff's exhibition of Seri portraiture, some artists take allegory to melodramatic extremes.

32. Agustín Basave Benítez employs this term with unfortunate zeal as he praises the indianism pertaining to some of Mexico's architects of national unity. See *México mestizo: Análisis del nacionalismo en torno a la mestizofilia de Andrés Molina Enríquez* (Mexico City: FCE, 1992).

CHAPTER THREE.
PIMPS, PROSTITUTES, AND POLITICOS:
MATILDE LANDETA'S *TROTACALLES*
AND THE REGIME OF MIGUEL ALEMÁN

1. As Rojas González commented to the press, he was pleased with the results of the filmic translations of his novels. See "Matilde Landeta: La cine-directora," *México Cinema* Aug. 1949: n. pag.

Carlos Monsiváis sees Landeta's *La Negra Angustias* as one of a few films about the Revolution that "shared a clear demystificatory impulse. . . ." Classifying *La Negra* with "Julio Bracho's *La sombra del caudillo* (The Shadow of the Caudillo, 1960), José Bolaños's *La soldadera* (1966), Paul Leduc's *Reed: México insurgente* (1971), and Carlos Enrique Taboada's *La guerra santa* (The Holy War, 1977)," the critic regards Landeta's reworking of Rojas González's novel as useful "'betrayal.'" See Carlos Monsiváis, "Mythologies" in *Mexican Cinema*, ed. Paulo Antonio Paranaguá (London: BFI, 1995) 119.

2. Landeta tells this story often, but nowhere with as much detail as in this interview with Fernando Gaxiola. She reveals that Luis Spota brought her his *Vagabunda* for inspiration "and between the two of us we wrote the script." See "Entrevista con Matilde Landeta," *Otro Cine* July-Sept. 1975: 12–17. (Translation here and throughout the chapter mine unless noted.)

Since the voyeuristic gaze upon *Vagabunda*'s prostitute fetishizes the feminine precisely in the way Landeta decried—this is a novel celebrating bruised bare flesh, torrid sexuality, and death lust—it is clear that Landeta was indeed inspired, but her goal was to reshape Spota's work if not his world view. She not only constructed her own thesis for the film, but replaced the novel's overheated sensibilities with considerably more temperate ones. See *Vagabunda* (c. 1950; Mexico City: Libro Mex, 1959).

3. Other Mexican women, including Candida Beltrán, Eva Liminana, Adriana and Dolores Ehlers, Mimi Derba, and Adela Sequeyro, played key roles in earlier decades, directing and codirecting a few films. The Frenchwoman Alice Rahon worked in the late 1940s, but was unable to finish her experimental film. Of the hand-

ful of works that were completed and released, only a few remain in archives. Sequeyro's recently excavated, captivating '30s films are the subject of most new scholarship. See Patricia Martínez de Velasco Vélez, *Directoras de cine: Proyección de un mundo obscuro* (Mexico City: IMCINE and CONEICC, 1991).

4. These comments are culled from a speech Landeta delivered between 1954 and 1956. I found the talk archived with her mid-1950s writing, but, like other pieces, it did not have full publication data.

5. See María Cristina, "Culpa de ser mujer," *México Cinema* June 1945: n. pag.

6. These reviews issued from a number of sources: See Sara Moiron, "Al fin triunfadora," *Cinema Reporter* June 1948: n. pag. Dina Rico, "Cómo trabaja la mujer mexicana," *Paquita* 5 July 1948: n. pag. "Una mujer al megáfono," *Cartel* Aug. 1948: n. pag. Ángel Chevalier, "Adventures of a Woman," n.p., n. pag., 1948. José Gutiérrez Galindo, "Matilde Landeta, o el triunfo de la mujer mexicana en el cine," *El Universal* 2 Jan. 1950: n. pag.

7. "Indios en Churubusco," Landeta Archives (no publication data for this newspaper clipping).

8. "La angustia de *La Negra Angustias*," Landeta Archives (newspaper clipping without publication data).

9. "Tres films de una directora mexicana," *La nación* [Buenos Aires, Argentina] 4 Nov. 1951: n. pag.

10. Díaz Ruanova, "No idealicemos a las mujeres públicas," *El Universal* 3 June 1951: n. pag.

11. Emilio García Riera is even more emphatic on this point: *Las abandonadas* "has nothing of neorealism." See *Emilio Fernández: 1904–1986* (Guadalajara: U de Guadalajara, 1987) 70.

12. Carlos Monsiváis, "Sociedad y cultura," *Entre la guerra y la estabilidad política: El México de los '40,* ed. Rafael Loyola (Mexico City: Grijalbo, 1990) 270.

13. Tzvi Medin discusses the government's program in *El sexenio alemanista: Ideología y praxis política de Miguel Alemán* (Mexico City: Era, 1990) 30.

14. See Edmundo Domínguez Aragonés, *Tres Extraordinarios: Luis Spota, Alejandro Jodorowsky, Emilio "Indio" Fernández* (Mexico City: Juan Pablos, 1980) 29–30. This interview with Spota makes fascinating reading especially when juxtaposed with Elda Peralta's (the costar of *Trotacalles* and Spota's longtime *compañera*) biography of the late writer. See *Luis Spota: Las sustancias de la tierra. Una biografía íntima* (1989; Mexico City: Grijalbo, 1990).

15. Medin 172.

16. Monsiváis, "Sociedad y cultura" 263.

17. Domínguez Aragonés 30.

18. Monsiváis, "Sociedad y cultura" 263.

19. Monsiváis, "Sociedad y cultura" 264.

20. Sergio de la Mora details the restrictions that, since the policies of pre-revolutionary dictator Porfirio Díaz, separated houses of prostitution by their denizens' socioeconomic classes. Translating Porfirian law (cited in Monsiváis, 1980), which specified that "in the brothels there will only be women who belong to the same class, it being terminally prohibited to allow the mixing of diverse classes," de la Mora summarizes the implications: "These classifications underscore the fear of the potential erasure or crossing of social differences and class hierarchies. They also connote the bourgeois fear of the 'lower' classes infiltrating and contaminating the 'respectable' social body. Additionally, these categories function to differentiate and isolate the high from the low, the pure from the impure, the norm from the deviant, and the respectable from the criminal." Such pedigrees, I argue in accord with this cultural critic, are precisely the aspects of social reality that Mexican *noir*-inflected cinema sought to taint. See *Virile Nationalism: Cinema, the State, and the Formation of a National Consciousness in Mexico, 1950–1994*, Diss., U of California-Santa Cruz, 1999 (Ann Arbor: UMI, 2000) 86.

21. Spota reminds his interviewer that these sites were once the venue of politicians: "Where did these *señores* meet after a hard day's work? Well, in the House of La Bandida, the House of Ruth, in the great houses of prostitution, where generals, colonels, and senators . . . all the big politicos of the epoch met . . . to eat *menudo* and *burritas* and drink coñac, finishing up 'thundering bullets' at five in the morning, after which, hung over, they'd go meet with the President." See Domínguez Aragonés 84.

22. Nevertheless, as Sergio de la Mora points out in his comprehensive study of the "Midnight Virgins" of the prostitute genre, *Víctimas del pecado* unusually "posits solidarity across class lines and advocates for a family model not based on blood ties." See de la Mora 104; 62–120.

23. Luis Trelles Plazaola, *Cine y mujer en América Latina: Directoras de largometrajes de ficción* (Río Piedras: U de Puerto Rico, 1991) 219. Landeta also discussed this during our 1992 interviews in Mexico City.

24. Arturo Escobar delineates how these formulations differed from region to region. See *Encountering Development: The Making and Unmaking of the Third World* (Princeton: Princeton UP, 1995).

25. Michael Walker, Introduction, *The Book of Film Noir*, ed. Ian Cameron (New York: Continuum, 1993) 8.

26. R. Barton Palmer, *Hollywood's Dark Cinema* (New York: Twayne, 1994) 10.

27. Monsiváis, "Sociedad y cultura" 264.

28. World War II as a catalyst for the cycle is discussed by virtually every *noir* critic; Frank Krutnik contextualizes the phenomenon with regard to other stimuli. See *In a Lonely Street: Film Noir, Genre, Masculinity* (New York: Routledge, 1991) 65–72.

29. David Reid and Jayne L. Walker, "Strange Pursuit: Cornell Woolrich and the Abandoned City of the Forties," *Shades of Noir*, ed. Joan Copjec (London: Verso, 1993) 57–96.

30. Deborah Thomas, "How Hollywood Deals with the Deviant Male," *The Book of Film Noir*, ed. Ian Cameron (New York: Continuum, 1993) 60–62.

31. The notion of the confessing picaresque character (exemplified in the geographically distanced but thematically similar Flanders and Duarte) has been provocatively advanced by Anthony Zahareas in "The Historical Function of Picaresque Autobiographies: Toward a History of Social Offenders," *Autobiography in Early Modern Spain*, ed. Nicholas Spadaccini and Jenaro Talén (Minneapolis: Prisma, 1988) 129–62.

32. *Detour*'s fortuitously criminal Al tells narrative whoppers, for instance, and the 1944 *Murder, My Sweet*'s detective, Raymond Chandler's Philip Marlowe (Dick Powell), represents the essence of fogged perplexity.

33. Mary Ann Doane excavates this trope insightfully: "Freud's use of the term 'dark continent' to signify female sexuality . . . transforms [that] sexuality into an unexplored territory, an enigmatic, unknowable place concealed from the theoretical gaze and hence the epistemological power of the psychoanalyst. Femininity confounds knowledge while male sexuality is its stable guarantee. Yet, the pertinent question may not be 'What is the dark continent?,' but 'Where is it?' The fact that Freud himself borrows the phrase from Victorian colonialist texts in which it was used to designate Africa is often forgotten." This site-specific term, conflating all blackness with all femininity, travels and transposes to U.S. contexts with the rise of the "dark continent's" historical immigration to increasingly less-white, urban America. See Doane, *Femmes Fatales: Feminism, Film Theory, and Psychoanalysis* (New York: Routledge, 1991) 209.

Deborah Thomas traces this nineteenth-into-twentieth-century xenophobia as it manifests in representations of the city, a locus which "became progressively seen as the place from which civilization was *absent*, this alleged absence of civilization largely linked to a sense of the city as an alien place." Without sustaining interest in domestic darkness as personified by ethnic others, "the genre's main 'heavies' (its main representatives, that is, of an alien and threatening world) are not so much foreigners per se as women and criminals." See Thomas 60–62.

34. Thomas 59; 64.

35. Thomas 64.

36. Thomas 64.

37. Landeta and Spota's screenplay is thus annotated. Landeta Archive.

38. Peter William Evans, "*Double Indemnity* (or Bringing Up Baby)," *The Book of Film Noir*, ed. Ian Cameron (New York: Continuum, 1993) 169.

39. Thomas 59.

40. Ruth's melodrama, *but not its postmortem coda*, is clearly inspired by novelist Federico Gamboa's 1903 *Santa*. Representing the most conventional thinking in the film, her short narrative of seduction and betrayal links her to the novel's heroine and

to celluloid Santas from 1932 and throughout the century. Like them, Ruth is the mother/whore whose initial rape precipitated her fall from grace, her ascendancy as a courtesan, and her descent into streetwalking. Dying of highly infectious tuberculosis, she mimics the venereally diseased Santa whose contagion, as Sergio de la Mora points out, binds with her victimization to produce dual "measures of fear and desire" in those who contemplate her. If "the first image [Santa as victim] elicits the sympathy of the reader with the purpose of reintegrating the prostitute into 'respectable' social norms and affirming her human rights . . . the second image [Santa as infectious] is driven by an impulse towards containing and isolating the destructive powers attributed to her." Ruth differs from Santa notably when this emotional schizophrenia is as limited as the mariachis' last lament. Landeta's clear-sighted, if grim, social sensibility saves us here from mainstream melodrama's impossible dreams. For a complex reading of Gamboa's *Santa* and a contemporary reworking of the prostitute paradigm in Sara Sefchovich's *Demasiado amor* (1990), see de la Mora 62–120.

41. Monsiváis, "Sociedad y cultura" 272.

42. Monsiváis, "Sociedad y cultura" 279.

43. Medin 46.

44. Medin 45.

45. José Agustín, *Tragicomedia mexicana I: La vida en México de 1940 a 1970* (Mexico City: Planeta, 1991) 114.

46. Qtd. in Agustín 83.

47. Matilde Landeta, personal interview, 22 July 1992.

48. "I spent a lot of time at the Molino Rojo, the Bombay, and the Club Verde," Landeta tells Díaz Ruanova, "and among ladies of the evening and *mariguanos* I recorded fundamental details with which to document the film. . . . I discovered the 'Mamboletas' [the group of dancers]. . . . In the nocturnal streets I made observations that I tried to bring to the screen with subtlety, [understanding that] it is the depth of dramatic realism that justifies the crudeness of some scenes." See Díaz Ruanova, "No idealicemos a las mujeres públicas."

49. Agustín 85.

50. Agustín 72. Italics mine.

CHAPTER FOUR.
NEOMELODRAMA AS PARTICIPATORY ETHNOGRAPHY:
ALLISON ANDERS'S *MI VIDA LOCA*

1. Monsiváis writes of audiences' acceptance of "the mechanics of emotional blackmail" in which they willingly indulged in order to be more fully enfranchised as

citizens in the great post-revolutionary national project. See Carlos Monsiváis, "Mythologies" in *Mexican Cinema*, ed. Paulo Antonio Paranaguá (London: BFI, 1995) 117–27.

2. James Clifford outlines several problems regarding anthropologists' use of language relevant to our consideration of a filmmaker who works mainly in English. In addition to that language, which constitutes only one of the barrios' three linguistic registers, we not only have to consider how Spanish and the vernacular, Caló, function, but we must also account for a fourth "language." This fourth idiom represents the realm of communication Clifford calls "stranger talk, the specific kind of discourse used with outsiders." How, wonders Clifford, are we to understand the role of translators? And to apply his question to our case: What are we to make of *Anders*'s translations of *other* explicators' translations of the ever-changing *in-group codes* of Caló? See "Traveling Cultures" in *Cultural Studies*, ed. Lawrence Grossberg, Cary Nelson, and Paula A. Treichler (New York: Routledge, 1992) 99.

3. The official purpose of these raids, dubbed "Operation Hammer," was to eradicate gang drug activity in a ten-square-mile area in South Central L.A. Police made few drug busts, notes Mike Davis, but they arrested 1,453 young men and cited hundreds more, logging yet others' names into computers for future surveillance. See *City of Quartz* (1990; London: Verso; New York: Vintage, 1992) 268.

Joan W. Moore calculates that a total of 1,600 youth, or virtually "every male encountered on the street except those of advanced age," were thus harassed. See Moore, *Going Down to the Barrio* (Philadelphia: Temple UP, 1991) 3–4.

4. The best print challenge to media coverage of the L.A. Rebellion can be found in Robert Gooding-Williams's anthology, *Reading Rodney King/Reading Urban Uprising* (New York: Routledge, 1993).

5. Rosa Linda Fregoso appreciates the film's "unflinching treatment of Chicano masculinities" and "its shrewdly oblique refusal to romanticize the defiance of the masculine heroic figure." See *The Bronze Screen: Chicana and Chicano Film Culture* (Minneapolis: U of Minnesota P, 1993) 123.

Kathleen Newman perceptively links the feminization of *American Me*'s male protagonist and the film's deconstruction of gender with discourses that "gender the representation of violence" in art and nation formation. See "Reterritorialization in Recent Chicano Cinema: Edward James Olmos's *American Me* (1992)" in Chon Noriega and Ana M. López's anthology, *The Ethnic Eye: Latino Media Arts* (Minneapolis: U of Minnesota P, 1996) 95–106.

Sergio de la Mora, in an expansion of his examination of the film's new ways of understanding masculinity (as seen in his "'Giving It Away': *American Me* and the Defilement of Chicano Manhood," collected in *Cine Estudiantil '95* [San Diego: Centro Cultural de la Raza, 1995] 14), discusses the significance of sexual violence between incarcerated men such as the instances we see in the film. The prison, a place where "men become 'wives' of other men and are often subordinated by sexual and 'domestic' violence—enslaved by dominant prisoners—is increasingly becoming a key space where we can look at the way gender relations get produced throughout society." Sergio de la Mora, personal interview, 9 Sept. 2001.

6. Fregoso astutely wonders where Chicana subjectivity abides in *American Me*. "Who is this new subject, this Chicana who Edward James Olmos claims is the heroine of *American Me*, the hope of our barrios? His story ends before hers can begin," she asserts. Female protagonist Julie's "surviving and resisting" what Fregoso calls *"la vida dura"* is told only by the "final weathered look in her eyes," and by the symbol of her gang affiliation tattooed on her hand (which Julie carefully conceals with makeup). For Fregoso that (hidden) sign is as powerful and as muted as "the history of Chicana membership in gangs that unfolds not on the screen, but in my mind." Writing before she completed her analysis of *Mi vida loca*, Fregoso asks "why the story of Julie's oppression and resistance, why the pain of her rape, is not up there, on the Hollywood screen, looking at me." See Fregoso 133.

Carmen Huaco-Nuzum offers insight on the erasure of Julie, and asks just how "hopeful" an element she represents in the film. See Huaco-Nuzum, rev. of *American Me*, *Jump Cut* 38 (June 1993): 92–94.

7. In "Hanging Out with the Homegirls? Allison Anders's *Mi vida loca*," Fregoso argues that the filmmaker has constructed a "one-sided" vision of gang life that ultimately has more to do with Anders than with the Chicanas whose lives she portrays. See *Cineaste* 21.3 (1995): 36–37, a special issue dealing with "race" in contemporary U.S. cinema.

8. I respect my *comadres* and their friends and families' consent to be cited by their own first names, without their full names appearing in formal notes.

9. Mary Ann Doane elaborates theorists' paradigms that describe the impossibility of female desire vis-à-vis cinematic pleasure. Since "distance from the image is less negotiable for the female spectator than for the male because the woman is so forcefully linked with the iconic and spectacle . . ." and since "voyeurism . . . and fetishism . . . [are] also inaccessible to the woman, . . . [f]emale spectatorship, because it is conceived of temporally as immediacy (in the reading of the image—the result of the very absence of fetishism) and spatially as proximity (the distance between subject and object, spectator and image is collapsed), can only be understood as the confounding of desire." Given this unhappy scenario, Doane asks us to look for "stress points" where the paradigm fails to hold. In Anders's film we'll find these points precisely in the humorous, self-aware ways that melodrama reveals itself. See *The Desire to Desire: The Woman's Film of the 1940s* (Bloomington: Indiana UP, 1987) 12–13.

10. Doane's reading of *The Purple Rose* delineates "stress points" that "can be activated as a kind of lever to facilitate the production of a desiring subjectivity for women—in another cinematic practice." See Doane, "Subjectivity and Desire: An(other) Way of Looking" in *Desire to Desire* 1–13.

11. Monsiváis, "Mythologies" 118.

12. Monsiváis lists melodrama's "atmospheres," from the "rural innocence" of the countryside "in which primitivism and purity were one and the same," to the "moral hell and sensate heaven[s] of the cabaret, dance hall, brothel, and street of prostitutes, among other, more quotidian spots." See "Mythologies" 118.

13. She chose "Laramie," Anders told me, in homage to Anthony Mann's 1955 *The Man from Laramie*, an unusual western concerned more with moral dilemmas than action sequences. Personal interview, 28 Aug. 1996.

14. Yet as Clifford suggests, ethnographies—whether fictions of the self or constructions of the other—are in various degrees "experiential, interpretive, dialogical, and polyphonic." In the unequal exchanges between those who occupy these positions "serious fictions" are wrought. See *The Predicament of Culture: Twentieth-Century Ethnography, Literature, and Art* (Cambridge: Harvard UP, 1988) 1–92.

15. Peter Brooks, *The Melodramatic Imagination: Balzac, Henry James, Melodrama, and the Mode of Excess* (New Haven: Yale UP, 1976) 15.

16. B. Ruby Rich draws the most cogent parallels between Anders's *vida y obra*. See "Slugging It Out for Survival," in *Sight and Sound* 5 (Apr. 1995): 14–17.

17. The young woman's fantasy, recounted in *Paul is Dead*, is part of Anders's liberating autobiography: ". . . one minute I'm in the smog-filled San Fernando Valley being beaten by my stepfather, and the next minute I'm in London shopping at the Apple Boutique with Paul McCartney." See Angela Matusik in *Paper*, summer 1994: 43, and Rich 15.

18. Anders's work has netted numerous Independent Spirit awards; she has been voted Best New Director by the New York Film Critics Circle; and she recently became a recipient of the prestigious MacArthur grant.

19. Manohla Dargis offers the most complete local press review of *Mi vida loca*. See "Earth Angel," *L.A. Weekly* 22 July 1994: 24.

20. Allison Anders, personal interview, 28 Aug. 1996.

21. Dargis 24. The "white *cholo*," if not his female counterpart, makes his screen debut in Luis Valdez's *Zoot Suit* (1981).

22. Bette Gordon, interview with Allison Anders, *Bomb*, summer 1994: 16.

23. Gordon 17.

24. Dargis 24.

25. Sheila Benson, interview with Allison Anders, *Interview*, June 1994: 96.

26. Clifford, *Predicament* 11.

27. When Anders asked that her film, *Grace of My Heart* (1996), be opened as a benefit for Echo Park student scholarships, Gramercy Pictures responded by offering a large donation to the project.

28. Clifford, *Predicament* 10.

29. *Con safos*, abbreviated to C/S, is often written at the base of graffiti. Its purpose is to invest authorship "with safety," defying erasure of art and artists.

30. James Clifford elaborates this idea throughout "Traveling Cultures."

31. Clifford, *Predicament* 9.

32. Charles Freeman completed his 1994 mural with SPARC (Social and Public Art Resource Center) teen affiliates Hector Rodríguez, Adrian Tapia, and Ayne Velasques. "Dedicated to the children of the sun," the mural is entitled *Return to the Light.*

33. Clifford asks us to "rethink cultures as sites of dwelling *and* travel, to take travel knowledges seriously." See "Traveling Cultures," 105.

34. I am grateful to Anders and her assistant Maya Smukler for such a packet.

35. Sanford Schram's ground-breaking examination of welfare policy argues for ethnographers' "self-reflective criticism attentive to its own constitutive practices." The "confessional character of [useful] welfare ethnography" (or, we might say, of useful ethnographic melodramas that deal with people in the welfare system) can illuminate the very "practices that make a political economy of welfare possible" (and facilitate filmic representations about the ramifications of those practices). See *Words of Welfare: The Poverty of Social Science and the Social Science of Poverty* (Minneapolis: U of Minnesota P, 1995) 50.

36. Brooks's delineation of this mode informs his entire work, and is most clearly outlined in *The Melodramatic Imagination*'s first three chapters.

37. See Kevin Thomas, "The Road to *Mi vida loca* Paved with Good Intentions," *Los Angeles Times* 22 July 1994: F4+.

38. Brooks 25.

39. Brooks 27.

40. Brooks 28.

41. On just about any given day the media records such assertions. This one relates to a U of California–Santa Barbara study relating to welfare and teen mothers. See "Teen Pregnancies Raising Crime Costs," *Santa Barbara News Press* 22 June 1996: B22+.

42. These spaces, Brooks continues, "very often [present to us] at stage rear a locked grille looking out on the surrounding countryside or onto the highroad leading from the city." Bullet's garden provides such an escape from the tough urban areas he daily negotiates. See Brooks 29.

43. One way Anders recognizes her role in the "race" privilege paradigm is by casting whites as druggies, thus using Brooks's melodramatic "aesthetics of astonishment" to rewrite racist films that insist on stereotyping. She further dislodges complacency in her viewers by casting daughter Tiffany Anders as a desperate user.

44. In our discussion about her work, Anders revealed that both Peter Brooks's and Douglas Sirk's writing has influenced her aesthetics.

45. Brooks 35.

46. Martín Sánchez Jankowski's ten-year research with gangs debunks conventional social scientists' theories since Frederic Thrasher's studies in the late 1920s. Jankowski refutes popular wisdom that absent fathers and "bad" families make for gang membership. Not only did the sociologist find that kids in gangs represented an even split between male- and female-headed homes, but within these families there were "just as many members who claimed close relationships . . . as denied them." See *Islands in the Street: Gangs and American Urban Society* (Berkeley: U of California P, 1991) 39.

While Jankowski discusses the economic pressures that both male gang members and their families face, Joan W. Moore's *Going Down to the Barrio* takes a similar tack with girls' realities.

47. Fregoso, "Hanging Out" 37 and Fregoso, *The Bronze Screen* 133.

48. Moore and Jankowski explore how gang members rely on their groups when unemployment soars.

49. Schram contends that "contemporary welfare policy research is created by the government and has come to be written in a discourse that reinforces state interests about how to understand [in order to manage the behavior of] 'the poor.'" See Schram 4.

50. Leslie Felperin, rev. of *Mi vida loca, Sight and Sound* 5 (Apr. 1995): 48.

51. Leila Cobo-Hanlon, "Another Side of the 'Crazy Life,'" *Los Angeles Times* 21 July 1994: F1+.

52. Fregoso, "Hanging Out" 37. While older women's presence is valued in *Mi vida loca,* as the filmic evidence documents, their absence is also part of barrio reality, as Anders's personal experience sustains. When her adopted son Ruben's nineteen-year-old mother died, Anders told me, there was no "elaborate support network" of family able to care for him.

53. We have only to think, for instance, of the Texas Rangers' numerous legitimations of their turf wars, where the mere evocation of the patriarchal familial structure of white settlers put God on their side.

54. Frances Fox Piven, foreword, *Words of Welfare* xiii.

55. Ruth Sidel discusses how "America's war against the poor" depends on "us" and "them" discourses that "denigrate, dehumanize, and demonize" those whom policy-makers have categorized as "enemies within" in order to legitimate slashed budgets. Study of this timely text reveals how the moralizing of discursive, political melodrama functions. See *Keeping Women and Children Last* (New York: Penguin, 1996).

56. The Mexican film is Fernando Méndez's *noir*-ish *El Suavecito* (1950).

57. Brooks 2.

58. Brooks 9.

59. Monsiváis, "Mythologies" 118.

60. "The Question," like the film that employs the poem, is itself a confusion between life and melodrama. It was first published anonymously in 1952 in Italy. When Pablo Neruda acknowledged his authorship of the verses—they were written for his future wife—he wrote, ". . . I present this book . . . as if it were mine and not mine. . . . Now that I recognize it I hope that its furious blood will recognize me, too." Qtd. in Donald D. Walsh, introduction, *The Captain's Verses* by Pablo Neruda (New York: New Directions 1972). See also Pablo Neruda, "La pregunta," *Los versos del Capitán* (Buenos Aires: Losada, 1953). Translation here is mine.

61. This speech is wonderfully ironic. Anders was fully aware that the Echo Park kids thought of Suavecito as "just a ride." As barrio resident "Evil" remarked to *Times* journalist Leila Cobo-Hanlon, "A car is a car. Everybody has one." By registering Shadow's doubt, Anders self-reflexively comments on melodrama's great trope of forcing the seemingly insignificant to signify. See Cobo-Hanlon, F3.

62. In the 1950 film, the character "Suavecito" (Víctor Parra; however unusually "corpulent") is a ladies' man. See Emilio García Riera, *Historia documental del cine mexicano* 5 (Guadalajara: U de Guadalajara, 1992–1997): 316–17.

63. Brooks 32.

64. Personal interview.

65. Brooks 33.

66. Brooks 32.

67. Anders affirms this in numerous interviews, including our discussion.

68. Personal interview.

69. Thomas F4+.

70. Criminalization of the barrio residents always begins by classifying all behavior as "gang-related." Cops can thus vilify all gangs and all inner-city youth by extension. See Davis, especially Chapter Five, and Jankowski.

71. See Jankowski, especially Chapter Three.

72. We might recall the Fed's hysterical hedges against inflation that "require" high unemployment rates, for instance.

73. Schram analyzes how institutionalized narratives about "dependency" function to construct those problems of poverty that the government wishes to address—or that legislators even invent. The very terms of the "dependency question" determine how research will be funded, approached, and completed. "Given the ascendancy of ETM [economic, therapeutic, managerial discourses] in welfare policy research," he writes, "it is basically impossible to suggest that welfare taking may often be a commendable attempt by women in particular to cope with difficult domestic and economic circumstances." See Schram, 13, as well as his Chapter Two, "Discourses of Dependency."

74. Independent documentary filmmaker Ann Skinner-Jones's "Neither Insider nor Outsider" offers an extensive bibliography of reviews in addition to an interesting analysis of *Mi vida loca*. Albuquerque, unpublished essay, 1994.

75. Allison Anders, "Critics Shouldn't Dictate *Loca*'s Artistic Content," *Los Angeles Times* 15 Aug., 1994: F3.

CHAPTER FIVE.
THE LAST JUDGMENT:
MARCELA FERNÁNDEZ VIOLANTE'S
REQUIEM (FOR) MELODRAMA

1. Working with U.S. independent cinema directed by men, for example, film critic Ira Jaffe has theorized a new cycle of "slow" films whose purposeful minimalism resonates with the transcendent simplicity of the cinema by Ozu, Bresson, and Dreyer. See both Paul Schrader's *Transcendental Style in Film: Ozu, Bresson, and Dreyer* (1972; New York: Da Capo, 1988), and Ira Jaffe's *Slowly Out of Control* (in progress).

2. Organized by Elena Feder, a 1999 Vancouver, B. C., conference on Latin American cinema ("Nations, Pollinations, and Dislocations: Changing Imaginary Borders in the Americas") featured just such a film. The "Americas on the Verge" segment showcased Ursula Biemann's *Performing the Border* (1998), which, using both analytical and affective aesthetics, documents Ciudad Juárez assembly plant workers' struggles and pleasures. A text now accompanies the video project. See Biemann, *Been There and Back to Nowhere: Gender in Transnational Spaces* (New York: Autonomedia, 2000).

3. Between the summers of 1998 and 2000, as Mexican newspapers decried, some 785 migrating Mexicans died in the Arizona desert, many the victims of ranchers with rifles. Very little commentary about these egregious abuses of human rights has ever appeared in the U.S. press. See, for example, "Tras el inicio de la operación Salvaguarda: Relaciones exteriores," *La Jornada* 13 June 2000.

4. We owe this insight to Gloria Anzaldúa. See *Borderlands/La Frontera* (San Francisco: Spinsters/aunt lute, 1987) 3.

5. Qtd. in Julianne Burton-Carvajal, "Daughter of the Revolution: Matilde Soto Landeta," Part I of *Three Lives in Film: The Improbable Careers of Latin America's Foremost Women Filmmakers* (forthcoming in English and available in Spanish as *Matilde Landeta: Hija de la Revolución* [Mexico City: IMCINE and CONACULTA, 2002]) 90.

6. Josefina Villar has initiated such study, situating indigenous broadcasting in its recent history as a remarkably independent project subsidized by the INI (National Institute for Indigenous Affairs). See *El sonido de la radio* (Mexico City: U Autónoma Metropolitana-Iztapalapa. Mexico City: Plaza y Valdés, 1988).

Filemón Ku Ché, a Mayan investigative broadcaster, details his personal experience with a sort of "Radio Free Mérida" as well as with INI-backed XEPET in Peto, Yucatán. See Jaime Vélez's interview, "Violando el aire. XEPET: La voz de los mayas," *México indígena* 12 (Sept. 1990): 43–45.

Since this sound barrier has been breached, Internet sources now abound. In addition to the aforementioned Web sites, see "Congreso Nacional Indígena," available at http://www.laneta.apc.org/cni, and "Frente Zapatista de Liberación Nacional," at http://www.fzln.org.mx.

7. This devastation has been eloquently—if painfully—captured by border photographers dedicated to exposing the "violent realities of Free Trade." Charles Bowden, for example, recounts his experiences with Mexican photojournalists in Ciudad Juárez. Women there earning three to five dollars a day (where the cost of living is roughly the same as across the border in El Paso) are forced into an underground economy for survival's sake. Many of these women, selling their bodies in order to eat, end up victims of yet more violence. Of the underreported 520 dead in 1995, for example, authorities admitted that "'an important percentage of them were female adolescents.'" Bowden's haunting photographs of these women document almost too clearly the face of a two-tiered society. See "While You Were Sleeping," *Harpers* 293.1759 (Dec. 1996): 52; 44–52.

In "Muertas sin fin, Ciudad Juárez: Misoginia sin ley" Sergio González Rodríguez writes of the seemingly unending horror of violence against women and young boys and girls in circumstances that underscore the "difficulty of finding justice" that the marginalized poor face all over the Republic. *Letras Libres* 5 (May 1999): 40–45.

Filmmaker Lourdes Portillo's *Señorita Extraviada* (Missing Young Woman; Xochitl, 2001) documents the most recent horrors in Juárez: an official death toll of over 200 young women in the last decade, with estimates of unreported deaths that could reach a total of 400; a government and police force little able to solve the crimes; grieving families organizing to search for truths and find justice for their dead and disappeared daughters.

8. Marian Wright Edelman, president of the Children's Defense Fund, has lobbied continually against what she has called the "Welfare Repeal" of 1996. In addition to opposing the 54 billion dollar cut ("at a time when the Pentagon received 11.5 billion without even asking!"), she has also worked to seek health insurance benefits for the nation's nearly 10 million unprotected children. See Edelman, "Citizen Activists: Ethics of Caring and Community in a World Desperately Seeking Moral Leadership," Pacifica National News Broadcast, 30 Dec. 1996.

Commenting on the problems of the 1996 Personal Responsibility and Work Opportunity Reconciliation Act (PRWORA), Barbara Gault, Heidi Hartmann, and Hsiao-Ye Yi maintain little hope for marginalized women to escape poverty. See "Prospects for Low-Income Mothers' Economic Survival under Welfare Reform," in *Welfare Reform: A Race to the Bottom?*, ed. Sanford F. Schram and Samuel H. Beer (Washington, DC: Woodrow Wilson Center P, 1999) 209–27.

9. As a historian and film critic, Fernández Violante discusses the annals of legislation for the film industry from the first protections initiated in the 1949 *Ley*

de la Industria Cinematográfica to the decimation of safeguards occasioned in 1992 with the *Nueva Ley Cinematográfica* ordered under Salinas de Gortari. Writing in 1997, she berates the government's premature inclusion of its film enterprise in the Free Trade Agreement, which "robbed the industry of protective legislation in place since the earlier Law of 1949," permitting the national patrimony to become a denationalized *"tierra de nadie."* See "La ley de cinematografía (Opus, 1992)," *Archipiélago* 14 (Sept.-Dec. 1997): 44–45. (Translations mine here and throughout the chapter unless noted.)

10. When we consider what critic Leonardo García Tsao calls Cheadle's "demonstration of the indomitable gringo spirit" in the context of the pseudohybridity granted by the character's manifestly comprehensible linguistic skills, it is hard not to appreciate how Hollywood hegemony extends to Mexico and naturalizes, if not completely renationalizes, the U.S. imperialist impulse. See García Tsao, "Misión imposible," *La Jornada* 9 June 2000.

Earlier in spring 2000, during a Supreme Court session open to the public, more than 250 filmmakers condemned legislation that would assure the demise of Mexican cinema with the rise of dubbed Hollywood imports. See Raquel Peguero "Los argumentos pro doblaje, tramposos," *La Jornada* 5 Mar. 2000.

11. See Marcela Fernández Violante, "El melodrama, orígenes y tradición," *Estudios cinematográficos* 19 (June-Oct. 2000): 32–37.

12. The requiem mass honors the dead "present in body" if no longer in spirit. Fernández Violante captures this doctrine in the title of her eulogy for melodrama.

13. It is important to note that Fernández Violante does not try to manage this unwieldy body on her own. As her demonic documentary is made with the passive collaboration of more than eighty directors over some seventy years, so too is its present body constructed with the active collaboration of two filmmakers over several years, assistant scriptwriter Alfonso Morales Carillo and editor Ximena Cuevas (former assistant director on two Fernández Violante pictures). While the force of what Morales Carillo calls the "Frankenstein" impulse belongs to Fernández Violante, she makes it clear that the documentary is the fecund product of multiple progenitors.

14. Benedict Anderson, *Imagined Communities: Reflections on the Origin and Spread of Nationalism* (New York: Verso, 1983) 29.

15. The structure of *De cuerpo presente's* screenplay makes for illuminating reading. *Moral Body, Social Body* serves as the title of the Prologue, which consists of two subsections. Like the nine "Stations" of the film and their multiple subsections, title denominations appear only as formal categories in Fernández Violante's meticulous script. I refer to these divisions by italicizing Station titles and placing subsection designations in quotation marks.

16. Jorge Ayala Blanco discusses this film in his analysis of director/actor Valentín Trujillo's growing cinema. See *La disolvencia del cine mexicano: Entre lo popular y lo exquisito* (Mexico City: Grijalbo, 1991) 235.

17. Ersatz indigenist Ureta teams up with sharp-witted national chronicler Salvador Novo and serious nationalist composer Silvestre Revueltas to devise a vehicle for comic actors Medel and Cantinflas.

18. Emilio García Riera thus briefly characterizes this film in his encyclopedia of Mexican movies. See Vol. I of his *Historia documental del cine mexicano: 1929–1937* (Guadalajara: U de Guadalajara,1992) 181.

19. Francisco Sánchez updates his 1978 *Todo Buñuel* with interviews of twenty-seven artists and scholars who knew Luis Buñuel or appreciated the surrealist's cinema. Fernández Violante's contribution might be said to characterize her work as well as that of the famed filmmaker. See *Siglo Buñuel* (Mexico City: CONACULTA, 2000) 260.

20. See Alfonso Morales Carillo's "Cuerpo marcado: La violencia y el cine mexicano" in the unnumbered, introductory pages of the screenplay *De cuerpo presente*.

BIBLIOGRAPHY

N

Spanish-language journals and newspapers listed below were published in Mexico City unless otherwise specified.

Agrasánchez, Rogelio. *Beauties of Mexican Cinema. Bellezas del cine mexicano.* Harlingen: Agrasánchez Film Archive, 2001.

———. *Cine mexicano: Carteles de la época de oro, 1936–1956. Posters from the Golden Age, 1936–1956.* San Francisco: Chronicle, 2001.

Agrasánchez, Rogelio, and Charles Ramírez Berg. *Carteles de la época de oro del cine mexicano. Poster Art from the Golden Age of Mexican Cinema.* Harlingen: Archivo Fílmico Agrasánchez; Guadalajara: U de Guadalajara; Mexico City: Instituto Mexicano de Cinematografía, 1997.

Aguilar Camín, Héctor, and Lorenzo Meyer. *A la sombra de la Revolución Mexicana: Un ensayo de historia contemporánea de México, 1910–1989.* Mexico City: Cal y Arena, 1990.

Agustín, José. *Tragicomedia mexicana I: La vida en México de 1940 a 1970.* 1990. Mexico City: Planeta, 1991.

Alarcón, Norma. "Chicana's Feminist Literature: A Re-Vision through Malintzin; or, Malintzin: Putting the Flesh Back on the Object." *This Bridge Called My Back: Writings by Radical Women of Color.* Ed. Cherríe Moraga and Gloria Anzaldúa. Watertown: Persephone, 1981. 182–90.

———. "Traddutora, Traditora: A Paradigmatic Figure of Chicana Feminism." *Cultural Critique* 13 (fall 1989): 57–87.

Anders, Allison. "Critics Shouldn't Dictate *Loca*'s Artistic Content." *Los Angeles Times* 15 Aug. 1994: F3.

———, dir. *Gas Food Lodging.* Perf. Brooke Adams, Ione Skye, and Fairuza Balk. Cineville, 1991.

233

———, dir. *Mi vida loca*. Perf. Angel Aviles, Seidy Lopez, and Jacob Vargas. Cineville, 1993.

Anderson, Benedict. *Imagined Communities: Reflections on the Origin and Spread of Nationalism*. London: Verso, 1983.

"La angustia de *La Negra Angustias*." Mexico City: Newspaper Clipping. Landeta Archives, n. d.

Anzaldúa, Gloria. *Borderlands/La Frontera: The New Mestiza*. San Francisco: Spinsters/aunt lute, 1987.

Ayala Blanco, Jorge. *La aventura del cine mexicano, 1931–1967*. Mexico City: Era, 1968.

———. *La disolvencia del cine mexicano: Entre lo popular y lo exquisito*. Mexico City: Grijalbo, 1991.

———. "Matilde Landeta, nosotros te amamos." *¡Siempre!* 23 July 1975: n. pag.

Bartra, Roger. *The Imaginary Networks of Political Power*. Trans. Claire Joysmith. New Brunswick: Rutgers UP, 1992.

———. *La jaula de la melancolía: Identidad y metamorfosis del mexicano*. Mexico City: Grijalbo, 1987. Trans. Christopher J. Hall. *The Cage of Melancholy: Identity and Metamorphosis in the Mexican Character*. New Brunswick: Rutgers UP, 1992.

Basave Benítez, Agustín F. *México mestizo: Análisis del nacionalismo mexicano en torno a la mestizofilia de Andrés Molina Enríquez*. Mexico City: Fondo de Cultura Económica, 1992.

Berg, Charles Ramírez. *Cinema of Solitude: A Critical Study of Mexican Film, 1967–1983*. Austin: U of Texas P, 1992.

———. "The Cinematic Invention of Mexico: The Poetics and Politics of the Fernández-Figueroa Style." *The Mexican Cinema Project*. Ed. Chon A. Noriega and Steven Ricci. Los Angeles: U of California Film and Television Archive, 1994. 13–24.

———. "Figueroa's Skies and Oblique Perspective: Notes on the Development of the Classical Mexican Style." *Spectator: The University of Southern California Journal of Film and Television Criticism* 13.1 (fall 1992): 24–41.

Benson, Sheila. Interview with Allison Anders. *Interview* June 1994: 96+.

Bhabha, Homi K., ed. *Nation and Narration*. London: Routledge, 1990.

Biemann, Ursula. *Been There and Back to Nowhere: Gender in Transnational Spaces*. New York: Autonomedia, 2000.

Blanco, José Joaquín. *Se llamaba Vasconcelos: Una evocación crítica*. Mexico City: Fondo de Cultura Económica, 1977.

Blom, Gertrude. "The Jungle is Burning." *México: Through Foreign Eyes*. Ed. Carole Naggar and Fred Ritchin. New York: W. W. Norton, 1993. 144–53; 292.

Bonfil Batalla, Guillermo. *México profundo: Una civilización negada*. Mexico City: Secretaría de Educación Pública, 1987. Mexico City: Grijalbo, 1990.

———. *Pensar nuestra cultura*. Mexico City: Alianza, 1991.

Bowden, Charles. "While You Were Sleeping." *Harpers* 293. 1759 (Dec. 1996): 44–52.

Brooks, Peter. *The Melodramatic Imagination: Balzac, Henry James, Melodrama, and the Mode of Excess*. New Haven: Yale UP, 1976.

Burton, Julianne, ed. *Cinema and Social Change in Latin America: Conversations with Filmmakers*. Austin: U of Texas P, 1986, 1988, 1992. Trans. Gustavo García and José Felipe Coria. *Cine y cambio social en América Latina: Imágenes de un continente*. Mexico City: Diana, 1991. Chinese translation: Taipei Film Archive, 1996.

———. *Latin American and Latino Film and Video: An International Analytical Bibliography, 1930–2000*. Lanham: Scarecrow, forthcoming.

———. "La ley del más padre: melodrama paternal, melodrama patriarcal, y la especifidad del ejemplo mexicano." *Archivos de la Filmoteca* 16 (Feb. 1994) [Valencia, Spain]: 50–63.

———. *Matilde Landeta: Hija de la Revolución*. Mexico City: Instituto Mexicano de Cinematografía and Consejo Nacional para la Cultura y las Artes, 2002.

———. "Mexican Melodramas of Patriarchy: Specificities of a Transcultural Form." *Framing Latin American Cinema: Contemporary Critical Directions*. Ed. Ann Marie Stock. Minneapolis: U of Minnesota P, 1997. 186–234.

———, ed. *Mexican Movie Melodrama: New Critical Directions*. Austin: U of Texas P. In progress.

———, ed. *The Social Documentary in Latin America*. Pittsburgh: U of Pittsburgh P, 1990.

———. *Three Lives in Film: The Improbable Careers of Latin America's Foremost Women Filmmakers*. In progress.

Burton-Carvajal, Julianne. See Burton, Julianne.

Castañeda, Jorge G. *The Mexican Shock: Its Meaning for the U.S.* New York: New Press, 1995.

Castañeda, Jorge G., and Robert A. Pastor. *Limits to Friendship: The United States and Mexico*. New York: Knopf, 1988.

Chávez, Patricio, Liz Lerma, and Sylvia Orozco, eds. *Counter Colón-ialismo*. San Diego: Centro Cultural de la Raza, 1992.

Chávez Camacho, Armando. *Cajeme: Novela de indios.* Mexico City: Jus, 1948. Sonora: Gobierno del Estado de Sonora, 1987.

Chevalier, Ángel. "Adventures of a Woman." Mexico City: Newspaper Clipping. Landeta Archives: 1948.

Clifford, James. *The Predicament of Culture: Twentieth-Century Ethnography, Literature, and Art.* Cambridge: Harvard UP, 1988.

———. "Traveling Cultures." *Cultural Studies.* Ed. Lawrence Grossberg, Cary Nelson, and Paula A. Treichler. New York: Routledge, 1992. 96–116.

Cobo-Hanlon, Leila. "Another Side of the 'Crazy Life.'" *Los Angeles Times* 21 July 1994: F1+.

Cockcroft, James D. *Mexico's Hope: An Encounter with Politics and History.* New York: Monthly Review, 1998.

"Con el TLC, México perdió su cultura." *La Jornada* 22 Sept. 1998: Landeta Archives.

Covacevich, Álvaro J., ed. *Cuando la danza se vuelve rito: Los indios de México.* Mexico City: Madero, c. 1990.

Culture Clash. *Life, Death and Revolutionary Comedy.* New York: Theatre Communications Group, 1998.

Dargis, Manohla. "Earth Angel: Allison Anders Talks about Making Movies, Melodrama, and Peace with the Echo Park *Locas.*" *L.A. Weekly* 22–28 July 1994: 19+.

Davis, Mike. *City of Quartz: Excavating the Future in Los Angeles.* London: Verso, 1990. New York: Vintage, 1992.

———. "Uprising and Repression in L.A.: An Interview with Mike Davis by the *Covert Action Information Bulletin.*" *Reading Rodney King/Reading Urban Uprising.* Ed. Robert Gooding-Williams. London: Routledge, 1993. 142–43.

de la Mora, Sergio. "Gabriel Figueroa: The Master of Light." *Cine Festival Latino.* San Francisco: Cine Acción, Sept. 1997.

———. "'Giving It Away': *American Me* and the Defilement of Chicano Manhood." *Cine Estudiantil '95.* San Diego: Centro Cultural de la Raza, 1995.

———. *Virile Nationalism: Cinema, the State, and the Formation of a National Consciousness in Mexico, 1950–1994.* Diss. U of California-Santa Cruz, 1999. Ann Arbor: UMI, 2000.

de Lauretis, Teresa. *Alice Doesn't: Feminism, Semiotics, Cinema.* Bloomington: Indiana UP, 1984.

de la Vega Alfaro, Eduardo. See Vega Alfaro, Eduardo de la.

de los Reyes, Aurelio. See Reyes, Aurelio de los.

Dever, Susan. *Celluloid Nationalism and Other Melodramas: From Post-Revolutionary Mexico to Post-Rebellion Los Angeles*. Diss. Stanford U, 1997. Ann Arbor: UMI, 1998.

———. "Las de abajo: La Revolución Mexicana de Matilde Landeta." Trans. Susan Dever and Magali Roy Fequiere. *Archivos de la Filmoteca* 16 (Feb. 1994) [Valencia, Spain]: 36–49.

———. "Re-Birth of a Nation: On Mexican Movies, Museums, and María Félix." *Spectator: The University of Southern California Journal of Film and Television Criticism* 13.1 (fall 1992): 52–69.

Díaz, Patricia. Dir. *My Filmmaking/My Life*. 1992.

Díaz Ruanova, Oswaldo. "No idealicemos a las mujeres públicas." *El Universal* 3 June 1951: n. pag.

Dirección General de Estadística, México. *La Estadística a través de medio siglo de informes presidenciales*. Mexico City: Secretaría de Economía, 1951.

Doane, Mary Ann. *The Desire to Desire: The Woman's Film of the 1940s*. Bloomington: Indiana UP, 1987.

———. *Femmes Fatales: Feminism, Film Theory and Psychoanalysis*. New York: Routledge, 1991.

Domínguez Aragonés, Edmundo. *Tres Extraordinarios: Luis Spota, Alejandro Jodorowsky, Emilio "Indio" Fernández*. Mexico City: Juan Pablos, 1980.

Dunitz, Robin. *Street Gallery*. Los Angeles: RJD Enterprises, 1993.

Dunitz, Robin, and James Prigoff. *Walls of Heritage, Walls of Pride: African American Murals*. Rohnert Park: Pomegranate, 2000.

Edelman, Marian Wright. "Citizen Activists: Ethics of Caring and Community in a World Desperately Seeking Moral Leadership." Pacifica National News Broadcast. Albuquerque, KUNM. 30 Dec. 1996.

Escobar, Arturo. *Encountering Development: The Making and Unmaking of the Third World*. Princeton: Princeton UP, 1995.

Espinosa García, Irma Arcelia, ed. *Cine Latino Americano Años 30–40–50* (Conference Proceedings from the XI Festival Internacional del Nuevo Cine Latinoamericano, Dec. 1989, Havana, Cuba). Mexico City: U Nacional Autónoma de México, 1990.

Evans, Peter William. "*Double Indemnity* (or Bringing Up Baby)." *The Book of Film Noir*. Ed. Ian Cameron. New York: Continuum, 1993. 165–73.

EZLN (Ejército Zapatista de Liberación Nacional). "Communiqués." 29 Apr. 2001. Online. Internet. 30 Apr. 2001.

Feder, Elena. *Dying to Be Born: The Vicissitudes of Birth in Life and Culture*. Diss. Stanford U, 1997. Ann Arbor: UMI, 1998.

———. "A Reckoning: Interview with Gabriel Figueroa." *Film Quarterly* 49.3 (spring 1996): 2–14.

Felperin, Leslie. Rev. of *Mi vida loca*. *Sight and Sound* 5 (Apr. 1995): 48.

Fernández, Adela. *El Indio Fernández: Vida y mito*. Mexico City: Panorama, 1986.

Fernández, Emilio, dir. *Río Escondido*. Perf. María Félix. Producciones Raúl de Anda, 1947.

Fernández Violante, Marcela, dir. and script. *Cananea*. CONACINE and Churubusco, 1977

———, dir. and script. *De cuerpo presente: Las espirales perpetuas del placer y el poder*. In film anthology *Enredando sombras*. Producciones Amaranta, 1997.

———, dir. and adapt. *De piel de víbora*. Instituto Mexicano de Cinematografía, 2001.

———, dir. and script. *De todos modos Juan te llamas*. Dirección de Actividades Cinematográficas-UNAM, 1974.

———, dir. and co-adapt. *En el país de los pies ligeros; o, El niño raramuri*. CONACITE II, 1981.

———, dir. and script. *Frida Kahlo*. Centro Universitario de Estudios Cinematográficos-UNAM, 1971.

———, dir. and co-adapt. *Golpe de suerte*. Riat Asesores and Fondo de Fomento a la Calidad Cinematográfica, 1992.

———. "La ley de cinematografía (Opus 1992)." *Archipiélago* 14 (Sept.-Dec. 1997): 44–45.

———, dir. and script. *Matilde Landeta*. Secretariá de Educación Pública, 1982

———. "El melodrama, orígenes y tradición." *Estudios Cinematográficos* 19 (June-Oct. 2000): 32–37.

———, dir. and co-adapt. *Misterio*. CONACINE, 1980.

———, dir. and co-adapt. *Nocturno amor que te vas*. UNAM, 1986.

Fiol-Matta, Licia. "The 'Schoolteacher of America': Gender, Sexuality, and Nation in Gabriela Mistral." *¿Entiendes? Queer Readings, Hispanic Writings*. Ed. Emilie L. Bergmann and Paul Julian Smith. Durham: Duke, 1995. 201–39.

Fox, Claire F. *The Fence and the River: Culture and Politics at the U.S.-Mexico Border*. Minneapolis: U of Minnesota P, 1999.

———. "Hollywood's Backlot: Carlos Fuentes, *The Old Gringo*, and National Cinema." *Iris: A Journal of Theory on Image and Sound* 13 (summer 1991): 63–86.

———. "The Portable Border: Site-Specificity, Art, and the U.S.-Mexico Frontier." *Social Text* 41 (winter 1994): 61–82.

Franco, Jean. *Plotting Women: Gender and Representation in Mexico.* New York: Columbia UP, 1989.

Fraser, Nancy. *Unruly Practices: Power, Discourse, and Gender in Contemporary Social Theory.* Oxford: Polity, 1989. Minneapolis: U of Minnesota P, 1994.

Fregoso, Rosa Linda. *The Bronze Screen: Chicana and Chicano Film Culture.* Minneapolis: U of Minnesota P, 1993.

———. "Hanging Out with the Homegirls? Allison Anders's *Mi vida loca*," *Cineaste* 21.3 (1995): 36–37.

Fuentes, Carlos. *Myself with Others: Selected Essays.* London: Andre Deutsch, 1988. New York: Noonday, 1990.

———. *Zona sagrada.* Mexico City: Siglo Veintiuno, 1967.

Gallegos, Rómulo. *Doña Bárbara.* Barcelona: Araluce, 1929.

Gamboa, Fernando. "Antoine Tzapoff." *Cuando la danza se vuelve rito: Los indios de México.* Ed. Álvaro J. Covacevich. Mexico City: Madero, c. 1990. 13–16.

Gamio, Manuel. *Forjando patria.* Mexico City: Porrúa, 1916.

García, Gustavo. *El cine mudo mexicano.* Mexico City: Secretaría de Educación Pública, 1982.

———. "Melodrama: The Passion Machine." Trans. Ana M. López. *Mexican Cinema.* Ed. Paulo Antonio Paranaguá. London: BFI; Mexico City: Instituto Mexicano de Cinematografía, 1995. 153–62.

———. "Tengo una tumba donde llorar. Ismael Rodríguez contra el melodrama." *Archivos de la Filmoteca* 16 (Feb. 1994) [Valencia, Spain]: 30–35.

García Canclini, Néstor. *Culturas híbridas: Estrategias para entrar y salir de la modernidad.* Mexico City: Grijalbo, 1989. Trans. Christopher L. Chiappari and Silvia L. López. *Hybrid Cultures: Strategies for Entering and Leaving Modernity.* Minneapolis: Minnesota, 1995.

García Canclini, Néstor, Patricia Safa and Lourdes Grobet. *Tijuana: La casa de toda la gente.* Mexico City: U Autónoma Metropolitana-Iztapalapa; INAH/ENAH, 1989.

García Riera, Emilio. *Emilio Fernández, 1904–1986.* Guadalajara: U de Guadalajara, 1987.

———. *Historia documental del cine mexicano.* 18 vols. Guadalajara: U de Guadalajara, 1992–1997.

———. "The Impact of *Rancho Grande.*" Trans. Ana M. López. *Mexican Cinema.* Ed. Paulo Antonio Paranaguá. London: BFI; Mexico City: Instituto Mexicano de Cinematografía, 1995. 128–32.

———. *Julio Bracho 1909–1978.* Guadalajara: U de Guadalajara, 1986.

García Tsao, Leonardo. "Misión imposible." *La Jornada* 9 June 2000. Online. Internet. 18 Jan. 2001.

———. "One Generation—Four Film-makers: Cazals, Hermosillo, Leduc and Ripstein." Trans. Ana M. López. *Mexican Cinema.* Ed. Paulo Antonio Paranaguá. London: BFI; Mexico City: Instituto Mexicano de Cinematografía, 1995. 209–24.

Garduño, Blanca, and José Antonio Rodríguez, eds. *Pasión por Frida.* Mexico City: Bellas Artes, 1992.

Garfias, Ramírez, Betty. "Matilde Landeta, toda una vida entregada al cine." *El Universal* 22 Oct. 1995: n. pag. Landeta Archives.

Gates, Jr., Henry Louis, ed. *"Race," Writing and Difference.* Chicago: U of Chicago P, 1986.

Gault, Barbara, Heidi Hartman, and Hsiao-Ye. "Prospects for Low-Income Mothers' Economic Survival under Welfare Reform." *Welfare Reform: A Race to the Bottom?* Ed. Sanford Schram and Samuel H. Beer. Washington, DC: Woodrow Wilson Center P, 1999. 209–27.

Gaxiola, Fernando. "Entrevista con Matilde Landeta." *Otro Cine* July-Sept. 1975: 12–17.

Gómez-Quiñones, Juan. *Mexican Nationalist Formation: Political Discourse, Policy and Dissidence.* Encino: Floricanto, 1992.

González Rodríguez, Sergio. "Muertes sin fin, Ciudad Juárez: Misoginia sin ley." *Letras Libres* 5 (5 May 1999): 40–45.

Gooding-Williams, Robert, ed. *Reading Rodney King/Reading Urban Uprising.* New York: Routledge, 1993.

Gordon, Bette. Interview with Allison Anders. *Bomb.* Summer 1994: 16–18.

Graham, Richard, ed. *The Idea of Race in Latin America, 1870–1940.* Austin: U of Texas P, 1990.

Gutiérrez Galindo, José. "Matilde Landeta, o el triunfo de la mujer mexicana en el cine." *El Universal* 2 Jan. 1950: n. pag.

Hernández, Fortunato. *Las razas indígenas de Sonora y la guerra del Yaqui.* Mexico City: J. de Eliazalde, 1902.

Hernández-Truyol, Berta Esperanza. "Reconciling Rights in Collision: An International Human Rights Strategy." *Immigrants Out! The New Nativism and the Anti-Immigrant Impulse in the United States.* Ed. Juan F. Perea. New York: New York UP, 1997. 254–76.

Hershfield, Joanne. "The Construction of Woman in *Distinto amanecer.*" *Spectator: The University of Southern California Journal of Film and Television Criticism* 13.1 (fall 1992): 42–51.

———. *Mexican Cinema/Mexican Woman, 1940–1950.* Tucson: U of Arizona P, 1996.

Hershfield, Joanne, and David Maciel. *Mexico's Cinema: A Century of Film and Film-makers.* Wilmington: Scholarly Resources, 1999.

Heuer, Federico. *La industria cinematográfica mexicana.* Mexico City: Policromia, 1964.

Huaco-Nuzum, Carmen. *Mestiza Subjectivity: Representation and Spectatorship in Mexican and Hollywood Films.* Diss. U of California-Santa Cruz, 1993.

———. Rev. of *American Me. Jump Cut* 38 (June 1993): 92–94.

"Immigrants' Rights Protest." *Los Angeles Times* 10 Mar. 1997: Metro Section 1.

"Indios en Churubusco." Mexico City: Newspaper Clipping. Landeta Archives, n.d.

Islas, Arturo. *Migrant Souls.* New York: William Morrow, 1990.

Jacobowitz, Florence. "The Man's Melodrama: *The Woman in the Window* and *Scarlet Street.*" *The Book of Film Noir.* Ed. Ian Cameron. New York: Continuum, 1993. 152–64.

Jaffe, Ira. *Slowly Out of Control.* In progress.

Jaffe, Ira, and Diana Robin, eds. *Redirecting the Gaze: Gender, Theory, and Cinema in the Third World.* New York: State U of New York P, 1999.

Jankowski, Martín Sánchez. *Islands in the Street: Gangs and the American Urban Society.* Berkeley: U of California P, 1991.

Jiménez, Arturo. "Una biblioteca al mundo." *La Jornada* 23 Aug. 2001. Online. Internet. 26 Aug. 2001.

Kaplan, E. Ann. *Looking for the Other: Feminism, Film, and the Imperial Gaze.* New York, Routledge, 1997.

Ketchum, Martha M. de, *Mexicanos creativos:* Volumen II. Mexico City: EDAMEX, 1996.

King, John. *Magical Reels: A History of Cinema in Latin America.* London: Verso, 1990.

King, John, Ana M. López, and Manuel Alvarado, eds. *Mediating Two Worlds: Cinematic Encounters in the Americas.* London: BFI, 1993.

Knight, Alan. "Racism, Revolution, and *Indigenismo:* Mexico, 1910–1940." *The Idea of Race in Latin America, 1870–1940.* Ed. Richard Graham. Austin: U of Texas P, 1990. 71–113.

Krutnik, Frank. *In a Lonely Street: Film Noir, Genre, Masculinity.* New York: Routledge, 1991.

Landeta, Matilde. "Francisco Rojas González y su cine." *Homenaje a F. R. G., 1903–1951.* Guadalajara: Secretaría de Educación y Cultura, 1992. 18–20.

——, adapt. and dir. *Lola Casanova.* By Francisco Rojas González. Perf. Meche Barba. TACMA, under the supervision of Eduardo Landeta, 1948.

——, adapt. and dir. *La Negra Angustias.* By Francisco Rojas González. Perf. María Elena Marqués. TACMA and Eduardo Landeta, 1949.

——, dir. *Nocturno a Rosario.* Perf. Ofelia Medina and Patricia Reyes Spíndola. Consejo Nacional para la Cultura y las Artes, Instituto Mexicano de Cinematografía, and Fondo de Fomento a la Calidad Cinematográfica, 1991.

——, dir. *Trotacalles.* Perf. Elda Peralta and Mirsolava Stern. TACMA and Eduardo Landeta, 1951.

Landy, Marcia, ed. *Imitations of Life: A Reader on Film and Television Melodrama.* Detroit: Wayne State UP, 1991.

Lillo, Gastón. "El reciclaje del melodrama y sus repercusiones en la estratificación de la cultura." *Archivos de la Filmoteca* 16 (Feb. 1994) [Valencia, Spain]: 64–73.

List, Christine. "Self-Directed Stereotyping in the Films of Cheech Marin." *Chicanos in Film.* Ed. Chon A. Noriega. Minneapolis: U of Minnesota P, 1992. 183–94.

López, Ana M. "Celluloid Tears: Melodrama in the 'Old' Mexican Cinema." *Iris: A Journal of Theory on Image and Sound* 13 (summer 1991): 29–51.

——. "A Cinema for the Continent." *The Mexican Cinema Project.* Ed. Chon A. Noriega and Steven Ricci. Los Angeles: U of California Film and Television Archive, 1994. 7–12.

——. "Tears and Desire: Women and Melodrama in the 'Old' Mexican Cinema," *Mediating Two Worlds: Cinematic Encounters in the Americas.* Ed. John King, Ana M. López, and Manuel Alvarado. London: BFI, 1993. 147–63.

López Bárcenas, Francisco. "Por qué renuncio al INI." *La Jornada* 22 Aug. 2001. Online. Internet. 22 Aug. 2001.

Loyola, Rafael, ed. *Entre la guerra y la estabilidad política: El México de los '40.* Mexico City: Grijalbo, 1986.

María Cristina. "Culpa de ser mujer." *México Cinema* June 1945: n. pag.

Martínez, Rubén. "Free Trade Art: The Frida Kahlo-ization of Los Angeles." *L.A Weekly* 17 Nov. 1991: 16–26.

———. *The Other Side: Fault Lines, Guerrilla Saints, and the True Heart of Rock 'n' Roll.* London: Verso, 1992.

Martínez de Velasco Vélez, Patricia. *Directoras de cine: Proyección de un mundo obscuro.* Mexico City: Instituto Mexicano de Cinematografía and CONEICC, 1991.

"Matilde Landeta. La cine-directora." *México Cinema* Aug. 1949: n. pag.

Matusik, Angela. Interview with Allison Anders. *Paper.* Summer 1994: 43+.

Medin, Tzvi. *El sexenio alemanista: Ideología y praxis política de Miguel Alemán.* Mexico City: Era, 1990.

Medina, Luis, and Luis González y González. *Historia de la Revolución Mexicana, 1940–1952: Civilismo y modernización del autoritarismo.* Mexico City: Colegio de México, 1979.

Mejía Piñeros, María Consuelo, and Sergio Sarmiento Silva. *La lucha indígena: Un reto a la ortodoxia.* Mexico City: Siglo Veintiuno, 1987.

México y la cultura. Mexico City: Secretaría de Educación Pública, 1946.

Mistral, Gabriela. *Lecturas para mujeres.* 1922. Mexico City: Porrúa, 1976.

Miyoshi, Masao. "A Borderless World?: From Colonialism to Transnationalism and the Decline of the Nation State." *Global/Local: Cultural Production and the Transnational Imaginary.* Ed. Rob Wilson and Wimal Dissanayake. Durham: Duke UP, 1996. 78–106.

Moiron, Sara. "Al fin triunfadora." *Cinema Reporter* June 1948: n. pag.

Molloy, Sylvia. "The Unquiet Self: Spanish American Autobiography and the Question of National Identity." *Comparative American Identities: Race, Sex, and Nationality in the Modern Text.* Ed. Hortense J. Spillers. New York: Routledge, 1991. 26–39.

Monsiváis, Carlos. *Escenas de pudor y liviandad.* Mexico City: Grijalbo, 1988.

———. "María Félix: Pabellón de la imagen." *Intermedios* 6 (1993): 12–17.

———. *Mexican Postcards.* Trans. John Kraniauskas. London: Verso, 1997.

———. "Las mitologías del cine mexicano." *Intermedios* 2 (1992): 12–23.

———. "Mythologies." Trans. Ana M. López. *Mexican Cinema*. Ed. Paulo Antonio Paranaguá. London: BFI; Mexico City: Instituto Mexicano de Cinematografía, 1995. 117–27.

———. "Se sufre, pero se aprende (el melodrama y las reglas de la falta de límites)." *Archivos de la Filmoteca* 16 (Feb. 1994) [Valencia, Spain]: 6–19.

———. "Sociedad y cultura." *Entre la guerra y la estabilidad política: El México de los '40*. Ed. Rafael Loyola. Mexico City: Grijalbo, 1990. 259–80.

Monsiváis, Carlos, and Hermann Bellinghausen. "Marcos: 'gran interlocutor.'" *La Jornada* 8 Jan 2001. Online. Internet. 18 May 2001.

Monsiváis, Carlos, and Carlos Bonfil. *A través del espejo. El cine mexicano y su público*. Mexico City: Milagro, 1994.

Monsiváis, Carlos, and Julio Scherer García. *Parte de guerra: Tlatelolco 1968. Documentos del general Marcelino García Barragán. Los hechos y la historia*. Mexico City: Nuevo Siglo/Aguilar, 1999.

Montoya, Richard, Ricardo Salinas, and Herbert Sigüenza. *Culture Clash: Life, Death and Revolutionary Comedy*. New York: Theatre Communications Group, 1998.

Moore, Joan W. *Going Down to the Barrio*. Philadelphia: Temple UP, 1991.

Mora, Carl J. *Mexican Cinema: Reflections of a Society, 1896–1988*. 1982. Berkeley: U of California P, 1989.

"Una mujer al megáfono." *Cartel* Aug. 1948: n. pag.

Morales Carillo, Alfonso. "Cuerpo marcado: La violencia y el cine mexicano." Unpublished essay. *De cuerpo presente*. Marcela Fernández Violante (with Alfonso Morales Carillo.) Unpublished screenplay. Mexico City: 1997.

Mulvey, Laura. *Visual and Other Pleasures*. Bloomington: Indiana UP, 1989.

Naggar, Carole, and Fred Ritchin, eds. *México: Through Foriegn Eyes*. New York: W. W. Norton, 1993.

Neruda, Pablo. "La pregunta." *Los versos del Capitán*. Buenos Aires: Losada, 1953.

Newman, Kathleen E. "Reterritorialization in Recent Chicano Cinema: Edward James Olmos's *American Me* (1992)." *The Ethnic Eye: Latino Media Arts*. Ed. Chon A. Noriega and Ana M. López. Minneapolis: U of Minnesota P, 1996.

———. "Steadfast Love and Subversive Acts: The Politics of *La Ofrenda: The Days of the Dead.*" *Spectator: The University of Southern California Journal of Film and Television Criticism* 13.1 (fall 1992): 98–109.

Noriega, Chon A., ed. *Chicanos in Film: Representations and Resistance*. Minneapolis: U of Minnesota P, 1996.

Noriega, Chon A., and Ana M. López, eds. *The Ethnic Eye: Latino Media Arts*. Minneapolis: U of Minnesota P, 1996.

Noriega, Chon A., and Steven Ricci, eds. *The Mexican Cinema Project*. Los Angeles: U of California Film and Television Archive, 1994.

O'Neill, John P., and Kathleen Howard, eds. *Mexico: Splendors of Thirty Centuries*. New York: The Metropolitan Museum of Art, 1990.

Palmer, R. Barton. *Hollywood's Dark Cinema*. New York: Twayne, 1994.

Paranaguá, Paulo Antonio, ed. *Mexican Cinema*. Trans. Ana M. López. London: BFI, 1995.

Paz, Octavio. *El laberinto de la soledad*. Mexico City: Fondo de Cultura Económica, 1950. Trans. Lysander Kemp. *The Labyrinth of Solitude*. New York: Grove, 1961.

———. "Will for Form." *Mexico: Splendors of Thirty Centuries*. Ed. John P. O'Neill and Kathleen Howard. New York: The Metropolitan Museum of Art, 1990.

———. "Las páginas escogidas de José Vasconcelos [1941]." *México en la obra de Octavio Paz*, t. II. *Generaciones y semblanzas: Escritores y letras de México*. Mexico City: Fondo de Cultura Económica, 1987. 561–64.

———. "Pintura mural." *México en la obra de Octavio Paz*, t. III. *Los privilegios de la vista: Arte de México*. Mexico City: Fondo de Cultura Económica, 1987. 221–319.

———. *Xavier Villaurrutia en persona y obra*. Mexico City: Fondo de Cultura Económica, 1978.

Peguero, Raquel. "Los argumentos pro doblaje, tramposos," *La Jornada* 5 Mar. 2000. Online. Internet. 6 Mar. 2000.

Peralta, Elda. *La época de oro sin nostalgia: Luis Spota en el cine*. 1988. Mexico City: Grijalbo, 1989.

———. *Luis Spota: Las sustancias de la tierra. Una biografía íntima*. 1989. Mexico City: Grijalbo, 1990.

———. *Nocturno mar sin espuma*. Mexico City: Morgana, 1997.

Pérez Turrent, Tomás. "Luis Buñuel in Mexico." Trans. Ana M. López. *Mexican Cinema*. Ed. Paulo Antonio Paranaguá. London: BFI; Mexico City: Instituto Mexicano de Cinematografía, 1995. 202–08.

Pick, Zuzana M. *The New Latin American Cinema: A Continental Project*. Austin: U of Texas P, 1993.

Piven, Frances Fox. Foreword. *Words of Welfare: The Poverty of Social Science and the Social Science of Poverty*. By Sanford F. Schram. Minneapolis: U of Minnesota P, 1995. ix–xv.

Piven, Frances Fox, and Richard A. Cloward, eds., *Regulating the Poor: The Functions of Public Welfare*. New York: Vintage, 1993.

Podalsky, Laura. "Disjointed Frames: Melodrama, Nationalism, and Representation in 1940s Mexico." *Studies in Latin American Popular Culture* 12 (1993): 57–73.

———. "Patterns of the Primitive." *Mediating Two Worlds: Cinematic Encounters in the Americas*. Ed. John King, Ana M. López, and Manuel Alvarado. London: BFI, 1993. 25–39.

Poniatowska, Elena. *La noche de Tlatelolco: Testimonios de historia oral*. Mexico City: Era, 1971. Trans. Helen R. Lane. *Massacre in Mexico*. New York: Viking, 1975.

———. *Todo México*. Mexico City: Diana, 1990.

Portillo, Lourdes. Dir. *Columbus On Trial*. Xochitl, 1992.

———, dir. *Señorita Extraviada* (Missing Young Woman). Xochitl, 2001.

Pratt, Mary Louise. *Imperial Eyes: Travel Writing and Transculturation*. London: Routledge, 1992.

———. "Scratches on the Face of the Country; or, What Mr. Barrow Saw in the Land of the Bushman." *"Race," Writing and Difference*. Ed. Henry Louis Gates, Jr. Chicago: U of Chicago P, 1986. 138–62.

Ramírez Berg, Charles. See Berg, Charles Ramírez.

Rashkin, Elissa J. *Women Filmmakers in Mexico: The Country of Which We Dream*. Austin: U of Texas P, 2001.

Reid, David, and Jayne L. Walker. "Strange Pursuit: Cornell Woolrich and the Abandoned City of the Forties." *Shades of Noir*. Ed. Joan Copjec. London: Verso, 1993. 57–96.

Reyes, Aurelio de los, *Cine y sociedad en México, 1896–1930: Vivir de sueños*. Vol. I (1896–1920). Mexico City: U Nacional Autónoma de México, 1983.

———. *Medio siglo de cine mexicano, 1896–1947*. Mexico City: Trillas, 1987.

———. "The Silent Cinema." Trans. Ana M. López. *Mexican Cinema*. Ed. Paulo Antonio Paranaguá. London: BFI; Mexico City: Instituto Mexicano de Cinematografía, 1995. 63–78.

Reyes Nevares, Beatriz. *Trece directores del cine mexicano*. Mexico: Secretaría de Educación Pública, 1974. Trans. Carl J. Mora and Elizabeth Gard. *The Mexican Cinema: Interviews with Thirteen Directors*. Albuquerque: U of New Mexico P, 1976.

Rich, B. Ruby. "Slugging It Out for Survival." *Sight and Sound* 5 (Apr. 1995): 14–17.

Rico, Diana. "Cómo trabaja la mujer mexicana." *Paquita* 5 (July 1948): n. pag.

Robinson, Cedric J. "Race, Capitalism, and the Antidemocracy." *Reading Rodney King/Reading Urban Uprising.* Ed. Robert Gooding-Williams. New York: Routledge, 1993. 73–81.

Robles, Martha. *Entre el poder y las letras: Vasconcelos en sus memorias.* Mexico City: Fondo de Cultura Económica, 1989.

Rodríguez, Antonio. *Guía de los murales de Diego Rivera en la Secretaría de Educación Pública.* Mexico City: Secretaría de Educación Pública, 1984.

Rodríguez, Luis. *Always Running, La vida loca: Gang Days in L.A.* New York: Touchtone, 1993.

Rodríguez Savaria, Patricia. *De piel de víbora.* Mexico City: Sansores y Aljure, 1998.

Rojas González, Francisco. *Lola Casanova.* Mexico City: EDIAPSA, 1947. Mexico City: Fondo de Cultura Económica, 1992.

———. *La Negra Angustias.* Mexico City: Compañía General, 1944.

Rosaldo, Renato. *Culture and Truth: The Remaking of Social Analysis.* Boston: Beacon, 1989.

Ross, John. *Rebellion from the Roots: Indian Uprising in Chiapas.* Monroe: Common Courage, 1995.

Roy Feguiere, Magali. *Women, Creole Identity, and Intellectual Life in Early Twentieth-Century Puerto Rico* (forthcoming, Temple UP).

Rozado, Alejandro. *Cine y realidad social en México: Una lectura de la obra de Emilio Fernández.* Guadalajara: U de Guadalajara, 1991.

Sánchez, Francisco. *Crónica antisolemne del cine mexicano.* Xalapa: U Veracruzana, 1989.

———. *Siglo Buñuel.* Mexico City: Consejo Nacional para la Cultura y las Artes, 2000.

Sánchez, George J. *Becoming Mexican American: Ethnicity, Culture and Identity in Chicano Los Angeles, 1900–1945.* Oxford: Oxford UP, 1993.

Saragoza, Alex M. with Graciela Berkovich. "Intimate Connections: Cinematic Allegories of Gender, the State and National Identity." *The Mexican Cinema Project.* Ed. Chon A. Noriega and Steven Ricci. Los Angeles: U of California Film and Television Archive, 1994. 25–32.

Schaefer, Claudia. "'Monobodies,' Antibodies, and the Body Politic: Sara Levi Calderón's *Dos mujeres.*" Feministas Unidas Panel. MLA Convention. San Francisco. 29 Dec. 1991.

———. *Textured Lives: Women, Art, and Representation in Modern Mexico.* Tucson: U of Arizona P, 1992.

Schrader, Paul. *Transcendental Style in Film: Ozu, Bresson, and Dreyer.* 1972. New York: Da Capo, 1988.

Schram, Sanford. *Words of Welfare: The Poverty of Social Science and the Social Science of Poverty.* Minneapolis: U of Minnesota P, 1995.

Schryer, Frans J. *Ethnicity and Class Conflict in Rural Mexico.* Princeton: Princeton UP, 1990.

Sidel, Ruth. *Keeping Women and Children Last: America's War on the Poor.* New York: Penguin, 1996.

Skinner-Jones, Ann. "Neither Outsider Nor Insider." Unpublished essay. Albuquerque, 1994.

Sommers, Joseph. *Francisco Rojas González: Exponente literario del nacionalismo mexicano.* Trans. Carlo Antonio Castro. Xalapa: U Veracruzana, 1966.

Soto, Shirlene Ann. *Emergence of the Modern Mexican Woman: Her Participation in Revolution and Struggle for Equality, 1910–1940.* Denver: Arden, 1990.

Spota, Luis. *Vagabunda.* [c. 1950.] Mexico City: Libro Mex, 1959.

Stavenhagen, Rodolfo. *Derecho indígena y derechos humanos en América Latina.* Mexico City: Colegio de México and Instituto Americano de Derechos Humanos, 1988.

Taibo I, Paco Ignacio. *El Indio Fernández: El cine por mis pistolas.* Mexico City: Joaquín Mortiz, 1986.

———. *María Félix: 47 pasos por el cine.* Mexico City: Joaquín Mortiz, 1985.

"Teen Pregnancies Raising Crime Costs." *Santa Barbara News Press* 22 June 1996: B22+.

Thomas, Deborah. "How Hollywood Deals with the Deviant Male." *The Book of Film Noir.* Ed. Ian Cameron. New York: Continuum, 1993. 59–70.

Thomas, Kevin. "The Road to *Mi vida loca* Paved with Good Intentions." *Los Angeles Times* 22 July 1994: F4+.

Torres, Blanca. *Historia de la Revolución Mexicana, 1940–1952: Hacia la utopía industrial.* Mexico City: Colegio de México, 1984.

Torres San Martín, Patricia. "Adela Sequeyro and Matilde Landeta: Two Pioneer Women Directors." *Mexico's Cinema: A Century of Film and Filmmakers.* Ed. Joanne Hershfield and David Maciel. Wilmington: Scholarly Resources, 1999. 37–48.

———. Interview with Matilde Landeta. *Pantalla* 16 (1992): 26–31.

"Tras el inicio de la operación Salvaguarda: Relaciones exteriores." *La Jornada* 13 June 2000. Online. Internet. 15 June 2000.

Trelles Plazaola, Luis. *Cine y mujer en América Latina: Directoras de largometrajes de ficción*. Río Piedras: U de Puerto Rico, 1991.

"Tres films de una directora mexicana." *La Nación* [Buenos Aires, Argentina] 4 Nov. 1951: n. pag.

Trinh, T. Minh-ha. *Woman, Native, Other: Writing Postcoloniality and Feminism*. Bloomington: Indiana UP, 1989.

Tuñón, Julia. "Between the Nation and Utopia: The Image of Mexico in the Films of Emilio 'Indio' Fernández." *Studies in Latin American Popular Culture* 12 (1993): 159–74.

———. *En su propio espejo: Entrevista con Emilio "El Indio" Fernández*. Mexico City: U Autónoma Metropolitana-Iztapalapa, 1988.

———. *Mujeres de luz y sombra en el cine mexicano: La construcción de una imagen, 1939–1952*. Mexico City: Colegio de México and Instituto Mexicano de Cinematografía, 1998.

Tuñón Pablos, Julia. See Tuñón, Julia.

Vasconcelos, José. *Memorias I: Ulises criollo/La tormenta*. [*Ulises criollo*. Mexico City: Botas, 1936. *La tormenta*. Mexico City: Botas, 1936.] Mexico City: Fondo de Cultura Económica, 1983.

———. *Memorias II: El desastre/El Proconsulado*. [*El desastre*. Mexico City: Botas, 1938. *El Proconsulado*. Mexico City: Botas, 1939.] Mexico City: Fondo de Cultura Económica, 1983.

———. *La raza cósmica: Misión de la raza iberoamericana. Notas de viaje a la América del Sur*. Barcelona: Agencia Mundial de Librerías, c. 1925. Trans. Didier T. Jaén. *La raza cósmica/The Cosmic Race*. Los Angeles: California State UP, 1979.

Vega Alfaro, Eduardo de la, "Origins, Development and Crisis of the Sound Cinema, 1929–1964." Trans. Ana M. López. *Mexican Cinema*. Ed. Paulo Antonio Paranaguá. London: BFI; Mexico City: Instituto Mexicano de Cinematografía, 1995. 79–93.

Vega Alfaro, Eduardo de la, and Patricia Torres San Martín. *Adela Sequeyro*. Guadalajara: U de Guadalajara; Xalapa: U Veracruzana, 1997.

Vélez, Jaime. "Violando el aire. XEPET: La voz de los mayas." *México indígena* 12 (Sept. 1990): 43–45.

Villar, Josefina. *El sonido de la radio*. Mexico City: U Autónoma Metropolitana-Iztapalapa and Plaza y Valdés, 1988.

Villoro, Luis. *Los grandes momentos del indigenismo en México*. Mexico City: Colegio de México, 1950.

Walker, Michael. Introduction. *The Book of Film Noir*. Ed. Ian Cameron. New York: Continuum, 1993. 8–38.

Walsh, Donald D. Introduction and trans. *The Captain's Verses*. By Pablo Neruda. New York: New Directions, 1972.

White, Edmund. "Diva Mexicana." *Vanity Fair* 53.11 (Nov. 1990): 210+.

Wolfe, Bertram D. *The Fabulous Life of Diego Rivera*. New York: Stein and Day, 1963.

Ybarra Frausto, Tómas. "Rasquachismo: A Chicano Sensibility." *Chicano Art: Resistance and Affirmation, 1965–1985*. Los Angeles: California State UP, 1991. 155–62.

Ybarra Frausto, Tómas, and Shifra Goldman. *Arte Chicano*. Berkeley: U of California P, 1985.

Zahareas, Anthony. "The Historical Function of Picaresque Autobiographies: Toward a History of Social Offenders." Autobiography in Early Modern Spain. Ed. Nicholas Spadaccini and Jenaro Taléns. Minneapolis: Prisma, 1998. 129–62.

Zúñiga, Ariel. "De la madre en el melodrama mexicano (*Nosotros los pobres*, 1948)." *Archivos de la Filmoteca* 16 (Feb. 1994) [Valencia, Spain]: 20–29.

———. "Roberto Gavaldón." Trans. Ana M. López. *Mexican Cinema*. Ed. Paulo Antonio Paranaguá. London: BFI; Mexico City: Instituto Mexicano de Cinematografía, 1995. 193–201.

———. *Vasos comunicantes en la obra de Roberto Gavaldón: Una relectura*. Mexico City: El Equilibrista, 1990.

INDEX

To clarify the relationships between particular endnotes and occasionally unelucidated passages in the text, I have placed page numbers in parentheses within note phrases. Other note locaters without additional text references function independently or in conjunction with listed pages.